Ecotourism in Appalachia

Ecotourism
in
Appalachia

Marketing the Mountains

AL FRITSCH
and
KRISTIN JOHANNSEN

THE UNIVERSITY PRESS OF KENTUCKY

Publication of this volume was made possible in part by a grant
from the National Endowment for the Humanities.

Scholarly publisher for the Commonwealth,
serving Bellarmine University, Berea College, Centre College of Kentucky,
Eastern Kentucky University, The Filson Historical Society, Georgetown College,
Kentucky Historical Society, Kentucky State University, Morehead State
University, Murray State University, Northern Kentucky University, Transylvania
University, University of Kentucky, University of Louisville,
and Western Kentucky University.
All rights reserved.

Editorial and Sales Offices: The University Press of Kentucky
663 South Limestone Street, Lexington, Kentucky 40508-4008
www.kentuckypress.com

07 06 05 04   5 4 3 2 1

Library of Congress Cataloging-in-Publication Data

Fritsch, Albert J.
  Ecotourism in Appalachia : marketing the mountains / Al Fritsch and
Kristin Johannsen.
    p. cm.
  Includes bibliographical references (p.   ).
  ISBN 0-8131-2288-0 (Hardcover : alk. paper)
  1. Ecotourism—Appalachian Mountains Region. I. Johannsen, Kristin,
1957- II. Title.
G155.U6F72 2003
917.4'0068—dc21   2003014584

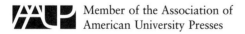 Member of the Association of
American University Presses

Contents

Acknowledgements

Many people and organizations have given us assistance and encouragement in the writing of this book. We are grateful to Kevin Millham for contributing his photographic and indexing skills and his unfailing support; to Mark Spencer for the meticulous maps and helpful suggestions; and to Jennifer Peckinpaugh, our editor, for her enthusiasm and vision. Paul Gallimore of Long Branch Environmental Education Center in Leicester, North Carolina, and Richard Baumann, provincial of the Chicago Jesuits, gave both financial and moral support.

Countless people gave us information and constructive criticism, and supported us in many other ways, including Richard Sambrook, David Zurick, Jennifer Gordon, Gene Wilhelm, Sherman Bamford, Joshua Bills, Martha Bond, Dan Bond, Peggy Pollard, and Belle Jackson.

We would also like to thank the staff and volunteers of: Appalachia—Science in the Public Interest (Mt. Vernon, Kentucky); the Cradle of Forestry in America (Brevard, North Carolina); the Blue Ridge Parkway Visitor Centers; the Appalachian Cultural Museum (Boone, North Carolina); Mt. Mitchell State Park (North Carolina); the Museum of the Cherokee Indian (Cherokee, North Carolina); the Folk Art Center (Asheville, North Carolina); the Friends of Great Smoky Mountains National Park; the state tourist offices of West Virginia, Pennsylvania, and Kentucky; the Appalachian Studies Association; our families and friends; and all of our traveling companions who helped us on the way.

Introduction

To anyone who has flown on a jam-packed airplane or stood in an endless car rental line in recent years, it will come as no surprise that travel is a booming business. The shock is in learning just how big it is.

Tourism is now the world's largest industry, creating $3.6 trillion of economic activity (directly and indirectly) annually, according to the World Travel and Tourism Council, an industry federation.[1] One out of every fifteen workers worldwide is employed in tourism, and tourism is the third largest household expenditure (after housing and food) in most industrialized nations.[2] Although the precise figures are debatable, there is no disputing that tourism is a major factor in the world economy and has a significant impact on the global environment.

And the tropical "paradises" of the Third World are hardly the only countries that depend heavily on tourism for income.[3] According to the Travel Industry Association of America (TIAA), travel and tourism directly generated over 7.8 million jobs in the United States in 2001. The travel industry ranks as the first, second, or third largest employer in twenty-nine states. It's a $545 billion sector of the American economy, with a multiplier effect alleged to extend far beyond that.[4]

Given the size of the tourism pie, it's not surprising that competition for the biggest slice is fierce among potential destinations. National tourism organizations are heavily funded by governments around the world, and U.S. states pour money into their respective tourism boards, spending nearly $686 million in 2000 in their attempts to lure tourists away from competing destinations. In that year, the Illinois Department of Tourism edged out Hawai'i as top spender, at a total of $61 million.[5]

Tourism is a major player in the states of Central Appalachia (Kentucky, Tennessee, Virginia, West Virginia, and North Carolina) as well. In 1998, North Carolina took in nearly $11 billion from domestic

1

tourists alone, while Tennessee collected almost $9 billion, though these states also have significant tourist attractions outside their mountain sections. West Virginia, whose territory lies entirely inside the mountains, received $1.58 billion of domestic tourist expenditures.[6]

In 2001, the state of Kentucky produced an informational video detailing the benefits of tourism for the local economy. According to their figures, tourist spending in the state amounts to $8.8 billion a year, making it the third-largest industry in Kentucky, and providing employment for one in every thirteen of the state's workers. Tourism has a total payroll of over two billion dollars and produces 11 percent of annual tax receipts. Despite this, Kentucky ranks only twenty-seventh among the states in the amount of tourist dollars it takes in—and twenty-ninth in spending for tourism advertising. Tourism promoters regard this as clear evidence that there is considerable room for expansion.

Vast amounts of time and money are expended to entice tourists, to study their tastes and preferences, and to package tourism "products" designed to separate them from their money. A half-dozen scholarly journals, with titles like *Annals of Tourism Research, Journal of Tourism Studies,* and *Leisure Sciences,* devote their pages to analyzing the behavior and preferences of tourists. The market has been minutely segmented, and trends of every sort pronounced and scrutinized.

Among the most visible of such travel trends is ecotourism—traveling to enjoy and learn about the natural environment. Tourist activities like whale watching, rainforest hikes, snorkeling, wilderness trekking, and "safaris" in places wild and not-so-wild have boomed in popularity in recent years. No less an authority than the World Tourism Organization has pronounced ecotourism the fastest-growing sector in the entire industry, and the United Nations named 2002 the International Year of Ecotourism. Estimates of annual growth in the ecotourism market range from 10 percent to 30 percent.

Almost from the time ecotourism first appeared, arriving at a precise definition of it has been tricky. In a 1991 paper calling for the foundation of a worldwide ecotourism organization, Megan Epler Wood stated, "The first task is to reach agreement on exactly what ecotourism is, and what it is not." More than a decade later, The International Ecotourism Society (TIES) is a large and influential organization—and there is even less agreement on the meaning of ecotourism.

One recent textbook entitled *Ecotourism: An Introduction* devotes an entire chapter to analyzing fifteen different definitions for this term proposed by various researchers and organizations.[7] These range from the microscopically precise (that author's own definition is an entire paragraph) to the hopelessly vague (the state of Texas defines ecotourism as "travel to natural areas" and considers hunting and fishing to be ecotourism). Of the myriad proposed definitions in circulation, we have chosen to use the one adopted by The International Ecotourism Society: *Ecotourism is responsible travel to natural areas that conserves the environment and improves the well-being of local people.*

We have chosen this definition because it is probably the most widely used—though it is also one of the least specific. A definition so nebulous can put a seal of approval on a very broad array of activities (and enterprises). In fact, it's hard to escape the conclusion that the continuing lack of a universally accepted definition for ecotourism suits many parties well, because it leaves them free to apply that label to anything that suits their purpose. In a paper entitled "Ecotourism: Ethics or Eco-Sell?" Pamela Wight states that the lack of a definition is due to "the many stakeholders involved in ecotourism who bring their own perspectives and motivations."[8]

In this book, we will use several different terms to talk about recreational travel in the outdoors. Our most general term is *nature tourism,* which we use to refer to any recreational travel that takes place in a natural setting. This is the broadest category; in Appalachia it includes such pursuits as sightseeing in natural areas, camping, houseboating, bird watching, rock climbing—every activity related to the outdoors. Some of these activities, like nature study and hiking, may be ecologically sound, while others, such as driving off-road vehicles (ORVs) through fragile areas, most emphatically are not.

We use *green tourism* to refer to a particular type of nature tourism that minimizes impact on the environment and increases travelers' understanding and appreciation of the natural world. In Appalachia, this includes bird watching, low-impact tent camping, and many outdoor activities.

Our narrowest category is *ecotourism,* which we use to mean a subcategory of green (low-impact, educational) tourism in which the environment is protected and the local community receives significant economic benefits. This matches the definition offered by The International Ecotourism Society, though few programs that call themselves "ecotourism" meet all—or any—of these loose criteria.

Not all green tourism is ecotourism. For example, a company based in New York could operate low-impact nature trekking programs in Appalachian national forests without employing any local people or purchasing any goods and services from local businesses, and funnel all of the profits straight back to New York. Though it may have an impeccable environmental record, we would not call it true ecotourism.

On the other hand, a business owned and operated by residents of a small mountain town could welcome visitors to its farmhouse bed-and-breakfast, arrange for local guides to take them on forest hikes focusing on history and ecology, and involve visitors in a project to count and identify local birds. Incorporating both environmental preservation and economic benefits to local people, this would meet our criteria for genuine ecotourism.

Ours is a very ambitious—even idealistic—definition of ecotourism. It excludes many types of nature tourism that do not incorporate environmental preservation and that can even be environmentally harmful (for example, houseboating and riding ORVs). It also excludes tourism products and programs that provide economic benefits mainly or exclusively to people outside the local community. In our view, true ecotourism involves three indispensable components: benefits to the environment, benefits to local people, and educational benefits to the traveler.

Unfortunately, few existing programs anywhere meet all of these criteria. As we will see, a bewildering array of tourism programs and businesses around the world now lay claim to the fashionable "eco" label: whale-watching tours, rainforest huts, luxury scuba cruises, hard-core backpacking trips, tribal treks, golf resorts that use organic fertilizers, ORV safaris, mountain biking expeditions, volunteer trail maintenance groups, helicopter-skiing companies, hotels that recycle those miniature plastic shampoo bottles . . . it's difficult to say what (if any) factors these endeavors have in common.

What is indisputable is the near-universal enthusiasm for the concept of "ecotourism"—however nebulously defined. Environmental groups, development agencies, the governments of what we will call, for brevity's sake, "Third World countries," national tourist boards, and travelers themselves are all heralding the rise of this new variety of tourism, asserting that it will preserve the environment while promoting a higher standard of living in economically backward areas of the world.

But among the most active and vocal supporters of "ecotourism" are bodies like the World Tourism Organization, a federation of government tourism offices; the World Travel and Tourism Council, composed of the CEOs of seventy major airlines, cruise ship companies, and hotel chains; the TIAA, whose members are 2,300 travel-related businesses; and the American Society of Travel Agents, which represents 26,000 travel agents worldwide.

This should raise questions about who, exactly, stands to benefit from projects labeled as "ecotourism"—the poor and powerless, and the endangered environments they call home? Or the corporations at the top of the tourism food chain? Too often an upsurge in tourism has brought little for local people but environmental degradation (as in Nepal), poorly paying and exploitative jobs (as in the Caribbean), or the collapse of traditional culture (as in the beach towns of Southeast Asia).

A key issue in current tourism development is how (and whether) it can be made sustainable—can development be carried out in such a way that it does not degrade the quality of natural resources, but rather preserves them for future generations? As one standard tourism textbook points out, "The environment is the core of the tourism product."[9] Without a reasonably clean, pleasant environment, no destination can hope to attract pleasure travelers.

Central to the issue of sustainability is the concept of carrying capacity. How many visitors can a tourist destination handle without bringing about unacceptable changes to the physical environment and a decline in the quality of visitors' experiences? Although the issue of carrying capacity pertains to all types of tourist destinations, it is particularly crucial in the case of areas where nature itself is the main attraction, such as wildlife reserves, national parks, and tropical beaches.

Environmentalist Tensie Whelan points out, "All protected areas have limited ecological and aesthetic carrying capacities. The ecological carrying capacity is reached when the number of visitors and characteristics of visitor use start to affect the wildlife and degrade the ecosystem. . . . The aesthetic carrying capacity is reached when tourists encounter so many other tourists, or see the impacts of other visitors . . . that their enjoyment of the site is marred."[10]

Clearly, places differ greatly in their carrying capacity. A large, well-developed, and affluent city like New York can absorb tremendous floods of tourists, while a poor village in the Himalayas may find its resources strained by a small group of adventure travelers. In fact, some environments may be so sensitive that even minimal development can cause serious damage. In her fieldwork in the Philippines, anthropologist Valene L. Smith concluded that on a small island, unplanned development of even small-scale, "alternative" tourism "can create such massive physical and social problems that a tourism industry based on 'alternative' tourism might not be sustainable."[11]

Tourism is emerging as a major economic force in Appalachia, as it is elsewhere around the world. Would the region and its people benefit from developing ecotourism? That is the central question we will address in this book.

Through our critique, we hope to encourage responsible tourism that preserves and protects the planet's resources while benefiting all who participate: tourists, businesses, and host communities. We aim to expose abusive tourism practices, offer steps to change them, and make the whole industry greener. And, lastly, in this discussion we hope to expand the concept of tourism to include not only the economically privileged and able-bodied but all portions of the American population.

Some environmentalists regard any skepticism about ecotourism as disloyal, because anything green is supposed to be beyond criticism. We'll try to redeem ourselves, however, by skipping ahead to our conclusion and stating that we want all tourism—whether blessed with the "eco" label or not—to be environmentally sound.

Everyone has biases, and we'll be honest about our own. First, we are biased in favor of Appalachia—and all regions that people call home. We all need to take care of our own backyards and learn to cherish them. Appalachia is our region, our home; it is incredibly beautiful, and it is part of a profoundly diverse bioregion with a tremendous number of plants and animals. This biological treasure lives within a geologically and culturally diverse region, fascinating to explore.

Our second bias is that getting around is a good thing, to be enjoyed and enhanced. We favor as much mobility as possible and feel concern for those who are prevented by personal circumstances from exploring new places; we disdain the enforced immobility that perpetuates isolation and lack of human interaction, whether it stems from physical disability or lack of economic opportunity.

Our third travel bias favors use of the automobile to the degree that it improves the quality of life. The curse of isolation remained on the people of Appalachia for decades, especially when mountain roads were too poor for year-round travel. Even today, school buses do not run in winter after the slightest snowfall, because many of the region's side roads remain icy long after the paved ones have been cleared. Vehicles and roads have linked people with the wider world; used with moderation, these enhancements cannot be faulted.

Along with apple pie and motherhood, we have a fourth bias in favor of sustainable development. While the term is open to a wide variety of interpretations, we use it in our discussion of tourism to mean improving the lives of tourists, the lives of people in the host regions, and the land itself—a three-legged stool. Visitors should have experiences that enrich their lives and expand their understanding; local residents need high-quality employment and good returns on the investment of their resources; and tourism development must not be exploitative, but should rather respect the current and future environment as well as the culture of the people. We favor a carefully controlled form of tourism development as both an environmental and an Appalachian solution, designed so that all parties benefit: travelers, host communities, and businesses.

At its best, the tourism industry helps people discover the wider world and renew themselves in doing so. In Appalachia, it can introduce travelers to scenes of rare natural beauty, diverse and fascinating ecosystems, and a proud traditional culture that flourishes to this day.

CHAPTER 1

The World's Biggest Industry

The Rising Star of Tourism

As with most smoothly functioning machines, the tourism industry received very little attention from its users—until it broke down. Following the attacks on the World Trade Center in New York City on September 11, 2001, most travel came to a sudden halt. Within the hour, tens of thousands of people found themselves pacing the floor in places they didn't want to be, as airports were closed and airplanes were grounded. Even after air transport was operational again, many Americans felt reluctant to travel.

The impact of these events quickly rippled through the global economy to its furthest reaches. Airlines in the U.S. and other countries saw their passenger loads decline steeply. Around the world, an estimated two hundred thousand airline employees were laid off from their jobs. Thousands of hotel rooms stayed empty while the parking lots at car rental companies stayed stubbornly full. Travel agents sat forlornly, waiting for their phones to ring. Club Med, the giant resort operator, shuttered seven of its properties, leaving workers in Tunisia, Egypt, and other countries unemployed.

The downturn in travel affected companies not often linked with tourism in the public mind. Sales of photographic film plummeted, as fewer people took vacation snapshots. A major U.S. paper manufacturer reported a sharp decline in revenue—a large percentage of its income was derived from sales of toilet paper and paper towels to airports and hotels. In Ireland, the parent company of Waterford Crystal laid off workers when purchases by tourists visiting the factory dried up.

Tourism has become an integral part of modern life and plays a key role in the economy of the U.S.—and the world. According to researcher Martha Honey, if the tourism industry were a country, it would have an "economy" second in size only to the U.S.[1] Where did this massive industry come from, and what are its key components?

The Old World: From Pilgrimage to Pleasure Tour

One of the most surprising discoveries you make if you travel extensively is that people have been moving around for a long, long time. A museum in Bergen, Norway, on the storm-swept fjord coast, displays pottery from Spain and Syria, found by archaeologists during their excavations of the city's medieval wharf district. On the beach near Ras al-Khaimah in the Persian Gulf, chips of blue and white Chinese porcelain from the fifteenth century still glitter in the sand. Native Americans in Florida during pre-history adorned themselves with ornaments of copper mined on the shores of Lake Superior. Viking mercenaries fought in the armies of the Ottoman Turkish sultans.

Granted, these early travelers were motivated mainly by economic gain rather than by curiosity or the simple human craving to see something different. The fact remains that people have traveled considerable distances for thousands of years, and many of the records they left behind show that curiosity about faraway places is hardly a modern innovation. The Greek epic poem *The Odyssey* records adventure and trade along the shores of the Mediterranean and Black Seas. Norse epics recount the voyages of the Vikings to unknown regions of Iceland, Greenland—even North America.

Our own ancestors before the twentieth century would have had a difficult time grasping the concept of "tourism." For them, a "journey" (derived from *diurnata*, or a day's work) was an arduous or dangerous venture, usually for exploration or for military, economic, or religious purposes. They did not connect travel with comfort, much less pleasure. To travel was to risk much and to suffer in order to reach the destination. Still, many early travelers reached the edges of the known world and beyond, leaving us fascinating chronicles of their journeys.

The Greek writer Herodotus, who lived in the fifth century B.C., was not only "the Father of History" but also the father of travel writing. His great *History* records the myriad wars and political developments of the era, set within the context of his own wanderings from Athens through Asia Minor, Egypt, Mesopotamia, and Babylon. He studied cultures that were ancient even then, and environments that were alien to him. He recorded local legends and customs, described everything he saw, and incorporated scandalous gossip into his narrative every chance he got—a precursor of the modern travel writer.

Travel in premodern times was generally for religious, scientific, or trade purposes, and often a combination of the three. But the written accounts we have now show that their authors possessed a lively curiosity about the unknown and derived great satisfaction from their wanderings.

The first great long-distance travel chronicle was written by Benjamin of Tudela, a rabbi in twelfth-century Spain who traveled to Palestine to learn about Jewish religious sites, as well as to gather information for use in trade. Over the span of fourteen years, he walked from Spain to Rome to Constantinople, then through Jerusalem and on to Baghdad, recording observations of the peoples he visited and their customs and beliefs. He also wrote down practical details for travelers, explaining how to find the Biblical pillar of salt into which Lot's wife was transformed (and mentioning that, despite being a favorite salt lick for local sheep, it was still growing).

Marco Polo's name is synonymous with adventure and exploration, and his exploits still boggle the mind. In 1272, at the age of seventeen, he set off with his father and uncle on an overland trading mission from Venice to the court of the Chinese emperor. After three years on the road, they finally reached China, where Marco became a favorite of Kublai Khan, serving as his emissary to India. For seventeen years he traveled across Asia, finally returning home through Persia and reaching Venice in 1295. Only a year later, he became a prisoner-of-war during a conflict with Genoa, and he dictated the story of his travels to a fellow prisoner during his captivity. That narrative became an enduring classic of travel.

Europeans were not the only noteworthy travelers of the era. Less known in the West but perhaps even more remarkable was the fourteenth-century Muslim geographer Ibn Battuta. From his home in Morocco, he roamed throughout Asia and Africa. He crossed the Sahara to Timbuktu, sailed to Ceylon and the Maldives, walked the shores of the Black Sea, and traveled as far as China and the Russian steppes. In his wanderings, he reached the boundaries of the Islamic world of his day—and beyond.

For the more typical traveler of this era, the main inspiration for long-distance journeys was religious. Pilgrimage was a central observance of medieval Christianity, with sites both near and far drawing men and women on quests of faith. Devout Norwegians journeyed to pray at the cathedral of St. Olav in Trondheim, while pilgrims from southern Europe traveled the long road to the tomb of St. James in Santiago de Compostela. Others traveled all the way to Rome or felt called to make the grueling journey to the Biblical sites of the Holy Land. For those unable to travel, the Stations of the Cross in a nearby church offered a symbolic pilgrimage to the sites of Christ's crucifixion and resurrection.

Pilgrims traveled to fulfill a vow, to do penance, or to be renewed and strengthened in their faith. To this day, the same motivations draw Christian pilgrims to sites such as Lourdes (in France), which receives an estimated seven million every year. And even larger numbers make pilgrimages to Rome and other holy places during Holy Year celebrations, which have taken place every fifty years since 1300. During the year 2000, about twenty million pilgrims went to Rome to take part in the various ceremonies.

The pilgrimage on the largest scale is the Islamic Hajj to Mecca, which every Muslim must make at least once in his or her lifetime, if physically able. When early Islam was developing on the Arabian peninsula the distance involved was not great, but as the new faith spread as far east as China and as far west as Spain, growing numbers of the faithful undertook arduous journeys of thousands of miles to the holy city. Today, for many Muslims in the Third World, an organized (and subsidized) journey to Mecca may be the only time they will ever travel outside their native countries—or even their native towns.

Travel to Mecca has had profound effects on traditional Islamic societies, bringing people of widely varying social backgrounds together in a setting of (theoretical) equality. At prayer time, a wealthy Turk might rub shoulders with a Malaysian farmer, a North African grandmother could pray next to her Indonesian counterpart. To minimize differences in wealth and status, all pilgrims wear identical plain white garments.

Pilgrimage is prominent in Asian religions as well. For centuries, Hindus from the massive Indian subcontinent have traveled thousands of miles to sites such as Varanasi, where they bathe in the sacred waters of the Ganges River. Buddhists make pilgrimages to sites connected with the life of the Buddha, such as his birthplace in Lumbini (Nepal), and Bodhgaya (India), where he attained enlightenment. Relics of the Buddha are said to be enshrined in eighty-four thousand shrines and stupas, each one a goal for devotion.

Doubtless there has always been an element of pleasure in travel undertaken for other purposes. Religious pilgrims surely enjoyed the new and varied scenery they passed through, and traders were clearly intrigued by the peoples and curious customs they encountered, recording them in their narratives. Given this, it is impossible to say when tourism—which we will define as travel for personal satisfaction—began. The word itself made its first appearance in the *Oxford English Dictionary* in its 1811 edition.

The English custom of sending young men of aristocratic families on a "grand tour" of continental Europe was already well established by the eighteenth century. A period of a year or so spent visiting the art masterpieces of Paris, the royal courts of the European capitals, and the monuments of ancient Rome was considered a nearly indispensable part of one's education, a sort of finishing school for the young gentleman.

Travel conditions were difficult, to say the least, and many areas of natural beauty were daunting obstacles, not tourist attractions. Even in settled areas, the roads were rutted and riding in a carriage was supremely uncomfortable. To cross the Alps, carriages had to be taken apart and carried across the passes by pack animals.

Nonetheless, thousands of young Englishmen (and a few Englishwomen) followed a well-beaten tourist track around the Continent. The first European travel guidebook was published in 1749, covering France, Italy, Germany, and the Netherlands. In addition to masterpieces and monuments, these travelers were drawn to "colorful" local customs. A standard stop for Protestant travelers in Rome was witnessing the ceremony in which young women were admitted to the convent—foreshadowing the twenty-first century backpacker gawking at a Balinese cremation ceremony.

Interest in nature tourism rose with the increasing popularity of landscape painting in the mid–seventeenth century. For the first time, people began to consider that a natural scene such as a mountain range or a forest had intrinsic beauty, rather than being merely an obstacle to travel. In the 1780s, an English minister named William Gilpin published a series of travel books on Wales, Scotland, and the English Lake District, emphasizing the most beautiful landscapes to be painted and how travelers could best appreciate them. The term "picturesque" was used, quite literally, to designate those scenes that would look most pleasing in a picture.

By the 1790s, the Lake District was the destination of choice for British travelers, and there were already loud complaints that the hordes of visitors were destroying the natural beauty that was its drawing card. Flotillas of noisy tour boats crowded the water, and entertainments such as mock naval battles were common. The discerning traveler abandoned the Lake District for the more remote Scottish Highlands, where the process soon repeated itself. One of the underlying themes of modern tourism was born—the quest for an escape from the beaten path, to get away from "one's detestable fellow pilgrim," as Henry James memorably put it.

Such detestable pilgrims, however, were still members of the tiny affluent class that could afford carriages and servants. Affordable travel for the masses had to await the development of the railroads, which began in the 1830s.

In 1841, a young English cabinetmaker and Methodist lay preacher named Thomas Cook had an idea. He felt that he could attract many more working people to his regional Temperance Society meetings if they didn't have to walk the long distance there, and it occurred to him that he might be able to negotiate a reduced train fare if he gathered a large enough group. On his first excursion, 570 traveling teetotalers rode with him the ten miles from Leicester to Loughborough, where they were greeted by a brass band.

The experiment was such a resounding success that he was soon organizing excursions for temperance groups and Sunday school classes all around the area. At the time, the railway network in England was a patchwork of small local lines with bad connections and unfathomable timetables. By planning the itineraries and selling a single ticket at an affordable price, he made it possible for the first time for working-class families to take short trips. He quickly branched out from his religious emphasis and began offering leisure excursions to the seashore and, of course, the Lake District.

Cook firmly believed that travel broadened the mind, and that spending time in clean environments and beautiful scenery was the birthright of all, not merely the aristocracy. His first overseas tour was to Paris in 1861, where he led a "Working Men's Excursion" for English laborers to meet their French counterparts. Over 1,700 travelers took part, staying in temperance hotels and following an arduous itinerary of monuments and museums. And the "working men" were not all men. One of Cook's unheralded achievements was giving Victorian-era women the opportunity to travel unescorted, by joining his eminently respectable groups.

Cook's business expanded rapidly in both scope and volume, attracting a rash of competing firms. He offered trips to Scotland, Italy, and Switzerland. He began leading groups to Egypt and the Holy Land, returning to his religious origins. He added tours to India, China, and New Zealand, and, in the 1890s, he began selling round-the-world tickets with complex steamship itineraries. Needless to say, only the well-to-do could afford these types of holidays, but numerous firms still offered brief trips to the Continent that even working-class families could afford.

By the end of the nineteenth century, mass tourism was firmly established in Europe, and an unprecedented number of people there had come to see pleasure travel, and time spent in nature, as an accepted part of their yearly routine.

The New World: Natural Wonders

Tourism developed differently in the United States. Lacking the history and cultural attractions of Europe, pleasure travel in America centered on natural attractions from its very beginning.

The first long-distance travelers in the young nation did not go to see sights but to escape from the "crowded" East Coast, to distance themselves from legal troubles, or to escape some intolerable personal situation. Remote areas such as the Appalachian Mountains beckoned to such people. Their main escape routes were rivers and slightly improved Indian trails. These "toll roads" also served as livestock-driving pathways. The early explorers of North America, such as Meriwether

Lewis, William Clark, and Alexander Mackenzie, explored, recorded descriptions, plotted locations, and struggled through the wilderness. While they doubtless knew the thrill of discovery, they were hardly pleasure travelers; they were too busy finding coordinates, collecting specimens, making maps, and determining the best trading routes. They were conscious of the overarching purpose of their journey: to expand their new nations.

Pleasure travel, however, began surprisingly early. The first white colonists liked to travel to mineral springs, both for the health benefits they associated with the water and the possibilities for socializing. As early as 1669, Bostonians were visiting Lynn Springs, while Berkeley Springs in (West) Virginia attracted people from the mid-Atlantic region, among them George Washington. Other early destinations drew visitors for their climate. Newport, Rhode Island, attracted throngs of visitors who sailed up from the southern colonies and the West Indies to spend every summer. Its fresh ocean breezes provided a respite from the stifling southern heat, and people spent their time walking on the dunes, collecting seashells, and attending endless social events.

Recognizing Appalachia as a place to visit—and not to avoid—is a recent phenomenon. In earlier times, the difficult travel conditions and forbidding terrain made primitive and mountainous areas unattractive destinations—in Appalachia just as in the Alps. On the other hand, the same qualities made Appalachia a refuge for those trying to escape the crowded East Coast or evade debt, disgrace, or other ties and bonds. The settlers who followed Daniel Boone in the 1770s did not want to be bothered, and they chose the region precisely for its inaccessibility. Independence and a desire to be left alone characterized the temperament of the early settlers, traits still manifested in a variety of religious and cultural expressions today. Anyone who tries to organize modern Appalachians around some pressing issue will soon discover the independence and individualism of mountain people, who are "born to be free."

By the early 1800s, advances in transportation began to make some inland journeys easier. Although Appalachia remained inaccessible, canals were created to link major waterways, and turnpikes connected many cities along the East Coast. But travel was almost unbelievably slow. In 1802, it was possible to go 1,200 miles by direct stagecoach service from Savannah to Boston—but it took three weeks.

This did not deter Americans from traveling. The price of passage to Europe made it a once-in-a-lifetime trip for all but the extremely wealthy, so there soon developed an American version of the "grand tour," centered on the country's most imposing scenery. The classic circuit of the early 1800s ran from New York City through the Catskill Mountains to the Hudson Valley, across to Niagara Falls, and then back to New York by a slightly different route. Some travelers added a loop through the White Mountains of New Hampshire and on to Boston.

Patriotic Americans insisted that the natural wonders of their young nation were the equal of anything in Europe. They compared the Hudson Valley to the Rhine and the Catskills to the Alps. And, of course, nothing in Europe could compare to Niagara Falls, which many visitors viewed as concrete evidence of the power of the Almighty. The Falls were already a prime honeymoon destination in the early nineteenth century—and already equipped with souvenir stands selling Indian crafts.

With the advent of railroads in the 1830s, moderate- or long-distance trips became a bit more comfortable. Instead of a misery to be endured, mechanized transportation made travel an opportunity to look out the window at a changing landscape. Travelers could enjoy the view while the engineer sped the iron horse along the rails. The singing of the wheels on the tracks provided a rhythm to the trip to go with the pleasant countryside, deserts, and mountains. Relative safety (despite the serious railroad accidents and train robberies) was assured to most passengers by the mid–nineteenth century. Thus, for the first time railway passengers became sightseeing "tourists," able to enjoy the ride across the Great Plains and through the Rockies. And the development of the Pullman sleeper car allowed the tourist to go to bed and wake up hundreds of miles away.

As in Europe, the spread of the railroads opened the way to mass tourism. In 1869, the Union Pacific and Central Pacific lines were linked to form the first transcontinental railway. In the next decades, five other transcontinental lines were built. To drum up business, the competing lines began offering cheap summer excursion fares to families, and they prepared guidebooks detailing the attractions of the areas they served.

All of these attractions were nature-based. The Northern Pacific boasted its service to Yellowstone National Park, which was quickly developed with hotels, tent hostels, and wagon roads to make possible a five-day loop tour. The Great Northern Line followed suit by touting the marvels of Glacier National Park, while further north the Canadian Pacific brought tourists to the Canadian Rockies. The Southern Pacific featured Crater Lake (which became a national park in 1902) and the sunny climate of southern California, while the Santa Fe Line advertised the glories of the Grand Canyon and the cultural heritage of the Southwest.

It was in this era that John Muir wrote, "Thousands of tired, nerve-shaken, overcivilized people are beginning to find out that going to the mountains is going home; that wilderness is a necessity; and that mountain parks and reservations are useful not only as fountains of timber and irrigation rivers, but as fountains of life."[2] The Sierra Club, which he founded, began organizing group treks for its members in the Sierra Nevada Wilderness in 1901.

Automobile touring began on a small scale almost as soon as the car was invented. The first coast-to-coast drive took place in 1903—and required fifty-three days! With the advent of the National Highway System in the 1920s, the vision of crossing the country on the Lincoln Highway became a practical reality.

Over time, travelers abandoned their goggles, leather gloves, and vast stocks of spare parts for emergencies. They purchased heavier vehicles with relatively more room and trunk space, packed the bags in back and on top, and set off to see Yellowstone, Pike's Peak, and points beyond. U.S. Route 66 from Chicago to Los Angeles became one of the main routes for sightseers and for people seeking jobs in the Golden State. Some touring cars were convertibles, some were equipped with rumble seats in the rear, some had front windows that cranked open, and some had running boards on the sides with a spare tire attached. Automobile touring was seen as adventurous. Filling stations and country stores dotted the routes; tourist courts of one-room cabins became plentiful, and road maps showed the way. Roads and cars were tying America together—and the public loved it.

With the advent of better roads and the U.S. highway system, Appalachia, along with other previously isolated regions, began to become more connected to the rest of the nation. An account written by W. M. Likins in 1929 tells in detail of a trip along newly finished Kentucky Route 15, "The Appalachian Way." He traveled from Winchester through Whitesburg, Kentucky, crossed the border to Virginia, passing through Norton, Coeburn, and ending up at St. Paul, Virginia. Though today it would be a drive of only several hours on the improved highways, seventy years ago it took days of slow travel. The writer spoke of the picturesque beauty of the landscape and towns, described the Hazard No. 4 coal seam, and mentioned the schools he saw along the way.[3]

Many of the most popular destinations for these early automobile travelers were nature-based. In 1920, nearly a million tourists visited the country's national parks and monuments. Motorists often stayed in the newly established campgrounds in areas where no hotels were available. The first RVs—truck bodies with homemade wooden houses built on the back—made their appearance in the 1920s, and before long, people were getting "back to nature" with incredible amounts of baggage—tents, cots, mattresses, cookstoves, iceboxes, and all the other comforts of home.

Satisfying leisure trips, generally covering less than a hundred miles a day, became increasingly common with the spread of the motorcar. Many roadways were dirt paths for the most part, studded with obstacles such as puzzling road signs and creeks requiring fording. The first cars were real adventures in themselves, with their cranks for starting the engine, the trusty spare tire, and the scattered filling stations with their precious hand-pumped ethyl gasoline. Dust and chickens were always flying in every direction. Young kids scampered and waved at them while dogs chased behind. With time, auto touring became somewhat less of an adventure, as roads became first macadamized and then paved with smooth concrete. But with the increased number of cars and the popular Model T and Model A, the problems of horse manure and road dust were supplanted by congestion and air pollution.

During the 1920s, a prosperous period in the United States, an increasing number of Americans crossed the Atlantic for pleasure. Inflation and economic hardship in Europe made prices there more affordable for Americans, and 437,000 of them traveled overseas in 1928.[4] But the Depression of the 1930s, followed by the outbreak of World War II, put a stop to most recreational travel for a decade and a half.

You Are Here: The Rise of Mass Tourism

One little-remarked aspect of World War II was that, during their military service, ordinary people were exposed to some very extraordinary places. American troops served from the jungles of Burma to the glaciers of Greenland, and GIs in Europe went on leave in towns and scenic regions that had previously been visited only by the wealthiest of Americans. This contact with intriguing, unknown places may be one factor in the upsurge in international travel that has continued ever since then.

The post–World War II period was the era in which opportunities for international travel reached the middle class. As national and international airlines grew, competition between them intensified, and airlines began concentrating on using tourists to fill the seats not occupied by business travelers. And the traffic was two ways, with wealthier Europeans beginning to cross the Atlantic for pleasure.

There was also an economic factor that drew American tourists to Europe. Following the war, the shattered European economies were desperate for U.S. dollars, so for the first time governments opened tourist bureaus overseas to attract visitors. U.S. government policy encouraged Americans to tour Europe, using the slogan, "Trade, not aid."

But the main factor supporting massive growth in international tourism was improvement in air transport. Some long-distance routes had been introduced in the 1930s, but they involved numerous stopovers, and because they relied on seaplanes, they could not operate when temperatures were below freezing. The first scheduled transpacific service in 1935 took a total of sixty hours to get from San Francisco to Manila.[5]

Aviation technology developed during the war made flying dramatically faster—and cheaper. In 1945, flying from New York to Paris took twenty-two hours. Only four years later, that time had been cut to twelve hours, and many airlines were competing to offer luxury service—including sleeping berths! The advent of commercial jet service in the 1960s transformed plane travel from a once-in-a-lifetime luxury to a common vacation choice for middle-class families in the developed world.

International travel has increased exponentially in recent decades.

The number of international arrivals increased from 25 million in
1972 to 528 million in 1996, according to the World Tourism Organization.[6] In 2000, according to data collected by the International Air
Transport Association, over 1.4 billion passengers traveled on scheduled flights of its member airlines—an increase of 5.2 percent over the
previous year. And these passengers were traveling ever greater distances—the number of international passengers up 9 percent from
than the year before.[7]

Travel closer to home is booming as well. In 1999, U.S. residents
made over 346 million pleasure trips, staying an average of 3.7 nights
away from home and spending a total of $426 billion. The top tourist
magnets in 1998 were California, Florida, and Texas, but even last-
place North Dakota took in over a billion dollars in tourist expenditures.

There is simply no question that tourism in Appalachia is ripe for
further development. The challenge of merely getting around has since
subsided, as better roads, including tollways and interstates, crisscross
the region. One can get within fifty or a hundred miles of most places
in the region on higher-speed highways, though driving the smaller
highways may still be an adventure—especially if a logging or coal
truck blocks the way. Regional tourism is rapidly becoming big business, and states like West Virginia and Kentucky are banking heavily
on the industry.

The Spiraling Scope of Travel

An underlying theme in the history of travel is the ever-broadening
range of travel as recreation. Social and technological changes have
made journeys once undertaken only out of practical necessity now
comfortable enough to undertake for pleasure.

Tourism began at the local level, in an era when all but the shortest
journeys were too expensive or arduous to be undertaken lightly. In
that era, pleasure travel included such activities as Sunday or weekend
strolls, local wedding, funeral, or festival processions, the Way of the
Cross (for those Christians who could not travel to the Holy Land in
the late Middle Ages), hunting and fishing for sport, berry- or nut-
gathering expeditions during the growing season, and visits to relatives.

For centuries, most touring was no more than strolls and family outings on a Sunday afternoon. Little wonder that earlier vacations consisted of visiting relatives and friends for short periods of time when they lived nearby, or for occasional longer stays at a greater distance. Visiting another farm was about as far as tourism went for most rural people, while a trip downtown was the limit of big city touring.

Footpaths, canoe routes, traces, turnpikes, canals, railroads, and then surface roads all increased the scope of touring, making it first regional, then national, and ultimately global. The barrier of the oceans was first traversed by clipper ships and then steamships and ocean liners; then in the last century there was the leap over the vast distances by airplanes, bringing people distances in a matter of hours that had taken weeks in ocean vessels.

Today, except for refugees or hard-core "adventure" travelers, travel seldom holds the danger and discomfort that it did for our immigrant ancestors who braved the holds of sailing ships. Now, simply getting there is no longer challenge enough; for many people, adventure means touching the last remote reaches of a well-trodden globe. Our thoroughly explored world has been "discovered" by almost all peoples, and present-day tourists will find traces of previous visitors in virtually every deep cavern and craggy mountain they explore.

Missing out on the thrill of being there first may discourage some travelers, and other motivations will have to develop. However, some would-be "discoverers" are turning their attention to outer space, hoping to find there some place to land and explore on some heavenly body.

Pleasure travel may now be reaching that level. In 2001, a wealthy American named Dennis Tito paid the Russian space agency $20 million for a ride to the new space laboratory being built in outer space. He called himself the "first space tourist," but even that has been contested. On December 2, 1990, Toyohiro Akiyama, a reporter for the Japanese television network TBS, traveled on the same type of Soyuz rocket that Tito did and docked with Mir—at a cost of tens of millions of dollars.

However, it is not just the Russians who have sold flights into space. In 1985 NASA launched Senator Jake Garn aboard the space shuttle Discovery. It can also be argued that Senator John Glenn's second ride in space was nothing more than pleasure travel under public subsidy. Space agencies are now thinking in commercial terms, and in a short while the rich and famous will be blasting off to outer space—largely at taxpayer expense. It was just such high-rolling benefactor/tourists who were on an American naval submarine distracting the crew in 2001 when it accidentally struck and sunk a small Japanese fishing expedition near Hawai'i and killed nine, some of them young students.

Wouldn't it be fun to cavort about a cabin in a space suit, without the normal drag of gravity pulling you down? Space tourism is attractive, and yet it is so very costly, even when subsidized by the government. Still in its early development, it is indeed a "journey" with many difficulties, rather than a mere tourist trip. Columbus's voyages, the Lewis and Clark expedition, and other such voyages of discovery involved risk to human safety and the possibility that disaster could occur—as did happen in travels such as Amelia Earhart's flight around the world.

Space claims to be that last "frontier"—but is that appeal to pioneer courage and independence really justified? In space, all travelers live on artificial life-support systems, all need immensely expensive rocket send-offs, and all must have technical backup from programs and agencies that cost the taxpayers billions. Why should a few thrill-seekers be subsidized at the expense of the taxpayer, and why should the various international agencies allow this practice, especially since they should know that such elitism will not enhance the popularity of financially strapped space programs?

Today, the very notion of adventure travel is changing. Reading a catalog from a high-end adventure tour operator can be a profoundly depressing experience. Travels that even twenty years ago would have been regarded as a once-in-a-lifetime experience are now commonplace events, baseball cards to collect and show off. Angkor Wat, Mount Everest Base Camp, canoeing the Amazon, and gorilla safaris are all depicted in succulent adjectives to tempt the most jaded traveler. In an effort to increase sales, tourism promoters are in a heated competition to package and sell new and ever more alluring types of travel, and in touting their offerings of "unspoiled" destinations, they unwittingly underline their own negative impact. As geographer David Zurick points out, "The adventure tours unwittingly confront the disturbing fact that in their search for authenticity, the tourists dispel the very qualities which they seek."[8]

A Look Inside the Tourist Machine

As we have seen, tourism is often proclaimed to be the "world's largest industry." Some components of this tourist machine are familiar names to anyone who has ever driven an interstate highway or flown from an American airport. A single major airline—United, American, Delta, Northwest, and British Airways—may fly to airports on every continent. Hotel chains like Hilton, Marriott, and Best Western have properties overlooking Alaskan glaciers and Arabian deserts. Major car rental chains, including Hertz and Avis, offer identical cars from identical offices around the globe. Other high-profile tourism participants are cruise lines, rail lines, travel agency chains, tour operators, and amusement parks.

Needless to say, there are also smaller regional and local companies, such as hotels, rental car services, and restaurants. And at the bottom of the tourist food chain are the mom-and-pop motel, the family-owned restaurant, and the quirky local tourist attraction advertised only by word of mouth.

But who, exactly, runs the industry? In this era of increased globalization, it should come as no surprise that many of the major players are international trade organizations and huge transnational corporations (TNCs). For a quick snapshot of the tourism industry, it's worth looking at the major industry bodies and who participates in them.

The main international organization in travel is the World Tourism Organization (sometimes referred to as WTO-OMT, adding its European name to distinguish it from the World Trade Organization). It originated as the International Union of Official Tourist Publicity Organizations in 1925, in The Hague, and was later renamed the International Union for Official Tourism Organizations (IUOTO) and expanded to include not only government tourism agencies but also tourism-related companies. In 1967, it became an intergovernmental organization. The IUOTO was renamed the World Tourism Organization in 1975 and signed a formal cooperation agreement with the United Nations two years later. It is an executing agency of the United Nations Development Program.

What is highly unusual about the WTO-OMT, now headquartered in Madrid, is that membership is open not only to government agencies, but also to corporations. The WTO-OMT boasts in its own literature that it is "the only intergovernmental body that offers membership to the operating sector and in this way offers a unique contact point for discussion between government officials and industry."

In 2001, membership of the WTO-OMT consisted of the tourist boards of 139 countries, along with over 350 "affiliate members," divided into the Education Council (ninety university-level training and research institutions) and the Business Council. The Board of Directors of the Business Council represents many big-name corporations, from Japan Airlines to MasterCard International, and the membership list is a virtual roll-call of entities that stand to profit from people's desire to go somewhere else: from the Association of Brazilian Travel Agencies to VISA International. Conspicuously absent, however, are non-governmental organizations (NGOs) and activist groups promoting fair or sustainable tourism. Though in theory there is nothing to prevent them from joining, the basic annual membership fee is $1800, which few grassroots activists can afford.

WTO-OMT's primary role is promoting the growth of tourism. The organization's analysts carry out a tremendous amount of research on the scope of tourism and its impact on the world economy. They are a prime source of widely quoted factoids like the one about the "world's largest industry." Though activist groups have questioned statistics such as these, they lack the money and resources to carry out this type of wide-ranging research.

This emphasis on the significance of tourism in the economies of countries around the world has a highly self-serving purpose. Through it, the WTO-OMT argues for government policies favoring the industry and portray any opposition to tourism development as a threat to people's livelihood. In their view, the cure for economic underdevelopment in the Third World can be summarized in two words: *promote tourism*. Of course, their main thrust is not family-run guesthouses, but massive corporate-owned resorts.

Another important body is the World Travel and Tourism Council, made up of the CEOs of seventy major international corporations involved in the tourism industry. Though the roster of members includes some predictable people (the CEOs of Marriott International, the

Hertz Corporation, and five of the world's ten largest airlines), others represent companies not generally linked with tourism in the public mind: Boeing, MasterCard International, Yapi Kredi Bank of Turkey, AIG Insurance. This should give some idea of the economic heavy-weights attempting to promote and benefit from the growth of tourism.

The WTTC, too, hires armies of statisticians and analysts to chart and predict the future of tourism, with similar results, and similar aims. A WTTC report produced in 2001 stated that worldwide travel and tourism was expected to generate $4.5 trillion of economic activity that year, a figure that would grow to $9.3 trillion by 2011—an annual growth rate of 4 percent in real terms.

Its philosophy is similar, too. Its 2000 report *Linking the Past With the Future* asserted, "Travel and tourism can be an engine, and sometimes the engine, for generating jobs and wealth in the world's emerging economies."

These industry organizations have their domestic counterparts within the United States. The Travel Business Roundtable, headquartered in Washington, D.C., was formed in 1995 "to educate legislative leaders—on the national and state levels—of the importance of the industry to the nation's economy." Its seventy-plus members, all top executives of travel-related corporations, are each asked to spend one day a year in Washington meeting with "lawmakers and policy makers" and also to "develop relationships with elected officials in their home districts." Underlining the burgeoning scope of the industry, membership includes executives not only of Delta Airlines and Walt Disney Attractions, but also of Coca-Cola Corporation, Diners Club, and the National Football League.

The main national industry body is the TIAA, which produces a vast amount of PR material tying the economic well-being of the United States to a flourishing tourism industry. In the aftermath of the World Trade Center attacks in 2001, it produced TV and radio campaigns, posters, information kits, and a jazzy logo promoting Americans' "Freedom to Travel."

While the scope of the tourism industry has expanded to encompass an ever broader range of businesses and activities, many well-known tourism-related companies have themselves branched out into an ever-growing range of activities.

Thomas Cook, the British firm that began by organizing temperance picnics, now owns the largest chain of travel agencies in the UK, with over seven hundred offices. It operates six different tour companies as well as its own charter airline, and has subsidiaries in India, Egypt, and Canada. It sells travel insurance and issues credit cards and only recently sold its huge travelers' check and currency exchange businesses, which will continue to operate under the Thomas Cook brand name. Not bad for a Methodist lay preacher.

American Express, which though founded in 1850 didn't even enter the tourism industry until the early twentieth century, is even more astonishingly diversified. Best known to tourists for its travelers' checks (which it likes to call "cheques"), it also issues a variety of credit and charge cards; sells mutual funds, insurance, and annuities; provides brokerage services, accounting, and tax preparation for businesses—and still claims to be "the world's largest travel agency."

Overall, the trend in tourism is for increasing integration of different areas of operation under the umbrella of a single corporation. With the globalization of the economy, ownership of the world's airlines, hotels, tour operators, and travel agents is increasingly concentrated in transnational corporations, overwhelmingly based in the developed world. For example, in 1995, nineteen of the twenty largest hotel chains in the world were based in North America or Europe.

"Hosts" and "Guests"

One unusual feature of tourism as an industry is that it mimics and reflects a social relationship: that between a host and a guest. In fact, references to careers in the "hospitality industry" (specifically lodging and food service) are common.

Clearly, there are parallels between the commercial and noncommercial varieties of "hospitality," and in many cases the welcome that is given to tourists springs from genuine warmth and a desire to share the scenic and cultural bounty of one's hometown with visitors. However, it's important to keep in mind the differences between tourism and the genuine, noncommercial guest-host relationship.

For one thing, the tourism version of such a relationship is transitory. Unless a visitor comes back to the same town and the same restaurant year after year, his interaction with the waiter who serves his table will never move beyond the most superficial level. Furthermore, the relationship is unequal. Unlike true hosts who welcome guests voluntarily, tourism workers are generally less affluent than the customers they serve, and the "hosts" are at work, while the "guests" enjoy leisure. In all too many cases, low-paid tourism workers can't afford the enjoyable experiences that they provide for visiting vacationers. And, most importantly, the interactions between tourism workers and tourists are programmed, not spontaneous.

There has been a great deal of research on the relationship between tourism workers and tourists. Anthropologist Valene Smith points out, "Catering to guests is a repetitive, monotonous business, and although the questions posed by each visitor may be 'new' to him, hosts can become bored as if a cassette has been turned on. . . . As guests become dehumanized objects that are tolerated for economic gain, tourists have little alternative other than to look upon their hosts only . . . as objects."[9]

Smith and others have analyzed how relationships between tourists and local people change as the industry becomes increasingly developed. After fieldwork in Barbados and Canada, G. V. Doxey developed his widely cited "index of tourist irritation" to describe how communities react to increasing levels of tourism. His "irridex" covers four main stages. In the first, "euphoria," local people are enthused about tourism and its benefits and welcome the first trickle of visitors. In the next stage, "apathy," the community takes the presence of tourists for granted, and contact with visitors becomes more impersonal. In the third stage, "irritation," tourism nears the limit of carrying capacity, causing strain on the community. At the fourth stage, "antagonism," the tension becomes overt, and the community blames the tourists for all its problems. Beyond this is the "final stage," in which the environment is destroyed and cultural values lost.

Of course, not all people in a community will share the same opinion, and the process is hardly inevitable. It's easy to imagine well-planned tourism programs that produce a flow of visitors at a level tolerable (and beneficial) to the community. But Doxey's model suggests that the relationship between visitors and the visited is not a static thing—and is not always positive.

Furthermore, where the cultural difference between tourists and the residents of the destination is part of the attraction, the host culture itself becomes part of the commercial equation. In a paper entitled "Culture by the Pound," Davydd J. Greenwood discusses the example of a festival called the Alarde in Fuenterrabia, Spain. Every year, the population ceremonially reenacted the breaking of a historic siege of the town, with much pageantry and gunfire. When the government asked that it be performed twice in the same day so that more tourists could see it, the townspeople simply stopped participating, because the ritual lost its meaning for them.

Greenwood observes, "Worldwide, we are seeing the transformation of cultures into 'local color,' making people's cultures extensions of the modern mass media. . . . For the moneyed tourist, the tourism industry promises that the world is his/hers to use. All the 'natural resources,' including cultural traditions, have their price, and if you have the money in hand, it is your right to see whatever you wish."[10]

Room to Grow

Though the actual size of the tourism industry is debatable, there can be little question that tourism is big and growing bigger. An increasingly interconnected network of corporations is competing for opportunities for further expansion, trying to increase their sales and market share by packaging ever more profitable "travel experiences" and selling them to an ever larger market of travelers.

And one region with a high potential for expansion in tourism is Appalachia. Despite its array of attractions—natural, historic, and cultural—many parts of the Appalachian region receive only a small number of visitors. For example, West Virginia, despite its stunning mountain scenery, masterful traditional crafts, and world-class whitewater rafting, ranks only forty-fourth among U.S. states in annual receipts from tourism. At the same time, the state's unemployment rate and other economic indicators compare unfavorably with national averages.

Organizations such as the WTO-OMT and their corporate members proclaim that they can offer a sure cure for economic underdevelopment. What harm can there be in trying to get more people to come and visit and pump some cash into the economy? Plenty, as we will see.

CHAPTER 2

Mountain Mist

Appalachian Tourism Today

In 1908, a wealthy young easterner accompanied his uncle on a trip to
Harlan County, Kentucky. While the uncle spent long days researching
land titles in the county courthouse, his nephew had plenty of time to
write letters home, describing the area in rapturous terms: "The most
beautiful country we have seen yet. The sides of the valley going up
2000 feet, heavily wooded with great poplars, chestnuts and a dozen
or two other deciduous trees and every mile or so a fertile bottom with
fine crops and a stream of splendid water." He wrote about the "magnificent view" above Cumberland Gap, "the Cumberland River—one
of the most beautiful in the land", and "gorges that for sheer beauty
beat anything we saw in the Black Forest."[1]

   The writer was Franklin D. Roosevelt, traveling with his uncle
Warren Delano Jr. Delano was a railroad developer who had come to
Kentucky to buy up mineral rights along a new railroad route, paying
paltry sums to mountain people for a resource that would make mil-
lionaires of outsiders. Roosevelt was the first in a succession of distin-
guished visitors to Central Appalachia: JFK making a campaign stop in
Charleston, West Virginia, and Lyndon Johnson sitting on a front
porch in Martin County, Kentucky; Richard Nixon making his first
public appearance after his resignation in Hyden, Kentucky, and Bill
Clinton touring a factory in Jackson County, Kentucky. Like other less
famous tourists, they were taken with what they saw.

   Stories such as these encapsulate tourism in Appalachia, now as in
the early days. Visitors come to Appalachia and enjoy the region's scenic beauty and hospitality. They bring much-needed cash into the local

29

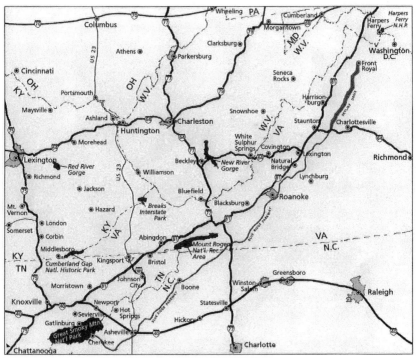

The central Appalachian region. Map by Mark Spencer.

economy. But these economic benefits can be outweighed by the negative impact of tourism on the land and on the culture. We will examine each of these issues—attractions, economic benefits, and impacts on the environment and the economy—in turn.

Appalachia's Drawing Cards

Prior to the development of air-conditioning and DDT, mountain retreats were extremely popular with people in the American South who wanted to escape from humid, mosquito-plagued lowland cities during the summer. This climatic advantage made Appalachian eastern slope destinations (West Virginia, Virginia, and North Carolina) summertime magnets during the nineteenth and early twentieth centuries. Needless to say, a tourist destination these days requires considerably more in the way of attractions to draw visitors. Present-day Appalachia has numerous features that make it well qualified to compete for a slice of the massive tourist pie.

Natural Attractions and Outdoor Activities

The most important feature of the region is obviously the mountains, which run in a long range from the Maritime Provinces of Canada to northeastern Alabama. Our focus here is on the Central Appalachian Mountains—namely, eastern Kentucky and Tennessee, western North Carolina and Virginia, and the whole state of West Virginia. Some would include southeastern Ohio in this area as well. This mountain range stretches northeast to southwest as the eastern spine of the continent; they are older mountains, often regarded as less impressive than the Rockies. Though they have a more smooth and worn look, they are covered with temperate forests, graced with verdant valleys and swift, clear-running streams.

The Appalachian Mountains are the heart of the eastern United States—and for the native-born, also a land with a heart. Mountain people conceive of the land as shaping their identity and, even when they are migrants in exile, look back on it as the place that somehow makes them who they are. Many Appalachian "émigrés" still maintain strong ties to their native place, in contrast to other U.S. regions. For example, the monthly magazine *Kentucky Explorer* advertises itself as being "for Kentuckians everywhere." It's difficult to conceive of a periodical published "for New Jerseyites everywhere." Without this land, there would be no Appalachian culture. Authors like poet James Still have waxed eloquent on the love of the people for their land, and no sensitive person could visit this region without noticing the intimate link.

One of the most famous recreational attractions of the mountains is the Appalachian Trail, running from Maine to Georgia through 2,100 miles of ever-changing terrain. Every year, a handful of hardy "through hikers" walk the complete distance, while countless others enjoy backpacking trips or shorter, single-day hikes. Campgrounds and hiking trails of state and national parks in the mountains draw visitors from the region and farther afield.

Appalachia is also blessed with many rivers and streams for water recreation and fishing. West Virginia is especially well known for its trout and bass streams, and the geologically unique New River, regarded as the oldest on the continent, is famed for its white-water rafting. North Carolina and Virginia have Appalachian east slope streams with plentiful fish as well. Tennessee is blessed with the valleys and craggy ledges of the Cumberland, Holston, and Nolichucky rivers. Kentucky, surprisingly, claims to have more rivers than any other state among the "lower forty-eight"—the Kentucky, the Rockcastle, and the Red are but a few. Those wishing to canoe, go white-water rafting, or hike near water find that the Central Appalachian region has an abundance of good locations, which are receiving an increasing influx of visitors.

Central Appalachia has a number of large lakes, which are generally man-made, unlike the more famous lakes of Minnesota and the upper Midwest. These extensive impounded reservoirs, especially in the Tennessee Valley Authority (TVA) region and in the lake region of Kentucky, draw visitors from surrounding cities such as Cincinnati, Dayton, Indianapolis, Memphis, Columbus, and Louisville. Motorboating and houseboating are two popular activities. Similarly, Virginia has Smith Mountain Lake and North Carolina has Fontana Lake. Many lovers of the outdoors are also drawn to West Virginia's Stonewall Jackson Lake in the central part of the state. Besides these large impounded lakes, the region is dotted with small private lakes and ponds, which allow fee fishing on a day-by-day basis. Such "pay lakes" are favorites of families with young children and with older people who want to fish in clean water and eat their catch.

Woods make up about 90 percent of the Appalachian region, and many of these areas are quite attractive for camping and hiking. Though numerous foot trails exist, the beauty of the forested areas is most easily accessible from public roadways and park areas. Stretching in a band from southwestern Pennsylvania to north central Alabama is what biologist Lucy Braun has termed the Mixed Mesophytic Forest, noteworthy for containing a greater variety of tree species than any other temperate forest in the world. The geographic center of that forest lies in east central Kentucky, near the border dividing Owsley and Clay Counties. The forest is the true Appalachian treasure, and its continuing presence must not be taken for granted. Opportunistic diseases that attack trees weakened by acid rain and other air pollutants are already affecting trees in the higher elevations of North Carolina and Virginia.

Central Appalachia has a number of geological formations that are of interest to sports enthusiasts as well as sightseers. Natural Bridge, in Virginia just off Interstate 81, has been called one of the seven natural wonders of the world. Kentucky's own Natural Bridge, in the northeastern part of the state, is spectacular in its own right, along with nearby Sky Bridge. The Cumberland Gap National Historic Park area, where Virginia, Tennessee, and Kentucky meet, is noted for its scenic beauty and rock overhangs, especially now that U.S. Route 25 East has recently been tunneled beneath the gap proper, and the landscape is being restored to its earlier appearance. The Red River Gorge in northeastern Kentucky is another site that is extremely popular for rock climbing, camping, and sightseeing. In fact, the carrying capacity of that wilderness area had been exceeded for a number of years; only recently has the Daniel Boone National Forest taken steps to preserve this rugged and fragile area.

Seneca Rocks in eastern West Virginia is a spectacular tourist attraction that can be reached from Elkins or by traveling from the East over some very scenic routes from Interstate 81. Other unusual rock formations can be seen at the side of Interstate 75 in Tennessee north of Knoxville, and along the sides of numerous small roads in the region. Several hours to the southeast, gorgeous mountain rock formations are accessible by traveling east on Interstate 40 from the

Tennessee border. Additional significant Appalachian rock features are the granitic domes found from Brevard, North Carolina, to northwestern South Carolina.

Many parts of the Appalachian Region have soft porous limestone formations, overlaid in parts with sandstone. These limestone areas contain deep fissures and sinkholes and are characterized by caves and underground streams. Though the famous attraction of Mammoth Cave National Park in western Kentucky is outside of the Appalachian region, every Central Appalachian state has less known but still intriguing caves, such as Luray Caverns in Virginia and Great Saltpeter Cave in south central Kentucky. Caving enthusiasts can explore such destinations as Smoke Hole Caverns and Scott Hollow Cave in West Virginia.

A final natural attraction of the region is its mineral springs. Hot Springs, North Carolina, has come back to life as a mineral bath location after experiencing a boom period in the nineteenth century and then falling into disuse for decades. Others, from Berkeley Springs in West Virginia, to White Sulfur Springs on the Virginia–West Virginia border, to Bluelicks in Kentucky, have a resort and tourist potential that goes beyond "taking the waters." Many of these historic places have motel capacity that can be utilized for tourists and for business meetings, and have nearby attractions worth a detour.

Popular Tourist Attractions

There are always some people who prefer to follow the crowd—and there are plenty of Appalachian sites that cater to them. The Tennessee towns of Gatlinburg and Pigeon Forge are well known to many Middle American tourists, with their catalog of "attractions" such as Ripley's Believe It or Not and the Star Cars Museum. Cherokee, North Carolina, has a similar array of facilities. Tourists who want to see the fall foliage at the most popular public location, Great Smoky Mountains National Park and its immediate environment, can find themselves caught in a massive traffic jam.

There are also package tours that take travelers through all the "must sees" of the region at a rapid clip. For example, an autumn foliage tour offered by Worldwide Country Tours (Greendale, Wisconsin) begins and ends in Nashville, but spends about half the time in

Central Appalachia, with such stops as Asheville, North Carolina, and the grounds of the Vanderbilt estate; a visit to Lookout Mountain and the scenic view of Chattanooga, the Oconaluftee Indian Village and the Cherokee heritage area; and Cumberland Falls, with its moonbow and the second-largest waterfall east of the Mississippi.

Many tourists are biased in favor of big cities and big-name attractions. A trip to New York "must" include Broadway plays, the Statue of Liberty, and on and on. However, if one overcomes the prejudice that certain places must be toured and certain snapshots taken, then the novel attractions of the mountains become more of a draw, especially to the large number of people who do not want to battle the seeming hostility of a distant urban metropolis, or the congestion involved in simply getting around. Once they overcome this bias in favor of the urban, travelers are more inclined to discover Appalachian scenic and recreational diversity in a multitude of features—festivals, natural areas, state parks, water activities, and cultural and historic sites.

A sometimes-overlooked attraction in Appalachian tourism is the potential positive value of isolation. Locations far from urban centers or resorts during the off-season can be valuable settings for conferences and business meetings. Organizers may put a premium on mini mizing distractions, so that participants will be able to give focused attention to the task at hand. An overly diverting location can sabotage the outcome of a conference. For example, attendance at meetings for public interest groups at the 1982 Knoxville World's Fair was high at the beginning, and then tapered off dramatically because the fair was luring participants away. On the other hand, when conferences are held at even the most popular winter resorts during the off-season, attendance at meetings is generally good, because there are few immediate outside attractions. Ski resorts such as Snowshoe in West Virginia host successful meetings from spring through fall.

Scenic Views

While outdoor sport enthusiasts choose vacation destinations on the basis of specific natural features—for instance, white-water rafters seek out challenging rapids—a large number of vacationers are interested in the natural environment as a scenic whole. By some estimates, sightseeing makes up over 40 percent of total tourist activity. It is relaxing, enjoyable, and easily accessible to tourists who are unable to participate in more strenuous activities, such as the elderly and people with disabilities. A high percentage of visitors seek out Appalachia expressly for its scenery—from the blossoming redbud trees of spring to the autumn colors in Great Smoky Mountains National Park.

As an example, with its curving roadways and low speed limits, the Blue Ridge Parkway is an ideal place to savor beautiful landscapes. The federal government owns only about a narrow thousand-foot strip along parkway routes and thus has not had to displace a large number of people, as occurred in some of the other parks in the region. The government bought longer-term renewable scenic conservation easements along the parkway from private landholders in order to keep the viewscape pristine. However, there is strong economic pressure to turn lands adjacent to the parkway into resort motels, summer homes, and other developments. Combined with these pressures is the dieback of high-elevation forested areas due to air pollution. Much of Central Appalachia affords sightseeing opportunities, provided that the routes are selectively chosen to avoid man-made disasters such as slurry ponds, forest clear-cuts and ugly road-cuts.

West Virginia, the Mountain State, is a perfect place to launch a sightseeing tour of the region, as it is easily approached from the populous Midwest and Northeast of the U.S., plus eastern Canada. The state's mountain beauty can easily be observed while traveling Interstates 64, 77, and 79, where one can see the verdant forested hills in summer, the flowering dogwoods and redbuds of spring, and visually appealing autumn colors. The side roads are even more spectacular. Rafting the many rivers of the state gives a different, and equally scenic, perspective.

In Virginia, the Heart of Appalachia Tourism Authority has prepared a visitors' guide to the most beautiful views of the mountains in southwestern Virginia. It lists a variety of scenic drives through the countryside and includes such sites as the Pinnacles Natural Area Preserve near Lebanon, Burke's Garden (with a scenic walk) in Tazewell County, and a section of the Trans-America Bike Route. Excellent roads link the attractions in one of the most beautiful sections of the state. More systematic tourists can follow the Daniel Boone Wilderness Trail from the starting point at the Netherland Inn in Kingsport, North Carolina, through Gate City, Duffield, and Jonesville to the

Cumberland Gap. At the beautiful and majestic gap, tourists are closer
to seven other state capitals than they are to Richmond.

Beyond Cumberland Gap, the Wilderness Road continues into
Kentucky; it was once the route over which nearly a million people
passed to begin America's westward expansion. The highway tunnel
under the mountains has allowed the original trail to be restored near
Middlesboro, Kentucky, offering a fine place for hiking and enjoying
mountain views. One may follow the trail into London and on over
Wildcat Mountain, the scene of a minor Civil War battle, to its destination at Fort Boonesborough or another branch in the middle of the
Bluegrass State. Visitors can also head east again into Harlan County
and take the Trail of the Lonesome Pine in the direction of Black
Mountain or Breaks Interstate Park. Taking back roads gives the full
flavor of the mountain scenery and the overhanging rock formations.

Mountainous eastern Tennessee has been well known to tourists
for some time, receiving the heavy traffic of visitors coming to
Gatlinburg and our region's most-visited national park, Great Smoky
Mountains, bordering North Carolina. Another scenic excursion is
westward to Norris, with a stop at the Appalachian Museum, which
can add a spice of mountain culture to the sights of the area. West of
Interstate 75 on the Cumberland Plateau are a number of sites showing
the beauty of the Volunteer State. These include the Catoosa Wildlife
Management Area north of Interstate 40 and Bledsoe State Park and
Fall Creek Falls State Park south of Interstate 40. Further east are the
many sites in the Cherokee National Forest.

North Carolina, the Tar Heel State, has been called the most diverse for scenery in all of America, since it stretches from beautiful
seacoast to rugged, forested mountains. While parts of this area are all
too well known to tourists, there are still many backroads areas to
discover: the New River, Mt. Jefferson, Lake James, Mount Mitchell
and Black Mountain State Parks, Grandfather Mountain, and, further
southwest in the corner of the state, the Pisgah National Forest. Lakes,
forests, and mountains intersect in that part of the state, which is being
discovered by more and more visitors each year.

A scenic forest that is a sightseeing destination produces a continuing and long-lasting stream of economic benefits, unlike the timber
harvested from an ugly clear-cut landscape. Scenic views are both aes-
thetically pleasing and economically beneficial. Retaining the Appala-

chian viewscape will require concerted effort on the part of public
agencies and private citizens.

Hospitality

Many visitors remark how Appalachian people pride themselves in
their genuine friendliness and courtesy to strangers. This stands in startling contrast to one of the stereotypes of the region's people as half-
crazed hermits who threaten intruders with their shotguns. In reality,
aggression is far less common in the mountains than in urban areas,
and gracious hospitality is nearly always the case.

> I once had the experience of driving in a borrowed pickup truck from
> Washington, D.C., to Kentucky, when the truck broke down in central
> West Virginia. Some local "good ole boys" took an interest in my
> predicament and got the truck going again. It took them several hours,
> so I offered them some money for their trouble. They were somewhat
> offended, and refused. They said that if they were in Kentucky and
> broke down, they would expect the same help from neighborly
> mountain folks. It's not by chance that Kentucky's board of tourism is
> promoting the state under the slogan "Kentucky: It's that friendly."
>
> —Al Fritsch

Managers of tourist facilities know that friendly staff will bring
satisfied visitors back again and again, and serve as advertising
through word of mouth. To fill the jobs, they select local people who
are outgoing, friendly, hardworking, knowledgeable about the area,
willing to interact with visitors, and serious about accomplishing good
work. This added flavor of dedication to work is considered a major
asset by the Appalachian tourist agencies—and they often focus on this
in the literature.

Accessibility

A day's drive from about half of America's homes—the region is
bounded by New York, Chicago, Atlanta, and St. Louis—puts travelers in Central Appalachia. This is a matter of easy driving on interstate
highways with convenient rest stops and an abundance of inexpensive
motels. Central Appalachia is directly linked with Atlanta and Detroit
via Interstate 75; Chicago, St. Louis, and the Virginia coast via

Interstates 65 and 64; Pennsylvania and New York via Interstate 81; Cleveland and South Carolina via Interstate 77; and Memphis and the North Carolina Piedmont via Interstate 40. Adding connector routes and a second day, another quarter of America is included, from Maine to Florida and from Minnesota to Texas.

Despite this proximity, Appalachia can seem almost a foreign country to people from other American regions—and this can, in fact, be a positive factor. Many Americans are reluctant to travel overseas, because of the difficulty—real or perceived—of dealing with foreign languages, strange currency, complicated airline tickets, and the bureaucratic headaches of passports and visas. Nonetheless, they still enjoy getting away to a culturally different place. Americans living near the Canadian border will find that Quebec and other parts of Canada fulfill such expectations, but crossing an international border still presents a psychological hurdle, and the prospect of dealing with French-speakers may also prove daunting. Central Appalachia can fill this craving for foreignness for more Americans than any other region of North America—and with lower travel and lodging costs. The highway network is convenient, motel accommodations are generally quite good, tasty food is available, and the language is the same—well, mostly!

Many blue-collar workers with limited vacation time are not interested in distant destinations, but prefer to spread their vacation days and dollars throughout the year, for weekends and short-term travel periods. For people in the Cincinnati, Columbus, Dayton, Indianapolis, Louisville, Lexington, Nashville, Pittsburgh, Atlanta, St. Louis, and Memphis urban areas, Central Appalachia is an attractive destination for short forays. Spending only moderate amounts of money, they can trail their boats or campers, camp out or stay with friends, and head home on Sunday afternoon in time to punch in on Monday morning.

These same metropolitan areas are the origin for weekend participants in activities such as caving, rafting, winter sports, hiking, camping and white-water rafting. Again, they may lack the money or inclination for exotic recreational activities requiring large amounts of money, such as gambling and coral reef scuba diving. Many outdoor enthusiasts welcome the opportunity to practice their sport closer to home on a regular basis, without having to budget the time or money required to go further afield. Busy professionals with very limited vacation or leisure time also find proximate tourist areas a great entice-

ment. State tourism boards are beginning to see the benefits of marketing to cash- and time-short weekenders, and to short-term visitors
wanting a change in scenery.

Economic Benefits—and Leakage

Tourism is Kentucky's third-largest industry, and it ranks equally high
in the economies of the neighboring Appalachian states. It is not easy
to calculate exactly what portion of the tourist dollar in each of these
states is spent in the Appalachian sections, except in the state of West
Virginia, which is entirely in Appalachia and has a $1.8 billion annual
tourist trade. The major portion of Kentucky's tourism industry is in
the non-Appalachian golden triangle (Louisville, Lexington, and
Northern Kentucky); Tennessee's tourist map includes the central and
western regions—the country music capital Nashville and Elvisland in
Memphis; Virginia's figures include the D.C. area and Mount Vernon
and its eastern shore and tidewater with Jamestown and Williamsburg;
North Carolina's Piedmont and Outer Banks are heavy tourist attractions as well. In fact, in these four partially Appalachian states, the
mountain regions do not exceed a quarter to a third of these states'
total tourist revenues.

However, this does not negate the vital role that tourism plays in
the Appalachian economy on a local scale. In economically depressed
areas, every low-paid service job has its own importance when people
cannot easily leave the region and lack higher-paying local opportunities. In many cases, service employment is a second household income,
and one that is seasonal, which permits other work in the off-season.
Because tourist services are not highly paid, outsiders may look down
on employment in tourist facilities such as motels and gas stations. The
actual workers, however, may see these as honest, satisfying, and often
pleasant jobs, though of a lower-paying variety.

Tourism in the Central Appalachian region may exceed five billion
dollars a year, and it is growing by several percent a year.[2] These cumu-
lative figures become more impressive when seen in the light of
Appalachia's extractive industries, coal and timber, which are devastating the mountains. Though such industries may at times offer higher
wages, it is too often a story of "boom and bust."

While tourism is big and growing bigger in the Central Appala-

Once, I was with a visitor at the county seat, and a friend of mine
stopped to tell me that she had found a job in a fast-food restaurant.
The visitor was incensed, saying that the poor service employee had
been taken advantage of in her new minimum-wage job. I challenged
the visitor, explaining that the job was really a position of dignity for
the local woman, who was proud to be employed.

—Al Fritsch

chian states, its impact has not been distributed equally across the region, with a few natural attractions drawing the lion's share of visitors. Driving the Blue Ridge Parkway during the time of the autumn leaves attracts people from far and wide, but there are other equally beautiful areas that receive few or no tourists. Recreation lovers are drawn to specific areas famed for sports such as hunting, fishing, winter skiing, white-water rafting, riding ORVs, hang-gliding, and rock climbing.

In contrast, Appalachian cities such as Charleston and Huntington in West Virginia and Knoxville in Tennessee draw far fewer visitors and are seen as lacking in attractions and activities. In listings such as the Rand McNally *Places Rated Almanac,* they are ranked towards the bottom of urban areas in the U.S. for the recreational facilities that are available. Nonetheless, they offer enough local museums, parks, and other attractions to satisfy those visitors who are enticed there. New attractions are being opened in some cities, one example being the Tennessee Aquarium in Chattanooga.

A key concept in examining the economic effect of tourism in Appalachia is *leakage.* Leakage refers to the percentage of the tourist dollar that is not retained in the local economy of the destination but rather goes to outside investors. In tourist destinations such as the Caribbean islands, where there is little local ownership of airlines, hotels, tour companies, retail outlets, and restaurants, as much as 90 percent of the expenditure of a traveler arriving on a package tour may be kept out of the local economy. (This estimate is for the Bahamas.)

For example, an American tourist taking a sun-and-sand vacation in the Caribbean may fly there on a U.S.-owned airline that flies on Venezuelan oil. The tourist might well stay at a French-owned resort, eating food imported from North America, drinking wine from France and whiskey from Scotland. For her excursions, she rents a Japanese-made car from a U.S.-owned agency. From this pricey vacation, the only money entering the local economy may be her share in the meager salaries of the local hotel employees and the souvenirs she buys. That is, assuming they're locally made—she could easily restrict her shopping to "bargain"-priced foreign luxury goods at the duty-free emporium. With this in view, it comes as no surprise that the vast influx of visitors in recent decades has brought little or no improvement in the standard of living for people in the Caribbean.

Furthermore, travelers arrive with different attitudes and plans for spending. At one end of the scale is the couple going to gamble for a weekend in Las Vegas, who will be prepared to spend large sums on travel, lodging, and the roll of the dice. At the other is the tent camper who plans to spend a week hiking in the woods and cooking over a campfire. A family with children who goes to Disney World will spend far more than the same family taking a fishing vacation—and state tourist boards are well aware of that.

The pressure is on for communities to offer enticements to get tourists to come and loosen their purse strings at glitzy commercial establishments. Such forms of entertainment may or may not be beneficial to the community. When Native Americans build casinos on their tribal lands, it often leads to friction within the community. Conflict results as some get rich fast and others become embittered by the entry of hustlers and developers looking to make a quick buck. Unstable employment further weakens the fabric of the community.

It seems logical that American tourist destinations would incur far less leakage than Third World sites. In developing countries, First World corporations own most accommodations and airlines, and the money is picked up quickly by those firms. However, leakage from Appalachian tourism can approach the rates seen in the developing world. Most vacation travel to and within the region is by car, bringing income to gas station chains and car rental companies, few (if any) owned within the region. Using corporate motel chains and patronizing big-name, outside-owned tourist attractions such as Dollywood also raises leakage rates.

Of course, individuals' vacation habits vary considerably, and this obviously influences leakage rates. Tourists in Appalachia could, if eating in locally owned restaurants and shunning the chain motels, have a leakage rate as low as 30 to 40 percent, much of that related to car expenses. The more outdoor activities are undertaken, the lower the amount of money going into the local area, raising the overall proportion of expenditure that ends up outside of Appalachia. In cases of hiking and camping, the expenditures are low, but in cases where the recreation involves motorized vehicles (planes, motorboats, and ORVs), the expenditure is high and the leakage rates are also high.

Some of the highest rates of leakage occur when people bring their own entertainment, drinks, food, and camping equipment. Thus, the frugal camper with a trunkful of groceries from home may pay only small campground fees for a weekend of enjoyment, contributing virtually nothing to the local economy.

However, there are even worse scenarios. Appalachia—Science in the Public Interest (ASPI) surveys of ORV tourism in Kentucky show that leakage rates from this type of visitor may approach 90 percent. People camp out and spend little on motels or other amenities because they are covered with dirt and stay outside much of the weekend. Of an average expenditure of over five hundred dollars, less than sixty dollars enters the local economy—pathetic compensation for the environmental degradation and other negative impacts on the community. We will examine this issue in detail in a later chapter.

While it is true that tourism does not exploit the countryside to the extent that clear-cut logging or surface mining does, it still has economic disadvantages for Appalachia that counter its economic benefits. Some long-term detrimental economic effects include the following:

- Few of the jobs created offer well-paying or year-round employment
- Tourism operators may focus on making the most in a given season, raising prices to a level where ordinary citizens find a hard time making a decent living. In some highly touristed regions such as Colorado, service workers are forced to pay exorbitantly high lodging and food prices along with tourists during the tourist season.
- Urban or rural sprawl in housing, park services, and billboards may result from an expanding tourism industry.
- A large number of tourists may exceed the carrying capacity of the particular place and physically damage the environment, thus eroding the economic base of the community.
- The quality of life can be eroded by heavy tourist presence—for example, in towns such as Gatlinburg, Tennessee, which have changed beyond recognition.

Tourism and Appalachia's Environment

All human activity has an impact on the environment, but the cave
dwellers who lived in Appalachia several thousand years ago left very
few traces on the landscape itself. Even the impacts of the first settlers
were small compared to the typical twenty-first century inhabitant of
this land. Today, virtually every one of our daily activities has serious
environmental impacts, and that includes recreation such as tourism.
We need to look carefully at what further development of tourism,
even a green tourism, will do to Appalachia.

The two authors of this book live near two major tourist sites of
eastern Kentucky. One author lives in Berea, which has become a center for traditional mountain crafts. Studios, galleries, festivals, and
activities at Berea College draw up to three hundred thousand visitors
every year, off of heavily traveled Interstate 75. The other lives twenty
miles away in Mt. Vernon, also near Interstate 75, in the vicinity of
Renfro Valley, the self-proclaimed birthplace of country music. This
music center is nationally famous for its Barn Dance radio program
dating from the 1930s, as well as bluegrass and other old-time music.
The typical short-term tourists to these two destinations will spend
between two and four hundred dollars per couple in a visit to the region, will not venture into natural environments, will stay in medium-
priced motels, and will eat at chain restaurants. They have some
environmental impact, but little more than local shoppers and TV
couch potatoes do.

It's easy to see that other types of tourists may not be so benign in
their impacts. Consider a recreational park where ORV enthusiasts
can ride their vehicles with no restriction—or, in a scenario envisioned
by some tourism planners, a thriving "ecotourism lodge" built in a
fragile forest area.

One must wonder whether some travelers who judge themselves to
be treading lightly on the earth are really doing so, and see how their
impact compares with that of the average inhabitant of the region or
that of the more typical Appalachian tourist described above. It is
highly likely that an increased but uncritical emphasis on ecotourism
in the region could result in greater—not less—environmental impact
and that the average ecotourist in Appalachia will do more—not less—
harm than the traditional tourist.

Tourists affect the environment in three main ways: through their transportation, accommodation, and choice of recreational activities. These areas must be addressed in considering any future development in Appalachia, whether a rustic campground or a massive theme park.

Transportation has a major impact. Over 90 percent of tourists arrive in the region by automobile. Airlines and railroad are far less important, with biking, hiking, boating, and horseback riding also playing a minimal role. Thus, many of the impacts of increased tourism are directly associated with increased vehicular travel. Use of public transportation (bus, airline, and railroad) would reduce air pollution caused by tourism to a major degree. A shift to such public modes could cut air pollution caused by tourist vehicles in half, but this would still not make a major difference in overall pollution due to so much nontourist travel. However, this would become a major factor in air pollution reduction, if the pass-through tourists ("snowbirds" from Canada and the northern U.S. to and from Florida) are also included. Many of these enter and leave the region via Interstates 75, 81, 64, 70 and 68 without making more than brief stopovers within the region, perhaps in still greater numbers than those who come to spend time here.

Another factor is lodging. Much depends on the type of lodging available in Central Appalachia. Luxury hotels consume prodigious amounts of water and electricity—the "green" campaigns of top hotel chains intended to reduce consumption (and, not coincidentally, reduce costs) testify to this. Such hotels also generate disproportionate amounts of garbage. However, there are relatively few facilities of this type in the region and many more mid-rate and economy motels, which are generally less wasteful of resources. Tourists coming to camp or engage in outdoor activities decrease their daily energy use from their normal consumption at home, so in terms of energy, the activity is an ecological benefit. However, if the campers drive an air-conditioned RV this is canceled out by the added fuel required to move it.

The types of activities a tourist engages in will make a major difference in the impact on the environment. Tourist pursuits range from activities with impacts smaller than daily life at home to activities so destructive to the environment that they should be banned, such as the unrestricted riding of ORVs. It is as difficult in Appalachia as elsewhere to fight the libertarianism that says "anything that is fun should be allowed." In some ways, it is even more difficult in Appalachia, because tourism-associated service jobs are scarcer and therefore more valued than in most other parts of America. For this reason, there is a tendency in Appalachia to soften criticism of ecologically damaging activities, even more so since the region has already been heavily damaged by resource extraction such as non-sustainable forestry and surface mining of coal. However, one can argue that Appalachian tourism that harms the environment is just a continuation of the exploitative practices of ripping out timber and coal, only with different machines and more scattered damage.

These facets of tourism produce a wide range of environmental impacts, some quite obvious—and others easily overlooked.

Air Pollution

For the most part, Central Appalachia's air has been traditionally considered relatively pure, except in areas downwind from coal-fired power plants and, to a lesser degree, areas of heavy chemical manufacturing. However, with the rise of acid rain levels due to sulfur and other acid-forming emissions from the multitude of power plants, that air purity is fading, and trees are showing the impact of acid rain in the region. Growth in tourism can be a factor if it leads to increased demand for electric power. In fact, pollution is already becoming a hindrance to tourism, as the higher elevations in the Blue Ridge and the Great Smoky Mountains lose their cover and the renowned autumn beauty fades to that of the denuded Frazier fir and other impacted species. Air pollution has taken its toll and will continue to do so. A number of repeat visitors have told how sad it is to drive the famous Blue Ridge Parkway in Virginia and see acres of countryside ruined by acid rain—while many native foresters remain in a state of denial. Obviously, all motorized vehicles contribute to air pollution, and a further influx of automobiles would only worsen it.

Water Pollution

Tourists can cause water pollution, especially through the use of motorized vehicles. Most visitors are aware of visible forms of water pollution, but do not know the quality of the water in areas that may look rather pristine but have toxic microorganism contamination. Since most motels and resorts obey basic environmental water regulations, one can expect that the water would be relatively clean. However, a "straight pipe" dumping wastewater from a tourist cabin directly into a stream is another matter. In 2001, over half of Kentucky's mountain streams and rivers were so polluted that they were unfit for swimming. Non-point source water pollution is caused by livestock and wildlife, and steps are being taken to contain the former. In his youth, one of the authors often drank from springs and small creeks, but that's risky behavior today.

Noise Pollution

The noise created by powerboats, ORVs, and other tourist-operated vehicles is also a factor. When the Catholic Diocese of Lexington, Kentucky, planned to build a retreat house on a hill overlooking scenic Herrington Lake, a favorite boating site, Appalachia—Science in the Public Interest (ASPI) conducted an environmental assessment. The site was extremely noisy due to the motorboats racing past and their engine noise reverberating off the denuded hillsides. Though ASPI's recommendations were not fully taken, after the retreat house was built much attention was given to wildscape, raised-bed gardening and some visual and vegetative barriers to keep sound from interfering with the contemplative atmosphere needed for a retreat house. Noise is an inevitable problem when waterways allow powerboats at any time, or the public uses ORVs, which disturb residents and wildlife alike. Noise, a growing menace throughout our country, can also result from tourism. Some activities are so quiet one does not know that anyone is present, while others are so overwhelming that the whole countryside is obliged to pay attention. Noisy relaxation would certainly seem to be an oxymoron.

Litter and Garbage

Litter is one of the most immediately visible impacts of tourism, and yet seemingly one of the most difficult to control. State anti-litter laws are virtually never enforced, and other solutions that have been tried are complex and ineffective. Near Williamsburg, Kentucky, the U.S. Corps of Engineers has erected a set of pylons in the form of a giant sieve halfway out into the normal channel of the Cumberland River, upstream from Cumberland Falls State Park. The purpose of this structure is to collect and strain out garbage, especially the "Kentucky ducks," the plastic gallon milk jugs that float down that river and mar the tourist attraction below. In the first year after it was completed, ASPI counted (along with the driftwood that has floated downstream from time immemorial) about twenty-five bags of actual garbage. Each bag of litter cost five thousand dollars to collect, including construction costs and lost interest—a fleecing of the taxpayers.

Litter and garbage are massive problems that harm the tourism industry in Appalachia, but the issues here are inadequate garbage pickup and lack of recycling programs. When local people dispose of trash haphazardly, it not only mars the scenery, but it also sends a signal to tourists that no one cares if they throw litter whenever the fancy strikes them. The most noticeable offenders are ORV riders, whose associations have sponsored cleanup days—as well they should, since riders dump enormous quantities of aluminum cans and food packaging each weekend in popular sites across Appalachia. Aluminum Anonymous, a Maryland-based citizens' group, found in their national roadside counts that Appalachia is above the national average for litter deposited—some, unfortunately, contributed by visitors as well as residents. When certain forms of recreation such as ORVs destroy the land—whether public or private—its participants regard littering as trivial in comparison. On that count, at least, they may be right.

Chemical Pollution

Industry is the principal culprit in chemical pollution in Appalachia, especially around Charleston, West Virginia, which is a major center for manufacturing. In comparison with the manufacture of chemicals or the use of pesticides by local residents, tourism is a minor contributor to Appalachia's chemical problems. However, motels catering to tourists may employ harmful chemicals in cleaning guest rooms and add to the environmental burden in some measure.

Wildlife and Wildflower Resources

Unregulated hunting has been the bane of many species, including the passenger pigeon, eastern elk, and bison, though the latter two are beginning to make a comeback through public and private management efforts. Today, hunting is more regulated and does not afford a threat to existing populations, especially since game animals (deer, rabbits, squirrels, and wild turkeys) are found in fairly large numbers and can be regulated on a county-by-county basis by the length of season and type of weapon used.

However, there are other sports besides hunting and fishing that can have an effect on Appalachia's wildlife and wild plant populations. The river orchids in Kentucky are suffering from the use of ORVs in fragile flora areas. It is extremely difficult to protect these and other endangered plant and animal species from the ravages of unregulated recreational vehicles. Campers in wilderness areas can also have an impact on both plants and animals, particularly through uncontrolled camping practices.

Energy Waste

America seems to be tied to the umbilical cord of the power companies, and there is a disproportionately large number of coal-, gas-, oil- and nuclear-fueled power plants in Central Appalachia. All travelers use nonrenewable energy when they drive a vehicle to and from the Appalachian region for a specific recreational activity. All types of tourists, whether conventional or green, will use about the same amount of energy getting here, except for those few exerting themselves pumping their bikes or walking on a trail. However, travelers who make a journey through the region starting at one end of the Appalachian Trail head in Georgia to the other end in Maine over two thousand miles away will use an extremely small amount of nonrenewable energy, in comparison with snowbirds driving a motor home with the size and gas mileage of a city bus. Campers, hikers, and bicyclists may actually use far less energy per day than do residents of the area.

Sprawl

We are aware that sprawl is a major detriment to the beauty of a countryside. Areas near interstate and other major highways are splattered with billboards, gas stations, parking lots, motels, fast-food chain restaurants, and other forms of human construction. Such agglomerations soon attract housing developments. With our insatiable appetite for more space, we see manifestations of sprawl cropping up everywhere in America. The spaces we use for residence, work, commerce, education, worship, and recreation have grown increasingly bloated in recent years, and Appalachia is no exception. Kentucky and West Virginia have fewer zoning restrictions and other codes to reduce or contain this phenomenon, which is affecting much of America like a cancer. Tourism can be a contributor to sprawl equal to certain other forms of industry or commerce, with clusters of chain motels and service stations mushrooming around even the most isolated interstate highway exit.

Visual Pollution

Sprawl eats up valuable farmland and contributes to visual pollution through its sheer ugliness. However, visual pollution can also be caused by a single structure in the wrong place that blocks an otherwise picturesque scene. The construction of the motel on top of the mountain near Boone, North Carolina, though not sprawl as such, certainly contributes to visual pollution. If construction along the approach road to that structure expands in the coming year, then the visual pollutant will give way to rural sprawl, which can be as disconcerting as the urban forms of blight. Any so-called green tourist who patronizes this type of location contributes to the problem. Every time we see a billboard advertising a place to eat or sleep and patronize that advertiser, we contribute to the visual pollution that is beginning to hamper the beauty of the very landscape we are traveling to enjoy.

Light Pollution

A new phenomenon that is being recognized in various parts of the developed world is light pollution—an effect comparable to having a full moon every evening. Now over half of the people of the United States are unable to see the Milky Way at night, due to the light glow from street and domestic lighting and vehicular traffic. There is evidence that this lack of darkness has a negative impact on human health. The effect is more pronounced in dense metropolitan areas and less so in rural America. The shading capacity of the Appalachian Mountains would have some effect in reducing the glare from such metropolitan areas as Pittsburgh, Charlotte, and Atlanta. On the whole, the problem of light pollution in Appalachia is not as pronounced as it is in the metropolitan strips of the East Coast, the Great Lakes and California—so far.

Vibrational Pollution

This type of pollution occurs wherever construction work is under-taken, and it is quite a serious problem in certain parts of the nation. The damage can be nearly permanent in places where surface mining of coal or rock quarrying operations occur. Quite often, as in those parts of Appalachia where mountain top removal is occurring (south-western West Virginia and eastern Kentucky), immense amounts of topsoil and overburden must be removed rapidly and efficiently in order to uncover the rich seams of coal, just like layers on a cake. Developers use waste oil and nitrate fertilizer to cause explosions as big as the Oklahoma City bombing on a daily basis. As surface mining has decreased in recent years, the amount of vibration damage to wa-ter wells and homes has dropped to a noticeable degree. Tourism can

Matrix of Recreational Activities and Environmental Impact

	air	water	noise	litter	chemical	wildlife	energy	sprawl	visual	light
sightseeing	X			X		X	X	X	X	
hiking	–	–				X				
hunting						xxx				
fishing						xx				
camping	X	X		xx		xx				
ORV use	xxxx	xxx	xxxx	xx		xxx	xx			
rockclimbing	X			X					X	
motorboating	xxxx	xxx	xxxx	xx		xxx	xx			
swimming	–		X							
golf	X							xxx		
tennis										
festivals	X		X	X			X			
rafting	–		–							

Scale of impacts: – negligible depending on particular practices
x some impact   xx medium impact   xxx+ large impact
Compiled by Al Fritsch, presented at Appalachian Studies Association 2001 conference

exacerbate this pollution through demanding more electricity from coal-fired facilities.

Other Forms of Environmental Damage

A possible threat that has been connected with tourism elsewhere is a competition between the tourism industry and local residents for water resources. One such place is the proposed 54,000-acre tourist ranch on the small island of Molokai, Hawai'i, where fewer than seven thousand local people are fighting a $200 million development and its $355-a-night rooms. Through both sabotage and court actions, native people have brought the Ranch project to a halt over competing claims for the limited amount of water available. The bitterness has broadened to a cultural conflict. As native opposition leader Walter Ritte says, "They were bulldozing through the bones of our ancestors, then offering us jobs like they were doing us a favor."[3]

Could a similar scenario be in Appalachia's future?

Comparative Environmental Impacts of Recreational Activities

All of our life activities have environmental impacts, including our recreational choices. By comparing the impacts in a number of areas, it is possible to rank the activities as more or less "green," both on an individual and a societal scale. The matrix summarizes the impacts of some common tourist activities, both in Appalachia and elsewhere.

Tourism and Appalachian Culture

The questions surrounding what form development should take in a given community are not only environmental: they are also cultural. The issue facing Molokai Ranch described above is more than just whether to bring money into a rather impoverished community. The hotel would involve radical changes to the way people live in order to supply a small number of them with jobs that don't pay much and provide little security. Visitors who come may have a relaxing time, enjoy a unique environment, and put some money into the community, but mistrust on the part of residents will keep tourists from having a genuine experience of the local culture. This is no different from a busload of Californians touring the Appalachian region to see poverty at its roots. No one enjoys being looked at like caged zoo creatures. At speaking engagements, it is hard to talk with candor and hospitality simultaneously. The culture of tourism at times clashes head-on with local culture, but does it have to? Are we compromising the integrity of a region in order to accommodate people who do not respect the local culture?

Cultural tourism is a booming business, especially among the more affluent sector of tourists. The TIAA reports that in 1997, 92.4 million of the 199.8 million adult travelers in the U.S. included a cultural activity during a one-way trip of fifty miles or more. The cultural activities included visiting a historic site (31 percent), visiting a museum (24 percent), visiting an art gallery (15 percent), seeing a live theater performance (14 percent), and other activities (16 percent). This is a group with higher incomes than average tourists. They also spend more money per trip—$615 per trip versus $425 for the general public—and so are of great interest to state tourism boards.[4]

Appalachian-based regional and local tourist agencies seek to attract these higher-spending tourists to this region—and they don't place too many preconditions in this race for customers. Granted, in Appalachia it would be difficult to satisfy the really big cultural spenders, those who would spend a week attending Broadway shows in New York. But there are opportunities available, which are sometimes overlooked. For example, the Appalachian Museum near Clinton, Tennessee, is one mile from the busiest highway (Interstate 75) in the region, and the nearby Knoxville area offers plenty of motels and other facilities. The Kentucky Music Museum near Mount Vernon, Kentucky, is another cultural attraction.

While Appalachians are proud of their culture and invite tourists to come and learn about it, there is still a tension between genuine hospitality and the fear that someone may make fun of what the region has to offer and term it "hillbilly." Partly, this is old-fashioned honesty, but there is a streak of defensiveness and diffidence as well. Too many people in the mountains can tell a story about helping an outsider, and then feel laughed at because of their own personal poverty or some amenities that the region lacks. Many fear that visitors will make disparaging remarks back home about the twang, the trash, the highwalls, or the cramped cottages on the flood plain. Appalachians, including tourist promoters, are haunted by a long history of out-migration, welfare checks, black lung, and chinks in the shanty walls.

Myths built around well-meaning but ill-researched documentaries and exposés feed on publicly perceived biases and stereotypes. One can imagine people in the mountains taking to task the well-intentioned liberal journalists who come to the region to write their stories. Some are based on fact, and some are embellished—all to the detriment of the people.

The stereotypical "Ugly American" is an affluent tourist who is contemptuous towards the host culture. Critics of tourism in many regions point to the clash between the economic concept "the customer is always right" and a native pride in one's culture. Some outsiders feel that if they spend money in Appalachia as a goodwill gesture to alleviate poverty, they deserve abject gratitude. That attitude may be more common to tourists than we care to acknowledge. On the other hand, there are other visitors who regard the Appalachian culture as worthwhile for its own sake and who accept the role of learner. They are willing to offer sincere thanks—but this person is certainly not in the majority. Theoretically, a visit to Appalachia could become an opportunity to learn and grow. But affluence, along with the sheer volume of tourists, is more likely to reinforce the ugly American syndrome—"In $$$ We Trust."

From a quarter century of sad experience, we can affirm that negative attitudes among visitors do exist, especially among wealthy young people. A single question often betrays inner attitudes. One visitor asked a goat farmer, "What do you *really* do to make a living?"—thereby offending the farmer and everyone in the vicinity. Another acquaintance gave as a gift a calendar containing monthly caricatures of drunken, barefoot "hillbillies." A more blatant example is the major newspaper that dispatched a reporter to stay with an Appalachian host family. Though he stayed only at their modest but respectable home while on his assignment, he returned to New York and wrote a story of how people defecated in the cracks of the floor—a gross fabrication. Over and over, mountain people have been subjected to biased reporting, which deflates the carefully produced tourist literature and enhances degrading stereotypes of our people.

Stereotypes must be squarely addressed, namely, that mountain people are inhospitable, drink moonshine, grow long beards, are incestuous, lie around sleeping all day, and live in shacks on mountainsides. The word "hillbilly" is still not seen as an ethnic slur, even by people who would never dream of saying "nigger" or "chink"—one feels guilt even writing them. As yet, there is no Appalachian Anti-Defamation League, and so the belittling of the culture, including the language and mountain ways, continues.

What the narrow-minded fail to understand before going to Appalachia is that although the region's isolation and long-term poverty continue to influence the culture, this is not always for the worse. For example, mountain music is authentic to the region, with people learning from neighbors or family members to play a variety of musical instruments in their earliest years. The exceptional number of musical talents found in isolated Appalachian places is amazing. Isolation and self-reliance have led to high levels of development in a large number of fields, including dance; crafts ranging from corn shuck dolls to cane chairs; cooking; storytelling; making do with little money; expressive language patterns; hunting, fishing, and trapping; knowledge of medicinal and culinary herbs as well as native fruits and vegetables; a spirit of caring for those who are plagued with misfortune; and the ability to stop and listen to others.

A potential attraction of Appalachia is the uniqueness of its music, language, and customs. Visitors would like to experience this difference from standard American English. Unfortunately, the unique flavor of Appalachia's dialect is being watered down and lost with each passing year. The modern highway system allows far more mobility than a generation ago. In a single hundred-mile drive on an Appalachian interstate highway, one can easily see cars from twenty-five states (and provinces). Though this influx of outsiders is a factor in the decline of traditional ways of speaking, it also contributes to the more cosmopolitan nature of Appalachia today.

The erosion of Appalachia's unique dialects is following the same pattern as the expected demise of up to 90 percent of the world's indigenous languages within the next century, according to the United Nations.[5] Cable television, personal computers, radio, and the extension of the Internet into schools, homes, and businesses add to the homogenization. As in other embattled cultures, one can observe the demise of tradition through modern communications and transportation systems. Chalk this up as part of the price of globalization.

Poor areas that are not isolated can lose their distinctive character quite rapidly. This is because hand-me-downs from outside (whether clothes, vehicles, or computers) goad the recipient into wanting more material comforts and pining to dress, ride, and be entertained like the rest of America. Even traditional cooking is affected. With the loss of family gardens, the increase in women's employment outside the home, and the spread of fast-food restaurants in smaller towns, more people in Appalachia are following the American pattern of cooking less and eating out more at fast-food restaurants for breakfasts, lunches, and even dinners several times a week. The soup beans, cornbread, stack cakes, and berry cobblers of the past are growing less common among younger Appalachians.

Those defending a native culture have often voiced complaints that outsiders dictate the art form itself through the tourist dollar. A craft item that was once tinted with pale native dyestuff might be brightened up for tourists by the use of non-native paint. If such a change makes the item sell in larger quantities, native artists may abandon their traditional technique. This is a common occurrence in the Third World, but is not limited to these areas. Increasingly, there are reports of the same phenomenon in Appalachia, where "traditional" quilt patterns must be made up in the latest fashion colors, dictated by the often bland copycat tastes of the tourist purchaser, if they are to be sold. The same can be found in many other crafts, from woodcarving to corn shuck dolls.

Factors Leading to the Erosion of Culture

Cultural erosion may be caused or accelerated by the following influences:

- Upward economic mobility of a deprived minority, which is willing to sacrifice ways of speaking or acting to gain acceptance in the dominant culture
- Media impact of contemporary American cultural and language patterns, which most Appalachian residents now have bombarded at them for about six hours daily (U.S. average) on radio and television
- Physical mobility of population, which results in out-migration to distant metropolitan areas with existing urban Appalachian populations, or to new centers offering employment

- The growing trend for many Appalachians to spend part of their career, education, or military service outside of the region
- Modern educational reforms, which lead to the consolidation of school districts and especially high school populations, as well as to the mixing of diverse clusters of local communities with larger ones, especially in academic, social, and sporting events
- Commercial homogenization through the "malling" of America, which also threatens the country store, the mom-and-pop diner, and other places where people used to meet and trade stories
- The divisiveness of entertainment through watching television, renting movies, playing computer games, or surfing the Internet. In the past, social and fraternal organizations, along with playing musical instruments together and telling stories at the country store, were major ways to spend free time. Academics speak of the erosion of the social capital in the communities of this country, as many civic organizations drop in membership and attendance.
- The power of the dominant entertainment culture from Hollywood, Broadway, Nashville, and other places. It is virtually impossible to stave off and reduce this influence. The people of Quebec know this all too well—as do the people of Appalachia.

Tourism is not the only cause of cultural erosion, and, conversely, erosion is not the only cultural effect caused by tourism. In fact, tourism also has some potential to check this erosion, if visitors' desire to see authentic old-time ways leads to their preservation. However, this type of tourist activity ranges in authenticity from watching the Amish riding unaffectedly in their horse-drawn buggies to seeing Native Americans dancing at powwows staged solely for the visitors.

But who determines what is authentic and worthy of preservation—the tourist "customer" or the host community? This contentious issue faces every community hoping to develop cultural tourism.

As we have seen, even in its current, relatively undeveloped state, tourism has strong impacts on the people and environments of Appalachia. In the next chapter we will look at a growing form of "nature" tourism that, if uncontrolled, could devastate the region.

CHAPTER 3

On the Wrong Track

ORV *Tourism in Kentucky*

The mist was all gone from the river now and the rapids sparkled and
sang. They were still young as the land was young. We were there to
enjoy it, and the great machines seemed far away.
—Sigurd F. Olson, conservation writer

Too often, the attitude of both government officials and residents of
Appalachia until now has been that tourism, all tourism, is an economic plus, and should be encouraged. As we have seen, Appalachia's
main attraction for visitors has always been nature—its majestic
mountains, peaceful forests, and untamed rivers. And in contemplating future development, the focus is largely on these natural features.
For example, in 2002, the Southern and Eastern Kentucky Tourism
Development Association sponsored an all-day conference on "Nature-Based Tourism Opportunities" for actual and prospective tourism
entrepreneurs. Their concept of nature tourism was broad enough to
include everything from farm tours to rock climbing to deer hunting,
and they planned to get publicity for the region by inviting crowds of
journalists on junkets to sample the golf, fishing, and houseboating.

But the term "nature tourism" covers a vast spectrum of activities,
from the educational and ecofriendly to those that are utterly devastating to the natural environment. Until now, there has been very little
proactive planning for the future development of tourism, and virtually no regulation of any form of activity that visitors choose to partake in. In this chapter, we will take an in-depth look at a fast-growing

and destructive type of nature tourism to highlight the threat that a laissez-faire approach to tourism can pose to environments and communities in the mountains.

The Situation

The term ORVs, off-road vehicles, includes all types of motorized transport designed for cross-country use, away from paved roads. There are several different categories of ORVs, such as sport-utility vehicles (SUVs), dune buggies, snowmobiles, motorized "dirt bikes," and all-terrain vehicles (ATVs), which are frequently seen in Kentucky. ATVs are small four-wheeled vehicles especially designed for use on rugged terrain. Originally sold in the 1970s as functional transportation to bring farmers, miners, and loggers to otherwise inaccessible work locations, during the 1980s they were increasingly used for recreational purposes. In 1998, there were 3.91 million ATVs in the U.S., ridden by an estimated 5.85 million people, 60 percent of them living in rural areas.[1]

In the last three decades, thousands of ATVs of every size and description have invaded the south central Kentucky countryside. The first ATV tourists in the 1970s were out-of-state visitors who came for summer and autumn weekends and holidays after their home states declared public lands off-limits to ATVs. Later they discovered that driving through slick, muddy areas during the winter and spring rainy seasons brought extra thrills, making it a year-round activity. The first riders were drawn by a small-time commercial ATV track operation, which opened at an easily accessible location a half-mile from exit 49 of Interstate 75. Many early ATVers came from Ohio and Indiana, but recently local people have also discovered "four-wheelers."

The ATV industry portrays these vehicles as a way to get close to nature, allowing one to roam in freedom through the beautiful backwoods. The reality is far different. In Kentucky, the influx of ATVs has terrorized wildlife, torn up endangered plants, plowed through and damaged the Rockcastle River (which is designated by the state as "wild and scenic" further downstream), and done untold devastation to public and private forestland—while local protest has effectively been silenced. Though the state has regulations on the books against the trespassing of motorized vehicles on private lands, they have gone unenforced. ATV riders regard themselves as "nature tourists," and in

Kentucky, the tourist is always right. Furthermore, this group has shown an uncanny ability to intimidate both state officials and local residents.

Present-day ATVs are big (weighing as much as six hundred pounds) and fast (some are capable of 65 mph). However, unlike other motor vehicles, regulations on their use vary drastically among states. For example, in Missouri, ATV operators must be over sixteen years of age. On the other hand, many other states have virtually no regulations at all—operators need not register their vehicles, have a driver's license, or even meet an age requirement. The regulations that do exist are often meaningless—in Utah, it is legal for an eight-year-old to drive an ATV at highway speeds.[2]

Owners of ATVs will haul their vehicles for long distances on trailers in order to practice the sport in states with fewer restrictions—such as Kentucky, whose few feeble laws are almost universally unenforced and unheeded. According to Kentucky law, riders may not operate on public land except where expressly permitted, and they are not allowed on private property without the consent of the landowner. But torn-up land is visible proof that dozens of sites that are theoretically off-limits are trespassed on a regular basis. Furthermore, Kentucky law says ATV riders under the age of sixteen "should" be under parental supervision, and that ATVs are not designed to carry passengers—but scores of children as young as two years of age have been treated at University of Kentucky Hospital for serious injuries received in ATV accidents.

Trespassing and environmental damage by ATVs are now being reported in virtually all rural Kentucky counties, with Laurel County probably the most seriously impacted. These ATVs harm Kentucky's environment in a number of ways. They are extremely noisy, as they can be heard for miles. They break through the thin forest undercover and cause devastating erosion. They compact the soil and flatten wild plants and contribute to air and water pollution. According to the California Air Resources Board, some ATV engines produce 118 times as many pollutants as automobiles. Even though they often operate far from roads within the wooded areas, they can't go unnoticed. Their increasing numbers and power, the "who cares" attitude of the operators, and the failure of law enforcement all contribute to serious problems in the areas where they have been most used. Other regions may soon experience these same negative effects.

Yet ATV enthusiasts argue vehemently that they have a right to enjoy nature in their preferred fashion, just as hunters, hikers, and sightseers do. They feel that nature is common property, and that no restrictions should be placed on their favorite form of recreation. They point to the contributions they make to the economy through their purchase of expensive vehicles and their spending on excursions.

Outline of an ATV Environmental Assessment

Together with Paul Gallimore of the Long Branch Environmental Education Center in Leicester, North Carolina, Al Fritsch has undertaken almost two hundred environmental resource assessments (ERAs) since 1982 for facilities operated by a wide variety of nonprofit organizations in all parts of North America. These ERAs involve on-site inspection and analysis and produce lengthy written reports containing a variety of suggestions for making programs more environmentally sound. This methodology can be applied to many fields, including recreational activity, in order to uncover related environmental problems and suggest solutions.

An ERA reviews all resources (renewable and nonrenewable) available for a given institution or locality. The assessment considers the impact on the environment through land disturbance, air and water pollution, noise, and natural resource depletion. If all factors are satisfactory or can be controlled effectively, then the venture can be considered environmentally sound. An ERA for a recreational activity (such as ORV use) includes data on the total environmental impact, the behavior of the recreation seeker, health and safety issues associated with the activity, and overall economic costs and benefits to the total community.

A full environmental assessment for ORVs would fill a quarter of this book, leaving little space for other pressing issues, so instead we present an outline of the approach and findings.

Environmental Impacts

> Keep up the effort. They [ATVs] are doing great damage to the environment in this part of the country."
> —Jim Cass, Area Development District,
> Appalachian Regional Commission[3]

A few years ago, a geologist (who asked to remain anonymous) visited the "909 Site," a popular southeastern Kentucky location for ATV riding. She had studied soil characteristics on three continents, but she said that this little patch of Kentucky was the most severely damaged land she had ever encountered anywhere.

Other visitors to the site just shake their heads in horror. Deep canyons have been torn through the fragile soil, and the few trees that remain cling precariously to hills that are nearly bald. Many observers get angry but do not know where to turn, especially when they discover the complexity of the land ownership pattern, a patchwork of federal, state, county, and private property. Private owners, especially, are too intimidated to speak out against the intruders who tear across their land.

Land Disturbance

Eroded landscape is the most immediately visible environmental problem caused by ATVs. Even a careful landowner tending livestock using an ATV will cause some damage to the farmland. If that same vehicle is used in fragile desert or forest terrain, the damage can mount up very quickly. The average ATV driver travels about two hundred miles off-road per month, or 2,400 miles per year. Under moist conditions, a hundred passes over forest understory will do grave damage; ten passes are enough to disturb the understory when it is dry. In very fragile terrain, even a single pass will have some impact. Land destroyed by ATVs is even more difficult and costly to reclaim than strip-mined land, because it is often crisscrossed with numerous trails, each producing compaction and erosion. For the most severely traversed terrain, no amount of effort may be enough to restore it to its prior condition. The cost of reclaiming land used by ATVs has been estimated at about $10,000 per acre for every fifty miles of traversed trail per acre—relatively light use. Others give much higher figures. Perhaps a half million acres are disturbed in some manner each year in the United States, with approximate reclamation costs of about five billion dollars per year.

Air Pollution

Fresh air is one of the things that ATVers claim to enjoy most about their sport. However, their very machines are a concentrated source of pollution. ATVs, like all vehicles with internal-combustion engines, produce unburned hydrocarbons, carbon monoxide, nitrogen oxides, and ozone. In national parks and other wilderness areas, the pollution caused by ATVs and snowmobiles is noticeable both in summer and winter. In California alone, the emissions from such small engines are equivalent to 3.5 million cars traveling a distance of sixteen thousand miles each. Small "dirty" two-stroke engines like those in ATVs and snowmobiles account for about 5 percent of total air pollution (sulfur oxides, ozone, carbon monoxide, and nitrogen oxides), according to U.S. Environmental Protection Agency estimates. The amount of fuel spilled in our country solely in filling these engines accounts for more than the total Exxon Valdez oil spill. The Natural Trails and Waters Coalition and other environmental groups are campaigning to tighten emission standards on ATVs, and California is clamping down on the areas where ATVs can operate and will most likely do the same for ATV emissions. Will the rest of the nation follow this lead?

According to an anonymous resident of Laurel County, Kentucky, "This used to be beautiful country, for I was born seventy-two year[s] ago right here in Laurel County. Once you run down the trees in these sandstone hills and break through the surface, the rain plays heck with the land. That's why these gullies on the off-roaders' trails are fifteen foot deep. They are wrecking the place."[4]

Water Pollution

ATVs affect streams in two ways: through the sediments that enter streams and rivers due to the land disturbance mentioned above and through the use of waterways themselves, especially scenic creek beds, as "trails." This last practice is devastating to plant and animal life within the streambeds, and has many biologists concerned over the inability of the streams to recover. In forested areas, it's easy to see in rainy weather where the ATVs have been: muddy creek water flows in otherwise clear waterways.

Endangered and Threatened Species

The increasing number [of ATVs] threaten wildlife and has become a nuisance for many sporting enthusiasts. Whatever you're doing, the tranquility of the setting is part of the reason you're doing it.
—Babe Winkelman.[5]

Scenic and fragile natural resource areas are targets for ATVers—forest understory, desert, tundra, coastlands, creekbeds, prairie, and salt marshes. These prime locations are rich in wildlife. ATV sites in south central Kentucky are home to threatened and endangered native plants and animals, including ten species of mussels, running buffalo clover, several bats, a number of birds, and a number of species of orchid. In the summer of 1990, a team from ASPI documenting ATV damage photographed a dead turtle; it had been deliberately run over on an ATV trail in the Daniel Boone National Forest. This occurred on the Sheltowee Trace—a Native American word meaning "Big Turtle."

Besides actual damage by running over plants, the disturbance caused by ATVs affects birds and mammals. Furthermore, communities of soil microorganisms are affected by the compaction and increased susceptibility to erosion. The recent fad for riding ATVs in rainy weather and in muddy conditions is even more hazardous to native flora and fauna.

Noise pollution

> ATVs are heard and seen everywhere, even in the remote locations. . . . The [ATV] noise is a real deterrent [to business].
> —Rick Egedy, Sheltowee Trace Outfitters,
> a Kentucky rafting operator[6]

While theoretically ATVs could be made far quieter, purchasers often prefer the louder vehicles, which they equate with power—and they enjoy the attention drawn by loud noise. The countryside is losing the natural sounds of birdcalls and crickets—they are drowned out by the roar of racing motors, which can be heard for miles around. Besides disturbing the tranquility of nature, these human-generated noises can damage riders' eardrums, and increase the stress levels of residents. In our country, nuisance noise often goes unchallenged, especially in rural areas. Like smokers, noisy people seldom admit to the disturbance they cause, and residents are reluctant to speak out, especially against people traveling in a pack on powerful vehicles. With more ATV activity occurring in winter, when deciduous trees are bare, complaints from local residents have increased considerably. And who can speak for the frightened birds?

Litter

> About half our tourists are doing something outdoors. . . . If tourists
> see . . . junk piles around the state, it really turns them off. They're not
> going to want to come back. Those who come here for outdoor
> recreation are the people who are going to be in the backwoods and
> along streams and places where they are going to see these dumps.
> —Ann Latta, Kentucky Tourism Development Cabinet Secretary[7]

Litter is a major problem in high-use ATV areas. Trashing the landscape and littering go hand-in-hand, even though Kentucky law decrees a $500 fine for littering. Older ATV gathering places are seen as
ruined due to erosion, soon become a dumping ground for riders' litter,
and then attract massive amounts of junk and tires.

In recent years, some of these illegal dumping areas have been
publicized in the media. A renewed determination to clean up these
sites, especially through the federally funded "Personal Responsibility
In a Desirable Environment" Program, also known as PRIDE, has
grown in Kentucky. Other Appalachian states are also making greater
efforts at cleaning up their sites as well. Recently, ATV trade associations have sponsored annual cleanup programs out of concern that the
dismal condition of popular ATV sites will give their sport a bad name.

Behavior

In 2000, *Audubon* magazine reported on a terrifying series of confron-
tations between a Michigan landowner, George Buchner, and a group
of ATV drivers. When Buchner discovered ATV operators driving
through his private trout stream, he demanded their names. One rider
attacked Buchner and broke his nose. When he later tried to fence his
property, ATVers just cut the wires (they often carry wire cutters).
When he continued to try to bar riders from his land, Buchner received
death threats, his street lights were shot out, his mailbox was smashed,
his driveway was seeded with broken glass, the fence on his farm was
cut in eighty-eight places, and his wife was run over. They subse-
quently moved to Arizona. "Basically, ATVs ran me out of Michigan,"
he told the reporter.[8]

ATV riders are very diverse: mature and immature, old folks and
youngsters hardly out of diapers, teetotalers and drunk drivers, the

thoughtful and the thoughtless, the careful and the careless, lone wolves and pack animals. Some act aggressively, fully aware that they have a powerful vehicle under their control, and assert their right to travel when and where they please, disregarding laws and "no trespassing" signs. Others are courteous and even pleasant—responsible riders who keep to designated trails and are careful to avoid disturbing the local community. For many of them, operating ATVs is a weekend family outing, not a daredevil contest—one rider described the activity as "a togetherness thing." Riders such as these are happy to travel on hard-surfaced trails, and are not interested in riding cross-country because of the different ages of family members and the desire to ride beside each other. They are looking for fun, not to impress others.

But a few bad apples can definitely spoil the barrel. Joshua Bills, a Kentucky environmental activist, estimates that about 10 percent of all ATV riders are responsible for most of the reckless acts and threatening behavior. Environmental groups who have observed ATVers over a dozen years have noted that there is a continuum of ATV behavior, sometimes within the same person. Some riders behave reasonably when alone but tend to show off in a group. Teenagers may drive responsibly around adults but undertake the most outlandish and risky stunts when with their peers. Al Fritsch once watched two youths on dirt bikes attempt repeatedly to ride up a nearly vertical slope, and repeatedly fall over on their vehicles. They finally reached the top, which only led them to look around for something riskier. The trail of beer cans in what are essentially "dry" counties indicates that many reckless riders have booze on their breath.

Many ATVers have social motivations, desiring companionship, tales to share with friends, bonding, and social interaction. And a lot of ATVers do seek out the most beautiful natural scenery—to the detriment of nature itself. Two of us were investigating ATV trails near Natural Bridge State Park in Eastern Kentucky when we found an incredibly scenic creek framed with overhanging hemlocks. The creek bed was torn up by ATV tracks, where these "nature lovers" had broken through in search of trails for an upcoming rally.

Astute observers have noted that many ATV riders are people who find it hard to participate in active sports and thus, by default, turn to motorized varieties. They are too overweight to backpack, too old to play basketball, or too unskilled to sail. Often they are hardworking people who prefer to spend weekends outdoors with friends. They want excitement and, to attain this end, use a powerful vehicle that generally requires little exertion. They like to congregate and socialize with those who reinforce their own values and tastes while claiming a need for fresh air and sunlight and an ability to enjoy nature throughout the seasons.

Some recreational activities involve a certain degree of risk, but for a thrill-seeking ATVer, danger and its anticipation are a major part of the fun. The prospect of relating one's exploits to peers is another driving force. When questioned, ATV riders readily admit that the hypnotic sensation and drug-like effects of hazardous trails and the danger of steep slopes and cliff areas are real and attractive. Seeking out more extreme places to ride, flirting with danger, and rehashing near misses are all part of the ATV thrill-seeking experience.

Any nature tourist may have mixed motivations, combining enjoyment of nature with other pleasures and pursuits. But does an ATV operator truly focus attention on the scenic landscape? On the contrary, the major focus is on driving a powerful vehicle at high speed on difficult terrain. The landscape becomes an object of conquest, even if ATVers attest that it is a source of beauty. Operators admit that diverting attention to the scenery may actually lead to accidents.

Certain situations provide outright invitations to ATV misuse. These involve factors such as permissive circumstances, lack of surveillance, and nearby onlookers to impress. In 1992, near Ashdod, in Israel, Al Fritsch observed teenage soldiers in the desert daring each other to race their jeeps over fragile sand dunes. These were the very dunes that preservationists from the Society for the Protection of Nature in Israel were proudly showing Al and his group as one of their legal victories over developers. When Al voiced a protest about the soldiers' activities, the guide said that nothing could be done and that "boys will be boys." Clearly, riding bronco fashion was destroying the only remaining seashore, but the preservationists considered the abuse to be an extension of the military exercises permitted on the seacoast— even though the commanding officer was absent. Certainly, normal boys will indeed be boys—especially in front of fifty sightseeing visitors. Youths anywhere else would have done exactly what those young Israelis did in showing off driving skills, exuberance, and power by sliding down a sand dune with a recreational vehicle; the jeep was a military vehicle and secondarily "recreational." Showing off is normal, but doing so within a delicate ecosystem is inexcusable. Typical ATV drivers can destroy a landscape in no time at all.

An ATV puts more horsepower at a child's fingertips than a Roman charioteer had in a large team of horses. Youths are enticed to use a powerful ATV in a cavalier manner, especially when police are absent. In the example just given, the Israeli military authorities did not know that the soldiers were joyriding over dunes, but the commander's absence encouraged such behavior. This example parallels many incidents in our ATV-ravaged countryside. The attitudes of operators, their exuberance and youthfulness, the power of the vehicle, and the lack of supervision are ingredients for major environmental disturbance.

Safety Issues

> Last summer [2000], I counted five helicopter evacuations of injured ATVers in our part of the county alone. They no longer fly the hurt riders to the nearby London hospital, in part because the Forest Service would come over and give out citations. Instead, they are flown to Lexington, some seventy miles away.
> —Peter Ayers, East Bernstadt, Kentucky, paramedic[9]

ATV sales and accident rates declined in the early 1990s, after production of the dangerous three-wheel variety was halted due to action by the Consumer Product Safety Commission and federal lawsuits. But since the mid-1990s, the number of ATV-related deaths and injuries has been steadily climbing again. Considering rider attitudes, ATVs are still inherently unsafe. In fact, even with the ban on new three-wheel ATVs, ATV-related injuries are fast approaching the high levels set during the three-wheel ATV period. By 1999 the annual deaths from (mostly four-wheel) ATVs had already exceeded the annual deaths from earlier period due to the increased number of riders, increased horsepower and speeds, and more driving on rougher terrain. By 2001 one manufacturer had introduced a four-wheeler with an engine size two and a half times bigger than the average four-wheeler in use in 1997.

ATVs can easily be misused, as is evidenced by the lengthy warnings printed near the operating panels of every new ATV. The ATV's center of gravity is high, so they are prone to overturning, especially when operators take them over rough terrain at excessive speeds, and with companions constantly encouraging risky maneuvers. Helmets are left behind, and quite often two or more people ride an ATV designed for a single operator. The resulting injuries can be horrific.

A study at the University of Kentucky Hospital in Lexington from 1996 to 2001 recorded 151 emergency room admissions of children aged sixteen and under due to ATV accidents. The youngest victim was two years old. Among the injuries they suffered were collapsed lungs, lacerated spleens, and numerous broken bones. Thirty-two of the children had fractured skulls. Five of the victims died, and two will spend the rest of their lives as paraplegics. Many of these accidents occurred while young children were driving these massive, powerful vehicles. "You wouldn't give your car keys to your eight-year-old, would you?" says Dr. Susan Pollock of UK Hospital. But too many parents do the close equivalent by permitting youngsters to drive ATVs.

Generally, youths are more inclined in under-policed areas to drive ATVs in a risky way, in order to impress others, to gain a sense of self-fulfillment, or to test a vehicle's power. Through extensive monitoring, ASPI found that some drive at high speeds in crowded areas, ride at night, traverse steep and remote hilly areas where rescue would be difficult, and drink while driving.

ATVs are promoted as a healthy outdoor activity giving the operator fresh air and sunlight, a certain amount of exercise, and a sense of exhilaration. But any such health benefits need to be weighed against safety risks as well—and the ATV is an awfully risky route to the healthy outdoors. According to the American Academy of Pediatrics, some forty thousand injuries related to these vehicles were treated in emergency rooms annually between 1994 and 1996. Assuming a conservative $5,000 per accident for medical costs and lost wages, then the annual cost would be $200 million, leaving aside the complex calculation of the hundreds of fatalities. Furthermore, about a third of ATV-related accidents involve persons not on the vehicle itself—onlookers or non-motorized users of the trail. Hikers and campers run to get out of the way of approaching ATVs, but they don't always make it to safety.

Young people often ride without any safety equipment, training, or licenses. In 2000, in a three-county area of Kentucky, there were three deaths and over a dozen major ATV-related injuries—most involving youths. In a recent eight-year period, there were sixty-four ATV-related deaths in Kentucky, of which over two-thirds were riders nineteen years old or younger. Only three were wearing helmets, and 45 percent of the total occurred when two or more people were on vehicles clearly designed for single riders. Sherman Bamford, an ASPI research associate, found ATV operators to be an ever younger group. Although ATV dealers are prohibited from selling larger ATVs if they believe that children will use the vehicles, manufacturers and dealers still target smaller ATVs to children as young at twelve. This encourages even younger kids to ride what they see as a toy. And it promotes the idea of ATV riding as innocuous play, even though it is a potentially life-threatening activity.

Health officials have consistently emphasized that adults respond better to driving situations, including emergencies, than youths. Many parents overestimate their child's capacity to drive high-speed motor vehicles. Over a third of serious ATV-related injuries occur among people under sixteen years old, and almost two-thirds of such injuries occur among those under twenty-five. However, older riders are not immune. From 1997 to 2000, injuries requiring hospitalization increased 85 percent among riders over 25, as compared to a 68 percent increase among those under 25. Other types of ORVs that pose a serious risk are growing in popularity too. In 2000, sales of off-road motorcycles rose 37 percent over the previous year's sales.

The federal government has refused to take any substantially new action on ORV safety since 1988. Urgently needed measures include banning the sale of ATVs for use by children; requiring manufacturers to install roll bars, speed governors, seatbelts, and other safety equipment to prevent injuries and save lives; and mandating devices, such as tamper-proof GPS transmitters, to track ORV riders who act illegally or are in need of rescue.

The Economics of ATVs

"Honda's ATV sales soared in 2000, ending the year at 211,152, an increase of 29.6 percent. Once again Honda exceeded the ATV industry's healthy growth rate of 18.8 percent, strengthening Honda's already dominant number one market share position of 32.6 percent," according to a press release.[10]

Sales of ATVs are at record levels and have been growing about 20 percent a year since the late 1990s. The exact amount of economic activity generated by ATVs is difficult to quantify, but is clearly significant. It's not a cheap hobby—an enthusiast may invest $20,000 or more to purchase an ATV and a vehicle capable of hauling it. Gasoline is purchased to transport and operate ATVs. Many enthusiasts travel hundreds of miles to ride in special locations, increasing fuel consumption. Events such as the national Jeep Jamborees near Natural Bridge State Park in Kentucky attract riders from as far away as Oklahoma and Florida

The total economic impact of ATVs includes manufacture, promotion, sales, and maintenance of ATVs and their hauling vehicles; the cost of travel to the site of activity; the food, fuel, and lodging at the site; as well as the cost of regulation, security, and liability for damages resulting from the ATV operation. Though most ATVs are made in Japan and other Asian countries, about a quarter of manufacturing is domestic. In addition, the ATV sales and service sectors amount to tens of millions of dollars. A further several hundred thousand Americans earn income directly or indirectly from the operation and maintenance of these vehicles.

Manufacturers and merchants tend to champion expensive and disposable goods and to encourage rapid obsolescence. The ATV industry revels in planned obsolescence, avoiding making more durable vehicles with components that can be replaced. The ATV enthusiast seeks an ever more powerful toy (and conversation piece), rapidly selling off older models for newer ones.

There is no doubt that sales and use of ATVs pumps significant amounts of money into the U.S. economy, but is ATV tourism really a meaningful source of income for our region? Leakage, as we have seen, is the amount of tourist spending that does not benefit the destination, but goes to outside businesses. For example, a typical tourist plans a trip to Appalachia to enjoy the beauty of the area and makes purchases at home of camping gear, groceries, and even a tankful of fuel, for a total of $105. The same tourist spends money for camping fees while in Appalachia, fills up with a tank of gas, and eats out three times while in the region, for a total of $45. The tourist has spent $150 on a trip to the mountains, but $105 of this, or 70 percent, is leakage— money that does not benefit the host region. The tourist derives benefits from Appalachia, but spends most of his or her money at home.

During the summer of 2001, ASPI conducted a survey to determine the amount of leakage in ATV tourism. Data collected included the state of ATV rider origin; money spent on meals, groceries, and fuel, and where purchased; lodging; and where and how much they paid for their ATV and related equipment. The survey found that out-of-state riders spent approximately $51 on meals, groceries, and gasoline in the local area (Laurel and Rockcastle Counties) and about $40 at home stocking up on gasoline, groceries, beer, and other items. Riders paid an average of $11,281 for each haul vehicle and an average of $6,335 for each ORV and related gear. The study calculates that ownership costs for the haul vehicles amounted to about $50 per trip, at eight trips per year, and the ownership costs for the ATV itself was $198 per trip. All told, the average expenditure for each ATV-riding trip to Kentucky was $339—with about $288 spent in the home state. Only 15 percent of the money spent by these tourists ever entered the local economy of the destination, with a portion of that going to outside companies such as the corporate owners of gas stations. The 85 percent leakage rate associated with ATV tourist spending in Kentucky is on a par with the most exploitative forms of tourism in so-called Third World countries, which receive little benefit from throngs of visitors.

By comparison, a survey on wildlife-related recreation by the U.S. Fish and Wildlife Service and the U.S. Census Bureau examined leakage rates for other types of nature tourism such as hunting, fishing, and wildlife watching. In the study, expenditures are broken down into trip-related expenditures, equipment, and other expenditures (such as camping gear, magazines, etc.). The statistics did not include information about where the various expenditures were made, so it was assumed that virtually all equipment and expenditures of that nature were leakage and that virtually all trip-related expenditures were not. Based on this method, it was estimated that in Kentucky, about 76.1 percent of all hunting and fishing expenditures are leakage, 78.9 percent of all wildlife-watching expenditures are leakage and 76.6 percent of all wildlife-related recreation expenditures together are leakage.[11]

The substantial ORV-related leakage rates do not take external costs into consideration, which would tip the balance even further. External costs are hidden costs to society that a purchaser does not pay for directly when he or she buys a good or service. For example, the price of cigarettes at the corner store does not include the cost of emphysema treatments ultimately paid for by insurance-holders or taxpayers. ATV riding entails higher external costs than many other forms of outdoor recreation, including soil erosion and loss, water pollution and associated cleanup and water filtration costs, air pollution, trash cleanup, property damage to landowners, energy use, and especially the costs of medical care and accidents. The Consumer Product Safety Commission found that the average cost of an ATV-related injury was $20,655 in 1997.[12]

Another form of cost associated with recreation is opportunity cost—the opportunities that are passed up in favor of a different choice. For example, if you spend $50 on concert tickets, you forgo the chance to spend that same $50 on video rentals, a fancy dinner, or any other activity you might have chosen. The opportunity cost of the concert is not seeing videos or eating a gourmet dinner. This concept pertains to ATV riding in both personal and societal terms. A family that pursues ATV riding is missing out on all the other opportunities they could pursue with the considerable amount of money that their chosen form of recreation requires—opportunities that may be more enriching and less environmentally damaging. And as a society, paying all the costs of ATV riding—repairing environmental damage, enforcing regulations, paying the medical costs of riders severely injured in accidents—draws money away from alternative uses. Dr. Roger Humphries calculated that the costs of treatment for juvenile victims of ATV accidents at University of Kentucky Hospital totaled $2.1 million in the period 1996 to 2001. And that was at only one hospital.

Controlling ATV Tourism

"When these ATVers are allowed to move about unlicensed, unregistered, and unpoliced, these 'free agents' can run amok—and they do," says Mark Spencer, Kentucky naturalist and video photographer.[13]

Al Fritsch once addressed an environmental club at a public high school in St. Louis, Michigan, the town where devastating industrial chemical contamination occurred in the 1970s. The discussion turned to recreational vehicles. While the environmental consciousness of the school was high, the majority of the students said that they wanted to buy ATVs and snowmobiles. Their teacher told Al afterwards that he had brushed on a touchy subject. The town's only industry had been closed down, and there was little chance of reducing the high unemployment rate except through developing tourism. These teenagers knew that snowmobiles and ATVs are popular and can bring employment opportunities, even if they drive away wildflower photographers or people fishing in rowboats. It's hard for low-impact recreation to coexist with higher-impact ATVs.

From their earliest years, Americans learn that their country is founded on the rights to "life, liberty, and the pursuit of happiness." How, then, can we justify restrictions on ATVers' liberty to travel cross-country, and their (noisy) pursuit of happiness?

Vulnerable public and private lands are a part of the commons, the natural environment that is the public property of all. In pursuing their preferred recreational activity, many ATVers infringe on their fellow citizens' equal right to their own vision of happiness—in peace and quiet. This amounts to a raid on the commons—expropriating public property for one's own use and precluding the possibility of its use by others. This is deemed unacceptable by civilized nations—but it has become all too common over time in instances such as the "privatization" of the American West by homesteaders, railroad barons, and mining companies. When raiders disregard the public good for their private gain, they often defend their actions by fashioning a political system to legitimize their claims. The ATV industry has justified its expropriation of wildlands by an appeal to Americans' love of liberty.

But the right to use a resource is not unconditional. In fact, the right to engage in a recreational activity is conditioned by a variety of competing rights and responsibilities, both on the part of participants and of others who are affected. Our public actions affect our environment, both social and natural. When these activities affect other people negatively, then one person's entertainment becomes another's burden. Society must stand up for the burdened and restrict the one being entertained. A certain type of person may enjoy beating up others for fun, but society decrees this must be confined to the boxing ring.

In our increasingly land-scarce world, the common good demands that we carefully consider competing uses for the limited recreational space that is available. Much of the available arable land is already cultivated or used for habitation. Remaining wildlands are generally rugged and fragile. Private motorized recreational vehicles are invaders, the unwanted but ever-advancing phalanx of modern land grabbers. ATV enthusiasts riding on a hard surface with safety gear, a driver's license, and the property holder's permission may be justifiable; those who harm the environment and endanger the riders and other people must be stopped.

Recreational activities can be subjected to different degrees of restriction. If land is held in common, if there are proper and improper land-related acts, and if the common good requires restrictions on improper activities, it follows that improper recreational use may be restricted or banned. Laws forbidding noisy parties and alcoholic beverages in public parks are already commonplace. In the case of ATVs, restriction could range from minor (placing only the most fragile areas off-limits) to moderate (permitting the activity only in specified areas) to severe (allowing only occupational use by trained and licensed adults). If children are easily hurt on ATVs, age limits need to be imposed. Gray areas exist in enforcement, making decisions more difficult. However, society may and should restrict recreational activities that harm fragile lands, both public and private. The goal is to create a pleasant natural environment where low-impact recreational alternatives may coexist and flourish.

There are a number of possible strategies to limit the damaging effects of ATVs but no guarantees of success. More and more ATVs appear each year, with a more powerful range of engines (increasing from 200 cc. to 680 cc. in recent models), and intimidated citizens and law enforcement officers are unable to act openly for fear of damage to property or their own police record. Here are some possible approaches.

Research and Monitoring

The public is largely unaware of the impacts of ATVs on their locality. A clear understanding of the rapidly emerging cluster of environmental, behavioral, safety, and economic issues related to ATV use has yet to emerge. Currently there is no easily accessible body of information on the volume of ATV use, infringement, operator practices, and other related data. The Natural Trails and Waters Coalition in Missoula, Montana, is seeking to coordinate educational and research efforts in all parts of the United States. Our own research center, ASPI, is now working to determine the exact amount of tourist leakage rates from ATV operators. Assessing the full scope of the problem is essential to raising public awareness.

Publicity

Many Americans subscribe to a libertarian position that allows those seeking recreation to do so in any manner of their own choosing—as long as it does not infringe on others' rights. There is an acute need for more reporting on the safety, economic, and environmental aspects of ATVs, especially the problem of youthful drivers. The media thrives on sensation, so a fatal accident or an incident of cemetery damage might be a front-page story until something even more dramatic comes along. However, publicity can never bring about change by itself, and it can lead to such harmful compromises as establishing "sacrifice zones" and writing off certain areas to be totally trashed by the ATVs. Consistent attention to ongoing problems and potential solutions is needed.

Obstruction

"Those riders were coming in, riding over the patch and popping my watermelons for the fun of it, so I strung piano wire across the gateway and that stopped them," said the late Albert Baldwin, Laurel County, Kentucky.[14]

In their frustration at repeated invasions by ATV riders, many property holders are tempted to resort to practices that could cause bodily harm. The degree of their resistance is a subject of discussion in many states, making this a complex issue. How far can one resist the trespasser? One local resident goes out and shoots his shotgun into the air in an effort to dissuade ATV drivers from trespassing on his property. He is visited five times by state police—but the police do not interrogate the ATV drivers. Other neighbors have spiked their trails with a variety of devices. In retrospect, Albert Baldwin was fortunate that he caused no decapitations with his piano wire. It may be better to create barriers where ATVs are being unloaded or driving at a slower speed. Trail spiking is generally regarded as a bad idea, because tire blowouts can cause serious accidents.

Some obstructionists use methods that are merely unpleasant but not dangerous. One Kentuckian said, "I bring ripe road-kill to spruce up their ORV wallowing hole." Few among us would ever think of making a citizen's arrest, for fear of violent resistance. Reporting vehicle license numbers of violators is possible only in those states that require registration—and only a handful do. Some protective methods, such as posting guards or using security dogs, are quite expensive and may have only a minor effect in hindering ATVers. "I would start by posting the 'Danger—Private Property' red-lettered sign for a week or two, and then I would proceed to sink some nice holes in the ground on either side of the roads and drive. Fill 'em with concrete and set a hasp into it. Get a nice big board, like a 2×12 cut to span between the two hasps. Drive some nice ten-pennies into them thickly, and then screw eyes at either end. Chain the boards to the hasps with padlocks. After they've lost a few tires, they may rethink their route," according to Julie Froelich.[15]

Education

Most schoolchildren, even those involved in environmental activities, think it's cool to ride ATVs cross-country. They see television ads of beautiful scenery, hear their friends boasting, and dream of the power of a revved-up engine. The children will collect cans for recycling and even patiently watch a slide show on preserving the environment, but they still want to ride ATVs like the rest of the gang. One fairly successful project was ASPI's three-year program targeting fourth and fifth graders. We spoke to fifteen thousand children about the need to help save our Mixed Mesophytic Forest in Appalachia, the oldest and most varied temperate hardwood forest in the world. The kids and their teachers responded warmly. All types of educational programs can raise awareness that ATVs are problematic. In 2001, Al Fritsch gave a formal talk on "Monitoring Environmental Damage from Off-Road Vehicles" at the annual Southern Appalachian Man and the Biosphere Conference in Tennessee.

Organizing

Local citizens opposed to ATV activity often feel isolated in enduring noise, trespassing, and intimidation. They need to be persuaded that they are not alone, and that they can come together and act as a group to take joint action. Individual citizens in affected areas are fearful of being singled out as ATV opponents. In fact, at one citizens' organization, neighbors agreed to attend a meeting only after they were promised that there would be no cameras. In meetings with both proponents and opponents of ATV use, we have found that common ground can exist. In upstate New York near Westport, John Davis and a group of landowners decided to post uniform signs reading "Wildlife Safety Zone." At one citizens' meeting at the Rockcastle Resource Center, both pro- and anti-ATV people agreed that "no trespassing" signs should be honored where posted. However, the people in attendance are not the ones who destroy the signs. This notifies ATVers that the community is resolved to stand together to prevent trespassing.

Enforcement

> I could never pursue an ATV for they would go cross-country and I would tear up my cruiser trying. Besides, my superior would reprimand me for running down youth who are all out to have a good time and not hurting anybody.
>
> —Kentucky State Police Officer[16]

In Kentucky, as in most other states, merely enforcing the existing regulations would be sufficient to control ATV use. Current law states that riders must have the landowner's permission to travel on private lands and are restricted to certain permitted areas on public lands. Four-wheelers may not be ridden on public highways for over a quarter of a mile at a time, and, where permitted, can only be driven by licensed drivers over sixteen years of age.

But enforcement of state and federal regulations is spotty and minimal at best. While the U.S. Forest Service has issued citations for violations on public lands, many other governmental agencies do not pursue violators. Even in the case of the Forest Service, the small number of officers means that many infringements go unchallenged. As for local police, it is virtually impossible to find county agencies willing to enforce laws against trespassing or littering. Attracting tourists, they feel, demands a certain leniency in enforcement.

Consumer Advocacy

The advent of motorized vehicle recreation (ATVs, snowmobiles, motorboats, airplanes, etc.) was not rooted in spontaneous demand on the part of consumers, but rather a heavily financed sales campaign by equipment makers who see this as a bonanza of profits. Though this popularity has hidden costs, the manufacturers and trade associations have a number of gimmicks that allow them to escape responsibility for environmental and safety costs. The corporations must shoulder the blame for placing these vehicles in fragile and scenic areas. Without ever explicitly saying so, their advertising invites riders to destroy fragile environments for recreation.

In addition, manufacturers play fast and loose with legal liabilities. The Consumer Product Safety Commission can cite any company that markets unsafe products. By offering "safety training," ATV manufacturers have sidestepped legal liability for injuries caused by use of their product. Holding these manufacturers accountable to the same statutes that regulate other industries could be one step in undoing the damage caused by ATV tourism.

Regulation

Both ATV proponents and opponents in south central Kentucky have agreed to the registration of ATVs, provided that the fees are not exorbitant. This would involve license plates or stickers clearly visible on the vehicles. Such a registration procedure permits easy identification of trespassers, makes it possible to fine unauthorized operators, gives additional information to insurers of ATVs, and allows penalties such as license suspension for drunken driving or other illegal activities. Tighter regulations involving training and proper age requirements could reduce illegal use of these vehicles and risky behavior. Licensing anticipates adequate policing and law enforcement. Regulation costs should be borne by ATV operators, not by the general public. Surplus funds from license sales could begin restoring land damaged by ATVs, but it is doubtful that license fees, no matter how high, could ever be sufficient to complete such a task.

Future Legal Routes

These days, many Internet ads entice ATVers to come and ride illegally in prohibited public areas and to trespass on private lands. Many people are unaware that such advertising over the Internet inviting groups and individuals to ride their ATVs in these favored sites is against the law. To counter this, some activists prefer such legal routes as pressuring state or federal agencies to enforce laws already in place. Others have been petitioning the Federal Trade Commission to put a stop to false and deceptive advertising that depicts recreation using motorized vehicles in fragile terrain. Furthermore, they demand that vehicles must not be described as an "overland" or "all-terrain" recreation vehicle when such phrasing is a clear invitation to

misuse. In due time the advertisers and the media carrying the advertisements will hear the message. ATV manufacturers are beginning to take
more pains to explain the dangers and the need for safety precautions.

Commercial Zones for ATVs?

In the future, providing public or commercial areas where ATV enthusiasts can practice their sport while minimizing environmental and
safety risks may be one way to deal with this problem. A number of state
and federal agencies are now providing regulated hard-surfaced ATV
trails. The Tennessee Valley Authority (TVA) designated for ATV use
an area in the Land Between the Lakes on the western Kentucky-Ten-
nessee border a decade ago, which is now under federal control. The
state of West Virginia has an ATV track that covers miles of ex–surface
mine areas in the southern part of the state. For the family-outing ATV
enthusiasts, these areas are ideal. For the reckless cross- country riders,
such commercial trails are anathema: they don't like to play follow-
the-leader. For them, pleasure and "freedom" go hand in hand.

As a youth Al Fritsch hiked cross-country with his gun over all the
neighboring farms in Mason County, Kentucky. He saw this as his
right as a resident and constitutionally protected bearer of firearms.
Few others were out on those Sunday afternoons, even in no-hunting
seasons. Such was people's misguided sense of the Second Amendment.
In retrospect, cross-country travel of any type cannot be condoned,
especially in more inhabited areas. We are no longer Daniel Boone
roaming his Kentucky hunting ground. A properly controlled ATV
recreation zone lets people enjoy their preferred recreational activity
with family and friends and have weekend leisure. But we cannot per-
mit a macho conquest of wilderness by free-ranging thrill-seekers.

Making ATV tourism more environmentally sound would require
a number of changes. Hard-surfaced tracks would be needed, ones that
could withstand ordinary use, and no cross-country riding would be
permitted. Users could follow each other over a single path or ride two
abreast on wider paths. Tracks would be closed during prolonged
rainy periods. All safety precautions would have to be strictly enforced, with all riders wearing safety gear. A driver's license should be
required to use ATVs. ATVers and their sport associations claim to
love nature. If that really is the case, then any move to protect the
natural environment should be welcome news to these groups.

Reflections

As we have seen, ATV operation is a highly problematic form of "nature tourism." Land is torn up by cross-country travel and by riding in muddy conditions, and wildlife is disturbed by the noise. Animals and plants are run over and killed, and air and water are polluted. Teenage riders run amok in zones that are not properly policed, and reckless and drinking drivers using inherently risky vehicles over rough terrain bring about numerous accidents. Local communities suffer a reduced quality of life, property damage, and loss of community cohesiveness; in addition, they miss an opportunity to develop more beneficial types of tourism. And to crown it all, the leakage rates from spending related to ATV tourism are so high that, despite all the damage they cause, these tourists put virtually no money at all into the host community.

This case study of ATV recreation in Kentucky highlights what can happen when local communities let others make tourism decisions for them. Through their advertising, ATV manufacturers have encouraged users to drive the vehicles cross-country; other states, by imposing (and enforcing) restrictions, have sent ATVers on a search for more lenient locales that will not interfere with their quest for "fun." Kentucky's environment and many of its rural people are now paying a heavy price for that fun.

Such a laissez-faire approach to tourism development virtually guarantees that the needs and wishes of local people will take a back seat to the profit motive of powerful corporate interests (such as the manufacturers of ATVs and their industry organizations) and to outsiders seeking to exploit weak laws and an economy in need of investment. Throughout this book, we argue that in order to benefit from tourism, communities need to take control of its development and proactively make decisions for themselves about what form it should take.

There are many possible forms of nature tourism that could be developed in Appalachia. One type that is currently in the spotlight is ecotourism. In the next chapter, we'll look at how ecotourism developed, who is involved in it, and where it may be headed.

CHAPTER 4

Going Green

Ecotourism as an Emerging Experience

Given the difficulty of pinning down a definition of ecotourism, it's hard to say who the first ecotourists were. Some likely candidates are the Sierra Club members who trooped off on the group's High Trips starting in 1901. Every year, upwards of a hundred members would spend days trekking together in the Sierra Nevada, getting to know the land that their organization was fighting to preserve. On the first trip, participants (including women in long skirts) hiked twenty miles and climbed four thousand feet—in one day! This was hardly "walking lightly on the Earth," though—porters, pack mules, and a whole team of cooks accompanied the huge groups.

As we have seen, nature travel became widespread in Europe during the nineteenth century and has been an important part of American tourism from the nation's birth. But apart from the first hardy visitors, this was generally not a matter of travel to remote, "unspoiled" environments, nor did it involve close interaction with the host cultures.

Where Did Ecotourism Come from?

The impulse to ecotourism has its origins in several intertwined late-twentieth century trends: backpacker travelers, the emerging environmental movement, and the growing affluence of North Americans and western Europeans.

Today, backpackers are everywhere—there are few international airports in the world that don't receive at least a trickle of long-distance independent travelers, most of them in their twenties, staggering under massive, scuffed backpacks and clutching battered guidebooks. The typical backpacker spends a month or more roaming through another continent on a shoestring budget, traveling on battered buses, sleeping at youth hostels or family-owned accommodations, and rubbing elbows with the locals at market stalls.

Backpackers are generally on a quest for new, "undiscovered" destinations—the mountain village with a dramatic religious festival, the empty beach lined with brightly painted fishing boats. But far from getting off the beaten track, these days backpackers have beaten a well-worn track of their own. There are international networks of backpacker hostels, closet-sized travel agencies selling cheap tickets on off-brand airlines to destinations listed on chalkboards out front, and untold thousands of backpacker restaurants serving standard menus of banana pancakes and fruit smoothies.

The backpacker phenomenon emerged during the countercultural explosion of the late 1960s in the U.S. and western Europe. Hippies began journeying eastward overland from Europe across Turkey, Iran, and Afghanistan to Nepal and India, in a quest for spiritual enlightenment, cross-cultural encounters, and cheap drugs. Even stodgy historical novelist James Michener noted and immortalized the trend. His would-be blockbuster *The Drifters* features a wooden depiction of a crowd of foreign dropouts in Morocco in the early 1970s.

The explosion of backpacker travel was not entirely due to cultural influences—there were also commercial factors. In 1968, the International Student Travel Confederation, which had been formed two decades earlier, began issuing its International Student Identification Card, which entitled any full-time student to hefty discounts on air and train fares in a number of countries. The cards were so valuable that counterfeit versions were soon produced for travelers who were not students. Today, despite the endless additions of holograms and other security features, fakes of varying quality are easy to find wherever backpackers congregate.

By the mid-1970s, airlines were beginning to capitalize on these low-budget, long-distance wanderers. At the time, many airlines were suffering from excess capacity, having ordered the new jumbo jets and then confronting the rise in oil prices. They gradually realized that young people would fill the empty seats on their long-haul routes if the price was right, and youth discounts became increasingly common.

The combination of discounts on services in western countries and the exceedingly low prices of the Third World made backpacker travel in the 1970s astoundingly cheap. One memoir posted on a travel website explains exactly how a British student could travel overland from the UK to Nepal and back on £50—all that was permitted by currency export restrictions at the time—and return home with a little cash left over. The author reminisces about his travels in Afghanistan (a great backpacker favorite) where he paid twenty-five cents a night for a cheap hotel, three cents for a bowl of soup, and thirty cents for the 300-mile bus ride from Herat to Kabul.

Growing streams of backpackers began beating their own beaten track around the world, with "hippie trails" emerging across Asia, Latin America, and, to a lesser extent, Africa. These tended to develop "backpacker centers," towns providing services travelers wanted, such as cheap travel agencies, restaurants with English menus, mail drops, and cafes where they could swap information with travelers just arrived from the town up ahead. Asia travelers spoke of the "three Ks": Kabul, Kathmandu, and Kuta (a beach town in Bali).

In 1973, two Australians got tired of answering questions about how they drove from England to Australia, and sat down to write a book giving all the necessary directions. Their book, entitled *Across Asia on the Cheap,* became the cornerstone of an empire. Maureen and Tony Wheeler's Lonely Planet publishing company now offers more than two hundred guidebooks to countries as far-flung as Malawi and Slovenia.

But these guidebooks were more a result of the growth of backpacker travel than a cause. By relying on local transport and accepting local standards of accommodation, backpackers broadened the sphere of travel. Rebelling against their parents' notions of travel, they scorned the Hilton Hotel in the capital city for a palm leaf hut in a friendly village and ate at a stall in the market instead of at a table swathed in white linen.

The goal of the first backpackers was to experience new cultures and environments directly, instead of mediated through the filter of the tourism industry. And for a time, this was quite possible. The first few white faces in a remote Indonesian village were certain to be met with open-mouthed curiosity and an eagerness to communicate. They could share a local family's home and take part in religious ceremonies.

But a thousand visitors later, travelers are almost inevitably faced with a row of hastily built guesthouses, cafés with noisy cassette players blaring last year's U.S. Top Ten hits, and a line of hustlers hawking souvenirs and treks to more remote, "unspoiled" locations—and the backpackers are off again on their ceaseless quest for authenticity.

These backpackers expanded the horizons of mass travel. Where backpackers go, the masses almost inevitably follow. As travel guru Arthur Frommer noted in a 2001 issue of his *Budget Travel Magazine,* "The vacation choices of penniless backpackers tend to become mainstream favorites in later years." Observations like this have been formalized into anthropological models of tourist behavior. In her path-breaking 1977 work *Hosts and Guests: The Anthropology of Tourism,* Valene L. Smith described a spectrum of seven tourist types. These range from the lone "explorer" who is among the first outsiders to visit a region and lives according to local norms, through the "unusual" tourist who takes an adventure tour and adapts somewhat to local norms, to the "charter" tourists who arrive by the planeload and demand all the amenities of home.[1]

Until the 1960s, international tourism was confined almost exclusively to North America and western Europe. Now, tour operators offer packages to the most remote corners of the globe, and Kristin Johannsen, one of the authors of this book, has met families with toddlers "doing" Indonesia, and busloads of retired Brits on the Silk Road. For example, Grand Circle Tours, which caters exclusively to the senior citizen market, has tours to Fiji, Thailand, and China's Yangtze (Chang Jiang) River.

Individual destinations can move rapidly from the private preserve of lone backpackers to a product worth packaging for mass consumption. In the early 1990s, Vietnam was territory only for the hardiest of independent travelers, those able to cope with its juddering buses and bare-bones hotels. Today, it's going mainstream, with package tours and luxury hotels.

At roughly the same time that the backpackers were beginning to cross continents en masse, a new political movement was focusing the public's attention for the first time on threats to the global environment. Though books like Rachel Carson's *Silent Spring* raised awareness of some specific environmental problems during the 1960s, it was the first Earth Day Celebration on April 22, 1970, that marked the first widespread public recognition that human activities threaten the survival of natural systems.

There followed a widespread reexamination of the impact of many human activities on the environment, and the more sensitive travelers began to consider the effect their presence had on the ecosystems they were visiting. Environmental groups established guidelines that called for travelers to minimize their use of resources by using energy-efficient transportation and consuming local food and other products. People became more aware of issues like garbage disposal. Travelers in Nepal began to request that trekking companies carry kerosene for cooking, rather than cutting firewood from the fast-disappearing forests.

According to The International Ecotourism Society, the first true ecotourism businesses emerged in the early 1980s, when more biologists began carrying out studies and filming documentaries on coral reefs and rainforests. Small local operators sprang up to provide services to scientists and filmmakers working in these areas, and later to amateurs interested in bird watching and other nature pursuits. Animal-watching safaris in East Africa may have been the first actual ecotours, though the name developed later. Costa Rica, in particular, soon evolved a large number of nature-tour specialists.

Travelers in remote areas could hardly help being captivated by the dramatic natural environments they saw—the rainforests of South America, the terraced mountainsides of Nepal, the coral atolls of the Pacific Islands. Later, some travelers began to consider the environment itself as an attraction, a worthy destination. Bird-watching enthusiasts have long searched for rare species to add to their lists, but new activities like whale watching, rainforest hiking, and coral reef snorkeling surged in popularity. Certain destinations, such as Belize and the Galapagos Islands of Ecuador, began to focus almost entirely on ecotourism in their marketing.

With tours to Antarctica now a not-uncommon occurrence, it's hard to imagine where the next frontier of ecotourism will be. The International Ecotourism Society lists Guyana, Cuba, Mali, and Togo as "up and coming destinations." The backpackers are already there, prowling around the rainforests and pointing their binoculars, and the tour groups are sure to follow.

A third factor in the rise of ecotourism, one that also provided the basis for backpacker travel and environmental activism, was the increasing affluence of many people in America and other western countries. In the latter half of the twentieth century, many workers earned ample money while working shorter hours, opening up the option of spending their time on long, aimless trips, or investing it in activities like public interest environmental work.

Furthermore, for the average person, work itself was getting less strenuous. In earlier eras, a vacation was seen as a well-earned respite from strenuous labor during the rest of the year. Farm and industrial workers would have found little attraction in arduous travel through difficult settings. But by the 1980s, the economy had shifted towards white-collar work to such a degree that an increasing number of Americans and Europeans found physically demanding travel to remote areas a refreshing break from the monotony of office work.

It was in the 1990s that ecotourism really took off during the longest period of economic expansion in U.S. history, which was fueled by the boom in technology. Working-class people continued to enjoy the same vacations they always had—visits to friends or family, trips to regional resorts or theme parks, and camping and outdoor activities, perhaps in a state park. Though the hardy backpackers can be considered the pioneer ecotourists, it was the affluent, sedentary "information workers" searching for new vacation worlds to conquer who really drove the ecotourism boom.

Industry analysts quickly ascertained that participants in ecotours were older, better educated, and more affluent than the general tourist. A 1994 study much quoted by the travel industry found that North Americans on ecotours were aged 35 to 54, and that 82 percent were college graduates (compared with 24 percent of the U.S. population in general). Most importantly, they have deep pockets: the largest group of those surveyed said they were willing to spend from $1001 to $1500 per trip, more than general tourists.[2]

It is this fact, more than any desire to preserve the environment or benefit local communities, that has led to the exploding number of tours and companies that label themselves "green" or "eco." As The International Ecotourism Society points out, "Many travel and tourism businesses have found it convenient to use the term 'ecotourism' in their literature, and governments have used the term extensively to promote their destinations, all without trying to implement any of the most basic principles" of actual ecotourism.[3]

For too many operators and travelers, ecotourism is merely a trendy product to be bought and sold. Rather than a mode of tourism that benefits the environment and the host community, ecotourism becomes a designer label to command premium prices in the tourism marketplace.

Selling Nature Tourism

Though it's all but invisible to vacationers, the tourism industry invests staggering amounts of money and effort in analyzing what travelers want and how to sell it to them most effectively. The nature tourism market, in particular, is a focus of attention for research because of its actual growth and its perceived potential. For example, a study carried out by Kenneth E. Silverberg and colleagues attempted to segment and analyze the market for nature tourism to the southeastern U.S. and pinpoint exactly what the different groups of tourists were looking for.[4] The study identified six "benefit-group profiles" of different types of nature tourists (classified by main interest, such as wildlife-viewing or relaxation), identified the unique demographic characteristics of each group (including differences in age and place of residence), and finally outlined the most effective advertising approaches to use with each group.

One introductory textbook on the industry presents the topic of tourism marketing by admonishing its naïve readers: "Tourists do not take vacations just to relax and have fun, to experience another culture, or to educate themselves and their children. They take vacations in the hope and belief that these vacations will satisfy, either wholly or partially, various needs and wants. This view of tourist motivations, while seemingly a partial one, is critical. . . . It is the difference between those travel agents who see themselves as sellers of airline seats and those who view themselves as dealers in dreams."[5]

Travelers, the text goes on to explain, think they are looking for a Caribbean cruise—but what they actually hope to buy is the esteem (and envy) of their friends. They think they are shopping for a discount airfare to go visit their parents, when what they are really trying to buy is love. The successful tourism marketer is the one who can persuade the potential customer that buying the experience on offer is the best or even the only way to satisfy these unconscious psychological needs. And nature tourism is no exception.

The first step in this type of marketing is to make potential customers feel dissatisfied with their current situation, awakening a "need" they may not have previously felt. An Appalachian example is a 2002 ad by the West Virginia Division of Tourism featuring a photo of a couple and a little girl bicycling down a leafy country road next to a creek and the caption "Get in touch with your family." The text reads, "Remember life before soccer schedules and video games? Get reacquainted with what really counts, in Wild and Wonderful West Virginia."

The girl appears to be about eight years old, far too young to remember (or care about) an era without video games. Clearly, the childhood being appealed to is the reader's own, a mythical time when pleasures were supposedly simple and the essentials of life were provided by nurturing parents. The photo in the ad is taken from such an angle that the adults appear to be the same size as the child—all three appear to be child-sized. The experience being sold is the impossible dream of retreating back to one's own childhood—and the way to do this is by vacationing in West Virginia.

People undertake pleasure travel for a wide variety of reasons, both conscious and unconscious. Some in the travel industry have analyzed these reasons using the framework of psychologist Abraham Maslow's hierarchy of needs.[6] Basically, Maslow's theory states that all human beings have the same underlying needs, which they try to satisfy from the most basic upwards.

In Maslow's scheme, the most fundamental are the physiological needs, those for food, drink, rest, and activity. Once these are satisfied, we turn our attention to safety—the needs for security and freedom from anxiety. Next comes belonging—we need to feel affection and a sense of relationship to others. The fourth level is esteem, both self-esteem and the esteem of others. The highest level is self-actualization, the need to fulfill one's potential.

All of this can be (and has been) neatly translated into the framework of travel. Some travelers are mainly trying to satisfy physical needs—for example, taking a lazy beach vacation to relieve the tension of a stressful job. Others may choose a spa vacation or some other health-related break, which satisfies the need for safety by ensuring our longevity. The need for belonging is satisfied by family-oriented vacations, trips to visit friends, and journeys to one's ethnic "roots." Trips to glamorous, exotic, or high-prestige destinations clearly appeal to the need for esteem—being "one up" on others. Finally, cultural, learning, and service-oriented travel address our need for self-actualization.

Of course, human beings have myriad possible ways to satisfy their various needs—but the travel industry wants to persuade them that travel is *the* way to do it. If nature tourism is perceived as the "flavor of the day," then it, too, will be reshaped and repackaged in its most salable form, aimed at people's underlying needs and desires.

Nature tourism can be targeted at people's physical needs, such as the stressed-out worker's desperate need for a respite from an overstimulating job. A 2002 ad for North Carolina tourism is a graphic example of this. Superimposed over a photo of a figure canoeing a mirrorlike mountain lake at sunset is a pink office-style phone-message slip printed with the words "While you were out." The handwritten message: "Worry called. Wondered where you'd been." In the wake of the 2001 terrorist attacks in the U.S., the travel industry got great mileage out of selling the "safety" of nature travel in particular locations—using "friendly" as a code word.

Innumerable ads tout nature travel as the way to heighten the sense of belonging in your family. An ad promoting Gulf Shores, Alabama, shows a family of four holding hands as they walk along a suspiciously empty beach. The text promises "sugar-white sand, emerald water, fewer crowds, and countless ways to get even closer to the ones you love." And if you are lacking in "ones you love," nature travel can supply that too. Windjammer Barefoot Cruises, an operator of sailing yachts in the Caribbean, claims to provide (in capital letters, no less) "small intimate groups of barefoot shipmates."

One of the most common messages employed in advertising nature travel is the appeal to the traveler's need for admiration from others—through the obscurity of the place visited. Some common terms applied to destinations are "unspoiled," "remote," "pristine"—all of which imply that the locale has been unvisited by the traveler's peers (or rivals). An adventure tour operator is not a mere tour operator but an "outfitter," equipping travelers to venture into hazardous unknown destinations. Never mind that almost certainly these places are home to entire communities who live there, raise kids, and earn their living by the daily grind.

Similarly, a trip is not a tour that anyone can purchase by plunking down money but rather a "journey," "trek," "safari," or even an "expedition." "Highly individualized private journeys to Africa's most pristine destinations," claims tour operator Explore, Inc. Costa Rica Experts says customers will "experience an endless variety of exotic adventures." Outer Edge Expeditions specializes in "the most remote wilderness and culture imaginable." Speakers at travel industry conferences emphasize that to be successful, adventure tour operators need to package and sell experiences that tourists will be unable to reproduce on their own.

The highest-level need on Maslow's hierarchy is for self-actualization, the realization of one's potential. To some extent, all nature tourism appeals to self-actualization, provided that there is a learning component involved. Even the largest group of whale watchers on a commercial tour boat can get a new appreciation of a magnificent and endangered species if meaningful information is well conveyed. Interpretive centers at national parks and other public outdoor sites teach about nature to a mass audience. "Learning vacations" of all types are a growing niche market in the travel industry.

True ecotourism (as opposed to general nature tourism) appeals to higher needs—for learning, generosity, and a sense of connectedness with the natural world. This combination is embodied in a program called Eco-Escuela de Español, located in San Andres, Guatemala, an isolated village in the Central American tropical forest. "Learn Spanish, Protect the Rainforest, & Explore Guatemala," proclaims their humble photocopied brochure.

The program is a joint venture between the village and Conservation International, an NGO operating in thirty countries. At the Eco-Escuela, participants study Spanish one-on-one with qualified teachers for twenty hours a week and spend their afternoons studying forest ecology and conservation and working on reforestation projects. All students live with local families, who supplement their income and broaden their worldview by hosting foreign travelers. The brochure says that participants can "become immersed in the language and culture of a region rarely discovered by tourists" and "gain a greater understanding of the threats facing Guatemala's tropical forest and traditional cultures." And if along the way you have an experience to impress your friends at home with, who can really complain?

Motivations for Tourism, and Motivations for Ecotourism

The driving forces behind ecotourism may be much the same as mainstream tourism, but with some key differences. Much depends on the lessons learned by the ecotourist through contact with the world around him or her—a world which is in itself quite healing and enriching, if we but stop and listen.

As we have seen, different people may go on the same trip for a variety of reasons—to de-stress from a draining job, to overcome boredom, to practice a favorite sport, to spend some extra money, to address health concerns, to one-up traveling friends, or to chalk up another "adventure." None of these motives seem elevated, though they could have some value under the right circumstances. What are some valid motivations for ecotourism?

We seek to experience the thrill of nature in all its wild beauty, and to put this experience to some deeper purpose. This thrill can be profound, or it can be merely a macho sense of conquest, namely, "conquering" high mountains, coral reefs, or tropical forests. Too often, the driving force is the desire to have an adventure that others have not yet experienced. This motivation may not differ too much from the thrills of the early conquistadors or the explorers of the great North American landscape. Much has been written about weaknesses of their motivation and how the biblical imperative in Genesis "to conquer" has been misapplied to a conquest of nature, rather than living with and having responsibility for all creatures. Here, the thrill is something akin to military combat.

A true ecotourist recognizes the fallacy of such reasoning and, in fact, may be philosophically committed to opposing it. However, we are all part of our society, and thrill-seeking is in our blood. We struggle within the prevailing culture's appetite for conquest in technical supremacy, sports, and political leadership. We strive to be number one, and there is a shared thrill related to the effort.

Another form of motivation is curiosity. We are driven to learn about the earth's diverse surface, the flora and fauna of the world, and all natural systems. This striving for knowledge is more salutary than mere thrill-seeking for its own sake. Here, the quest to learn about the unknown drives people to great lengths in researching and probing the planet's wealth of species. An added motivation for action now is that these species are disappearing at a tremendous rate, so the time is short to verify and observe those threatened with extinction. There is still a possibility that if we are observant, persistent, and perhaps lucky, we could make a new discovery, and do our part in preserving a threatened portion of the planet. For some students, a vital part of ecotourism is the ability to build one's résumé and improve one's professional standing. Education is a journey of discovery, one that can involve travel as well as study.

Some people view ecotourism through the lens of their own needs and well-being, and ecotourism can also be a quest for personal healing. Today much time and effort is spent on healing people, and any effort at taking a more natural approach should not be dismissed as a waste of resources. Ecotourism may not be a traditional form of healing, but alternative travel may have positive effects on the individual traveler. Health improvement here involves a participation in the earth rhythms of certain places. Writer Kenny Ausubel speaks of "ecological Medicine."[7] This means advancing public (and private) health by improving the environment. The goal of this type of medicine is to promote health, not to cure disease. Humans are part of their local ecosystems, and if a disturbed ecosystem can make people mentally ill, it can surely also make people physically ill.

Some ecotravelers feel that visiting places where the environment is relatively pristine will be a healing experience. Making trips for personal healing is not something new—visiting hot springs for health reasons has been practiced by those who could afford it since ancient times. Appalachia was a prime destination for this early on, at places like Montvale Springs, Tennessee, and White Sulphur Springs, (West) Virginia. "Taking the waters" was a form of healing (real or imagined) that involved soaking in and drinking water from mineral springs. In the heyday of mineral springs during the late nineteenth century, the number of such devotees at some resorts and springs ran into the tens of thousands, especially when railroads brought people in comfort to locations like Saratoga Springs, New York, or West Baden Springs, Indiana.

Finally, we may speak of a sense of healing presence. Many people are truly caring souls who are deeply concerned about the condition of the Earth. Rather than a concern with self, this is a concern about the suffering other. The planet is suffering through pollution, and caring people are convinced that part of the healing process is to do something about it. We all see the value of going to the bedside of an ailing friend, for a visit is salutary and quite beneficial to both parties. For those of us who contend that the Earth is a being with feelings, a concept found in the Bible, being present is a corporal work of mercy.

Of course, the motivations of a traveler may be mixed, and are often wholly unconscious. A letter written to a friend by a participant in an East African safari shows a whole range of driving forces:

> I had to take the trip to Kenya since Uncle Tom said before he died that I should use his inheritance in a way that would please him most, and he loved animals. The thrill of Africa beckoned me to come during my two month accrued vacation time; so I went over with Pat who knew a bargain when it comes along yet endured the heat to please me. Fun, fun, did I ever have fun and I learned more than any one year in college and that's without paying ten-thou in tuition. I'm glad I went for I identified with all the animals. Enclosed are six photos taken without telescopic lens. Yes they have bad breath, especially the flesh eaters. But I was glad I went. I found my Earth Spirit is all the wildlife. Uncle Tom's love for these poor threatened creatures was transferred to me. It was great. Wish you had been there too. [Personal communication to ASPI staff]

A critic of ecotourism may say that such mixed motives are hardly praiseworthy. The desires of this African-bound ecotourist could have been satisfied in far simpler ways than going on a 9,000-mile trip. Consider how much water could have been pumped to irrigate Kenyan agricultural fields with the fuel consumed in air travel, or how easy it would have been to simply see the lions at the local zoo. Playing with unwanted pets at the local animal shelter or feeding pigeons and squirrels in the park could have satisfied the concern for animals. Why a trip to Africa? Only the affluent could afford such a trip, or feel a supposed "obligation" to spend an inheritance in such a fashion.

An advocate of ecotourism would counter by asking: what activities do not have some mix of motivations, each with varying levels of merit? And isn't our journey in life an ongoing struggle to purify our motivation? One benefit of travel is that it makes real the symbolic journey of life. It becomes the symbol of the reality of life. In this sense, ecotouring that starts out as simple thrill-seeking may become, after deep reflection, an experience that teaches us much more about ourselves. We achieve something far more enriching than what we set out to do. The travel experience itself may prove instrumental in transforming motivation, by providing the time and emotional distance we need, and the healing process to remake ourselves.

Nature Travel to Exotic Places

For about five years, I was obsessed with scuba diving. I took it up when I was living in the Persian Gulf and the nearest coral reef was a short drive away, and it truly did give me an awe-stricken regard for the part of the planet that's underwater. At one point, I spent a month working extremely hard as a volunteer diver doing underwater surveys to establish a Marine Protected Area in Belize. But as a scuba diver, I was burning up vast amounts of fossil fuels to fly to tropical countries and to pilot the boats out to the reefs. I was benefiting from the low wages of the workers who made it all possible—the dive industry relies on having an endless supply of underpaid labor in Third World countries to keep it going. Can I pretend that the effect of my greater awareness of the marine environment outweighs that?

Kristin Johannsen

People are drawn to the exotic—to places far removed from the region where we grew up, or regions we later came to know. We yearn to see strange (to us!) flora and fauna, or unfamiliar climates like arid deserts or steamy rainforests, or dramatic geological formations—the highest mountains, the deepest canyons, the emptiest plains. These may be in Central America, or central Asia—the improved accessibility of travel now makes previously exotic places a mere day or two's travel away.

Exotic nature destinations are now not unapproachable or even particularly difficult to reach. Whole shelves of eco-guidebooks are published, with how-to details as well as information on flora and fauna. The *Ecotravellers' Wildlife Guide* series from Academic Press covers Tropical Mexico, Belize and northern Guatemala, Alaska, Hawai'i, Costa Rica, Ecuador and its Galapagos Islands, and Peru, with other titles projected to include the Caribbean Islands, Florida, East Africa, and South Africa.

Ecotourists in remote, exotic destinations are especially dependent on their tour guides and other information providers, who need to be both responsible and knowledgeable. These people should possess a deep understanding of a country's wildlife and conservation issues, and they should be committed to communicating this to visitors. Most recreational tourists will not have much background knowledge of the host country or its ecosystems. The visit may be relatively short, and so much information will need to be disseminated during the stay. Quite often distractions such as food, lodging, evening entertainment, and transportation details will crowd the day as well. For a really educational visit, literature, journals, and photographs may be necessary supplements to direct experience of the local ecosystem.

Travel to exotic places can be an opportunity to learn about the flora and fauna and the culture and ways of the people, or it can be just a way to rationalize extravagance. Educational trips to exotic destinations can benefit even those who don't go along, if the traveler keeps careful records about the place, its natural environment, and its culture, and brings the information back to share with others. But why must numerous individuals travel to truly fragile places such as Antarctica, and render them no longer exotic? The most avid globetrotter does not wish all of the world's people to follow suit. Okay, we might say, not all—then who? Are you documenting everything you see so that others can learn without destroying the place? Or are you saying that I can go but you must not, lest you become the straw that breaks the (endangered) camel's back?

One of the major problems with ecotourism arises when it says all the correct things and yet acts as though its own impact is immaterial. The Explorer II, an "eco-ship" taking tourists through the Galapagos Islands, advertises that all its compostable wastes and recyclables are air-freighted from the cruise ship to the mainland. But this is hardly ecological, in any sense of the word, but rather conspicuous consumption pretending to be ecological. We should instead be asking: Should tourists be there in the first place? What is the impact of their presence—including the expenditure of fossil fuel to ship their garbage—and is it really balanced by any amount of environmental learning? At what point does tourism weaken or strengthen the cultural bonds of the local people by defining them as the exotic? Is there not a covert elitism that hurts both the host community—and the tourist? Questions like these need to be considered before developing ecotourism—not after the fact.

The Major Players in Ecotourism

As the hottest trend in the travel market, so-called ecotourism is being marketed to ever broader categories of people by an ever-widening range of businesses. From hard-core backpacking trips where participants haul fifty-pound packs for weeks at a time to multinational hotel chains that place little cards asking guests to use their bed linens an extra day (not coincidentally cutting expenses for the corporation), everyone claims to be practicing ecotourism. Environmentalists allege that many programs claiming the ecotourism label are nothing but greenwashing—"conventional mass tourism wrapped in a thin veneer of green," as researcher Martha Honey succinctly puts it.[8]

Who is involved in promoting, marketing, and carrying out "ecotourism"? We can start our analysis by dividing organizations into two major groups: nonprofit organizations and businesses. The nonprofit organizations include some devoted exclusively to ecotourism, such as The International Ecotourism Society (TIES), based in the U.S. Founded in 1990 "to make tourism a viable tool for conservation and sustainable development," its membership includes researchers, consultants, and government officials as well as tour operators and lodge owners.

In Europe, there are a number of responsible tourism organizations that take a slightly different approach. Tourism Concern in the UK and the Arbeitskreis für Tourismus und Entwicklung (Foundation for Tourism and Development) in Germany both raise awareness of the impact of tourism on the environment and culture of the destination country, and produce codes of behavior for the responsible tourist.

Many environmental and development organizations have become involved in ecotourism, seeing it as a means to further their specific purpose. The United Nations Environment Program has been promoting ecotourism as a means of reducing the negative impact of tourism. Conservation International has developed twelve ecotourism programs in partnership with local groups in the Third World to protect environmental "hot spots."

Many business organizations have jumped on the ecotourism bandwagon. The World Tourism Organization, the hub of the mass tourism industry, was a major organizer of the 2002 International Year of Ecotourism program. Industry bodies such as the World Trade and Tourism Council and the Pacific Asia Travel Association have heavily promoted ecotourism.

A notable characteristic of these organizations is their penchant for holding numerous conferences, workshops, colloquia, and summits, both individually and jointly—and preferably in the most scenic and pleasant settings possible. For example, the run-up to the World Ecotourism Summit, held in Quebec City, Canada, in 2002, included regional meetings in Maputo, Mozambique; Thessaloniki, Greece; Cuiaba, Brazil; Male, in the Maldive Islands; Salzburg, Austria; Fiji; the Seychelles—not an ugly duckling among them.

All of these meetings were organized by the WTO-OMT in partnership with the United Nations Environment Program, and all charged fees for participation (attendance at the World Ecotourism Summit cost $300 per person) in addition to the travel expenses required to reach these inaccessible destinations. A spokeswoman for The International Ecotourism Society said that the budget was too low to bring actual ecotourism operators from Third World countries to the world meeting. One wonders why the same work couldn't be accomplished through online seminars, such as those successfully held by the Mountain Institute, an organization that links mountain-related environmental groups around the world, and Planeta.com, a responsible tourism website focusing on Latin America.

Some nonprofit environmental groups are also in the nature travel business. They offer trips for their members, both as a means of raising funds for the organization and as an educational program. The Sierra Club's "outings" are a well-known example, with trips to wilderness areas in the U.S. and overseas. Some of these also include a service component, such as trail maintenance and plant community restoration. The Audubon Society, the Nature Conservancy, and the Earthwatch Institute are among the groups that sponsor nature travel programs.

The second major category involved in ecotourism is tourism-related businesses, and here things get much murkier. How green do you have to be to count?

Generally, analysts divide international tourism-related businesses into the following categories. *Travel agents* work with individual travelers to make arrangements for travel (for example, "Getaway Travel" at your local mall). *Outbound operators* are companies in the traveler's home country that put together package tours (for example, "Tropical Expeditions" with a range of trips to Costa Rica, Belize, and Guatemala) for sale by travel agents. *Inbound operators* are businesses in the destination country that arrange services for travelers (for example, "Maya Ecotours" lines up the lodges, jeeps with drivers, and nature guides for customers of "Tropical Expeditions" and other outbound operators). Finally, at the bottom level are the *local service providers*, which actually supply the tourists' needs, including rooms, meals, and activities (example: "Jose's Rainforest Lodge"). Service providers range from the high-school student who guides tourists on weekends for pocket money, to the Accor Group, which owns 3,500 hotels in ninety countries.

Businesses in each of these categories come in every size—and in every shade of green. Given that one of the defining tenets of ecotourism is minimizing the environmental impact of travel, it seems clear that the smaller the scale of operations, the less the impact will be. However, it is some of the biggest mass-tourism providers that make the loudest claims to the "green" label. British Airways, for example, trumpeted that it had reduced emissions by passenger-mile between 1991 and 1993—conveniently ignoring the fact that because the number of people traveling farther had grown, its overall emissions increased by 6 percent.[9]

In the category of travel agents, few (if any) specialize in "ecotourism," since by their nature travel agents deal with a broad spectrum of customers. On the other hand, there are a large number of outbound operators who do specialize in nature travel. A 1996 study compiled data from a survey of eighty-two outbound operators in the U.S. that offered nature tours; it found that they sent a total of 119,810 clients on trips, with Central America ranking the most popular destination. The size of the businesses varied wildly, with the number of clients ranging from as few as twenty-five to as many as fifteen thousand, but the five largest had almost forty perecent of the total number of clients.[10] Again, we can be skeptical about whether nature tourism on a massive scale can really protect the environment, or give local people anything beyond a lot of poorly paid service jobs.

Inbound operators are generally located in the main urban areas of Third World countries. The choices they make in the services they purchase for tourists have a strong influence on how "green" a tour actually is. Do they put visitors in big resorts or family-run guesthouses? Is transportation to remote areas by plane or on foot with pack animals?

By definition, local providers for nature tourism are located in remote areas, mostly in Third World countries, so it can be very difficult to collect data about them. Though there are a few genuine ecotourism providers that are truly owned by and operated for the benefit of the whole community (for example, the Community Guesthouses in Belize), we can expect that the most affluent people of the country own many of the largest and most profitable service providers. Though some enterprises can be started with little or no investment (such as a one-person guide service), it takes a lot of capital to build a hotel or to buy a whale-watching boat.

Tourism businesses vary greatly in the depth and nature of their commitment to the principles of ecotourism, however they may define it. In a paper entitled "Ecotourism and Ethics," David Cruise Malloy and David Fennell outline a whole range of ethical stances that ecotourism (and other) businesses can take. These range from a "market culture" (promoting ecotourism as a means to make money by exploiting nature) through a "sociobureaucratic culture" (promoting ecotourism as a way to meet societal norms and expectations) to a "principled culture" (promoting ecotourism out of a commitment to ecological values). But they note that fundamentally, moving to higher-order ethical principles depends on a business's desire to transform its organizational culture and conclude, with a hint of despair, that "only some types of tourism or tourism operators may be interested in attaining the final level of the proposed model. To those not motivated in this way, it will be business as usual."[11]

How Green Is It? The Problem of Certification

How, then, can concerned travelers know whether a trip they are considering is bona fide ecotourism—or just the same old mass tourism with a trendy green label? It seems obvious that an objective system of standards and ratings is needed, to give a seal of approval (including a special logo) to businesses and programs that meet environmental criteria and benefit the local community.

In reality, certification is an extremely thorny issue. As we have noted many times, there is still no universally accepted definition of ecotourism. Even if one were adopted, a number of controversies would remain. Who has the authority to set the standards? What criteria should be used? How should they be weighted—for example, should approval be given to a program that is environmentally exemplary but employs no local people? Or one that provides revenue to the community but has only a weak educational component? Should certification be international, so that programs in two different countries can be compared? Or should it be national or regional, to target concerns specific to that geographical area?

Despite such uncertainties, environmental groups have hardly been waiting on the sidelines for these issues to be clarified. A study by the World Tourism Organization found no fewer than 104 competing (and incompatible) schemes for certifying environmentally sound tourism programs around the world. Of these, over fifty are based in Europe, while Africa has none at all. Most cover specific fields, such as hotels or beaches. Despite the proliferation of labels, the WTO-OMT study found that worldwide, only seven thousand tourism "products" (such as a tour or lodge) had received any form of certification at all.[12]

A major problem with these eco-certifications is that they are of two drastically different types. *Performance-based* certifications measure how well businesses meet a set of outside criteria. This provides a "yardstick," which makes it possible for travelers to compare different tours, hotels, and programs. For example, the government of Costa Rica has set up a program called the Certificate of Sustainable Tourism that specifies 153 criteria for hotels and guesthouses and ranks them in five categories.

Process-based certifications, on the other hand, measure how well a business is moving towards meeting targets that they set for themselves. For example, a hotel company may set a specific goal for reducing electricity consumption at its various properties, and then track changes at each one over a period of time. The problem comes when these internal standards are touted to the public as objective certifications. It is quite possible, for example, that a hotel that has greatly reduced its energy use may be damaging the environment with its excessive garbage production—or paying its workers miserable wages. Consumers have no way of knowing what's behind the labels that businesses choose to apply to themselves.

The tourism industry has a strong vested interest in planning and carrying out its own environmental certification programs, in order to head off the threat of outside scrutiny, specifically government regulation. The World Travel and Tourism Council, made up of the CEOs of the largest corporations involved in tourism, has invested a great deal of time and money in promoting its own Green Globe certification program. Rights to use the Green Globe logo in a business's advertising can involve as little as making a verbal commitment to "environmental improvement"—and paying a fee. The program does have several levels of certification, some of which do have measurable criteria—but how many members of the traveling public are aware of that?

Obviously, if these "ecolabels" are to have any significance at all, there must be some agreement as to who has the authority and what criteria they should use. But until there is a broadly accepted definition of ecotourism to base these on, certifying green travel programs will continue to be an exercise in rhetoric—and an excuse for more international get-togethers. In 2001, a group of big ecotourism players met at Mohonk Mountain House, a resort in New York state, and laboriously worked out an agreement to set up a body called the Sustainable Tourism Stewardship Council, a group that would accredit groups that want to run certification programs. Stay tuned for bigger and better international conferences, in ever more mouthwatering destinations.

Ironically, while the ecotourism industry is expending vast amounts of energy in arguing about certification, actual travelers have shown little awareness, or even interest, in ecolabels of any sort. Ron Mader, owner of Planeta.com, one of the largest and most comprehensive websites about responsible tourism, reported that he has never had a consumer specifically ask for a certified tour.[13] This could be a result of the confusing profusion of ecolabels—or an indication of the lack of real environmental concern among supposedly "green" travelers, who may only be grabbing on to the latest trend in travel.

Who Are the Ecotourists Today?

Though, as we've seen, there is a lot of debate about the exact size of the ecotourism market, few people would dispute the fact that it is growing—at 9 percent annually, according to WTO-OTM estimates. Who is taking all of these ecotrips—of every shade of green?

Again, it's difficult to pin down information, partly because there is so little agreement about what counts as an ecotour. The travel industry generally refers to the study discussed above, which found that ecotourists were about evenly divided between male and female, mostly between thirty-five and fifty-four years of age, well-educated, and with a higher than average household income.

But more recent studies have criticized the methodology of this research as faulty. It was carried out by surveying customers who had made arrangements for ecotours through tour operators, while ignoring the large number of tourists traveling independently and making their own arrangements.

A study that used a different approach found a very different pattern. The Rural Ecotourism Assessment Project, carried out in Belize in 2000, surveyed all passengers in the departure lounge of the country's only international airport on certain days and tallied the responses of twelve hundred travelers who said they had participated in ecotourism during their visit.

The picture that emerged was completely different. Less than half of these travelers had arranged their trip through a travel agent or tour operator in their home country—and so would not have been counted in other studies, which surveyed only the customers of such businesses—and 87 percent of them used the Internet to research or purchase travel. Most surprisingly, 57 percent were under forty years of age. Though 75 percent had stayed in a standard hotel or resort on the current visit, many indicated that they would prefer to stay in an ecolodge or community guesthouse on their next visit.[14]

This study showed nature tourists to be younger than previously thought, with many years of travel still ahead of them, and more open to true, community-based ecotourism than older travelers, who are increasingly demanding all the standard resort-style comforts in the heart of the jungle and skipping the nature walk to laze by the pool.

But we have to ask ourselves—how typical are international ecotourists in the first place? The startling fact is that less than 23 percent of the U.S. population holds a valid passport.[15] We are overwhelmingly a nation that prefers to travel domestically—to "see America first."

In the wake of the 2001 terrorist attacks, this pattern intensified, though the long-term result remains to be seen. A survey of "active travelers" carried out by the Away.com website in 2002 found that 62 percent of the respondents were more likely to travel within North America. The travel industry noted the increasing trends towards family vacations, outdoor recreation, and emphasis on personal growth.

Appalachia is perfectly situated, both geographically and psychologically, to capitalize on these trends. It is easily accessible by car from main U.S. population centers of the East Coast, Midwest, and Upper South; at the same time it is little known and somewhat exotic. It offers plenty of activities for family travelers, as well as preserving a distinctive culture in striking natural settings. At the same time, its environment is in dire need of protection, and local economies would almost certainly benefit to some extent from an increased number of visitors.

The time seems ripe to consider developing ecotourism in Appalachia. But what can we learn from the experiences of other places that have attempted this—both overseas and in the United States?

CHAPTER 5

Lessons for Appalachia 1

Ecotourism in Developing Countries

Though it seems that everyone in Appalachia has high hopes for the future of tourism, from state governors down to small-town dwellers, the fact remains that the industry is comparatively undeveloped here. The Appalachian states are relatively low on the list of U.S. tourist destinations. In 1998, the entire state of Virginia took in 2.8 percent of total tourist expenditures in the U.S., with only a part of that going to the mountain areas, and the rest to the suburbs of Washington, D.C., Williamsburg, and other major non-mountain areas. Other Appalachian states had much lower percentages of the total, down to West Virginia, with a minuscule 0.4 percent of the country's tourist spending—$1.5 billion, compared with California's $54 billion.

In considering the future development of nature-based tourism in the region, it's well worth looking in detail at the effects it has had on other destinations that have followed this path of development. In this chapter, we'll examine two very different countries, Nepal and Belize. Both have tourist industries centered almost exclusively on nature tourism, and both have experienced massive growth in nature tourism—and its consequences.

Tourism Takes Off in Nepal

Nepal is a small kingdom, roughly the size of North Carolina, on the southern face of the Himalayas. More visibly than most countries, geography has shaped its destiny. Nepal is overwhelmingly mountainous, with four of the world's eight highest mountains. Its farmers raise

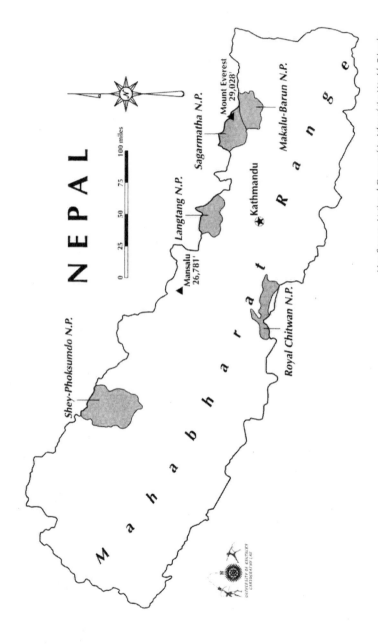

NEPAL

Shey-Phoksumdo N.P.

Mansalu
26,781'

Langtang N.P.

Sagarmatha N.P.

Mount Everest
29,028'

★ Kathmandu

M a h a b h a r a t   R a n g e

Royal Chitwan N.P.

Makalu-Barun N.P.

0   25   50   75   100 miles

Map Source: National Geographic Atlas of the World, 7th ed.;
Miriam-Webster Online

Nepal, including Mt. Everest. Map by Dick Gilbreath, University of Kentucky Cartography Lab.

potatoes and barley at altitudes equal to the highest peaks of the Swiss Alps.

By any measure, it's a poor country, consistently appearing on lists of the world's least-developed nations. The per capita GNP is only $210. Like many of the world's poorest nations, Nepal is landlocked, forced to rely on its sometimes-difficult neighbor India for access to the sea and for any chance of an economical transportation of goods. It has virtually no natural resources except for timber and the potential to generate hydropower from its mountain rivers.

Fortunately for Nepal, its rugged geography also makes it a magnet for tourism. The low latitude (28 degrees North—putting it south of both Cairo and New Orleans) combined with steep changes in elevation, from the low-lying plains of the south to Mt. Everest, only forty miles north, give it an astonishing range of climates, landscapes, and life forms. In the space of just a few miles, travelers pass through a tremendous range of environments. This remarkable variety of environments is home to an equally remarkable variety of cultures, with differing ways of life adapted to the small geographical regions where they live. A dozen different ethnic groups live in Nepal, from the Hindu farmers of the subtropical lowlands to the Tibetan-related Sherpa herders of the highest mountains. They wear a rainbow of different costumes, build different houses, raise different crops, and speak a babel of different languages. A day's hike along a mountain path can feel like a whirlwind tour of a whole continent.

Tourism is a fairly recent development in Nepal. For centuries, the country was closed to foreigners, and even when the first westerners were admitted, the numbers were extremely small. It has been calculated that between 1881 and 1925, only 153 westerners entered the kingdom.

This began to change when mountaineers set their sights on the world's highest mountain on the border between Nepal and Tibet. The first expeditions approached the mountain from the Tibetan side, but in 1950 an expedition was permitted through Nepalese territory for the first time. The Sherpa people who live near Everest (which they call Sagarmatha) had already made a name for themselves as skillful porters and guides since 1907, when they were first hired by British expeditions in India. When Edmund Hillary and Tenzing Norgay, a Nepalese Sherpa, reached the summit of Everest on May 29, 1953, the kingdom hit the front pages of the world's newspapers.

> No tumbleweeds here, but we've seen virtually every other plant known
> to humans, including banana trees, aloes, holly, cacti, lemon trees,
> bamboo, banyans, poinsettias, and I can't even remember the others—
> sometimes all within fifteen minutes or so. . . .
>
> This is not at all what I expected. . . . I knew there were people living
> around here, but I certainly didn't expect this many. It has been one
> continuous village since we left Pokhara, and the path is crowded
> with people cheerfully lugging the most enormous loads imaginable—
> firewood, baskets of vegetables, stacks of pans and water pots. . . .
>
> This feels like *Out of Africa*—all that's missing is the Victrola. We
> have a guide, a cook, and now five porters, for just the two of us.
> They're hauling everything from cauliflowers to camp stools for us.
> I've never felt like such a rich snot in my life—particularly when I see a
> tiny little boy, aged maybe five or six, struggling up a mountain in flip-
> flops, carrying a sack of rice on his back.
>
> —Kristin Johannsen, Nepal travel journal

Tourism developed very slowly at first. Kathmandu Airport
opened in 1954, and Thomas Cook offered the first organized tour of
Nepal for westerners the next year. In 1960, the kingdom received four
thousand tourists, but apart from mountaineers, none of them traveled
outside the capital, mostly for lack of transportation. As late as 1965,
the entire country had only 125 miles of paved roads. To this day, large
areas of the country have no roads usable by motor vehicles, and air-
strips accessible to only the smallest planes. In these regions, all long-
distance transport is on foot, and even the heaviest of goods are hauled
on the backs of porters, who carry loads approaching two hundred
pounds up steep mountain paths.

Kathmandu is a fascinating city, almost medieval in the variety of
activities performed in its streets, but it was only natural that hardier
travelers willing to travel on foot like the local people would want to
explore further into the countryside. The first organized trek took
place in 1966. Within ten years, Nepal was receiving a hundred thousand tourists a year, 10 percent of whom were trekkers. At the end of
the overland route from London through Asia, young travelers who
just couldn't quit at the end of their long odysseys would set out from
Kathmandu to see this "exotic," little-known country.

Today, trekking is the premier nature travel activity in Nepal, and Nepalese trekking organizers have refined it to an art. Typically, a small party of a half-dozen trekkers is accompanied by a staff consisting of a guide, a cook, and a team of porters who carry all the equipment in baskets on their backs. Some groups camp out, with the staff setting up a small city of tents for sleeping, cooking, and even a toilet tent every night. Others overnight in "tea houses," small locally owned lodges.

A trek in Nepal hardly qualifies as "roughing it." Trekkers are awakened with tea in their tents and basins of hot water to wash in, and then eat a huge breakfast before setting off. After walking all morning, there's a two-hour lunch break, during which the staff performs such culinary feats as cooking pizza over a campfire, followed by a shorter afternoon walk. The faster porters may even arrive at the night's stop before the trekkers, and have the camp set up and waiting. An equally sumptuous dinner is served, followed by reading, journal-writing, and other relaxing activities, and an early bedtime. On a typical two-week trek, it's easy to fall into the routine.

Trekking in Nepal is overwhelmingly concentrated in two areas. The region around Annapurna, in central Nepal, receives up to 38,000 foreign visitors a year (compared with a local population of 40,000). Access to the region is easy, with daily scheduled flights to the airport at Pokhara, and a wide variety of treks are possible, from the untaxing three-day "Royal Trek" (given this name after the Prince of Wales followed the route) to an arduous, month-long circuit of the region, crossing a pass at eighteen thousand feet.

The other main destination for trekkers is the Khumbu area around Mt. Everest in the northeast of the country, homeland of the Sherpa people. Despite the common misconception, "Sherpa" is not an occupation but the name of an ethnic group living at high elevations in the Himalayas. The opening of an airport at Lukla in Khumbu eliminated the need for a two-week walk merely to reach the Sherpas' homeland, making it far more attractive to tourists, though the more strenuous nature of the treks means that they appeal to a smaller audience. Around 20 percent of trekkers visit this region.[1]

Besides trekking, other types of nature-based tourism have been developed in Nepal. White-water rafting on the country's rivers grew greatly in popularity in the 1990s, on destinations like the Trishuli River near Kathmandu and the Sun Kosi River in eastern Nepal. However, most of the money paid by rafting tourists goes to the agencies in Kathmandu, so there is very little benefit to the local community.

And in the subtropical Tarai region, on the country's southern border with India, wildlife tour operators have developed large-scale operations at Royal Chitwan National Park, home to Bengal tigers, rhinos, and other high-profile species. Prior to the establishment of the park in 1973, the area was the private hunting preserve of the royal family. Its protected status has led to a resurgence in the populations of some endangered species and has helped to raise awareness of the value of protecting wildlife among the Nepalese.

But with the best-known resort there, Tiger Tops Jungle Lodge, charging $300 a night per person for luxury accommodation and only a tiny fraction of this money entering the local community, it's debatable whether this can really be called ecotourism even by the most lenient definition. And with a roster of guests (listed on their website) that includes Mick Jagger, Robert Redford, and the Prince of Wales, it seems questionable how much broad-scale environmental education such places really provide.

In the space of a few decades, tourism developed from virtually nothing into one of Nepal's biggest industries and its major source of foreign exchange. From a little-known and isolated country, Nepal had become a major destination on the world tourism scene.

Tourism and Nepal's Environment

Not surprisingly, the massive invasion of tourist trekkers had consequences for the fragile mountain environments, with popular destinations far exceeding their carrying capacity. One of the most immediately visible manifestations was garbage. Nepal is a densely populated country, with over twenty-four million people sharing the small percentage of the land flat enough to live in, but these people were traditionally subsistence farmers who wasted virtually nothing. The arrival of tens of thousands of foreign travelers with all their foreign garbage put a huge strain on traditional disposal systems. One study found that an average trekking group produces fifteen kilograms of nonbiodegradable, nonburnable garbage on a single trip.[2] Little if any of this is hauled back out of the trekking region.

Garbage was a particular problem in the Everest region, where

expeditions were notorious for the amount of rubbish they left behind—soon to be joined by the litter deposited by trekkers. In 1984, a
team of Sherpas removed one thousand bags of litter from the lower
elevations of Mt. Everest. Between mid-July 1995 and 1996, almost
two hundred tons of garbage were collected by the Sagarmatha Pollution Control Committee.[3]

Another impact was increased consumption of wood. Firewood is
the main source of fuel in the country—one study estimated that it
meets 87 percent of the country's total energy needs—and wood is an
important material in Nepalese building. For example, building a typical Sherpa-style house requires about eighteen cubic meters of timber—about fifty entire trees. Building tourist lodges in the local style
consumes proportionately larger amounts of wood. And trekking tourists are known to use far more firewood than the average Nepalese for
their exotic meals and hot showers.

The actual scope of deforestation in Nepal has been the subject of
acrimonious debate, starting with the release of a World Bank report in
1978 that asserted that the mountains would be nearly bare of trees
within fifteen years. Many later studies argued that these reports of
catastrophe were based on faulty assumptions. Nonetheless, it's clear
that an influx of foreign travelers is bound to add to consumption.

And considering that trekking and nature tourism are heavily concentrated in a few regions, even if the overall impact of increased consumption is not severe, people in tourist regions will feel the effect
much more strongly. Collecting firewood is a major daily household
chore for Nepalese families—the further the person needs to walk, the
more onerous the chore. Depending on the region, the average time
needed to collect a single load of firewood varies from three to eight
hours. It's easy to see that even a small increase in the distance people
need to travel would significantly increase this burden.

Even hiking itself, a seemingly harmless activity, was seen to
cause damage when concentrated in limited areas. The endless
tramping of feet on the most popular routes led to soil erosion, root
exposure, deep ruts, and excessive trail widths. This results in a vi-
cious circle, wherein low-quality trails become difficult to walk on,
leading hikers to start new trails that run parallel, which contributes
further to degradation.

Taming Tourism

In the first years of its development, nature tourism in Nepal was completely unregulated, and environmental damage was becoming increasingly obvious in heavily used areas. In an attempt to preserve these threatened mountain environments, two very different programs were established in main trekking regions.

In 1976, the government of Nepal established Sagarmatha National Park in the Khumbu area around Mt. Everest. The area of around a thousand square kilometers is home to about 3,500 Sherpa people, who traditionally made their living by herding and through trade with Tibet. But the park was set up without consulting with the residents, and without any overall plan for the development of tourism.

The basic approach was to ban environmentally damaging activities inside the protected area, including cutting firewood and littering. In 1979, new regulations required trekking parties to carry kerosene instead of burning firewood. But since this ban did not apply to lodges, the rule merely caused a shift away from camping to staying in lodges. Since all cutting of firewood was banned inside the park's boundaries, people turned to sources just outside them, leading to severe deforestation in specific limited areas.

Without any real structure for enforcement in place, similar regulations that required trekkers to carry out all nonburnable garbage were largely ignored. Some estimates put the amount of trash carried out at less than 10 percent of the total. One study found that a single lodge in Namche produced fifteen thousand empty beer bottles a year![4]

According to some observers, the biggest problem is that park authorities have not been given enough funds to carry out meaningful environmental projects, nor do they have the authority to regulate tourism development within the park. Little of the revenue from tourism goes back into the operating budget of the park. Despite tourists' willingness to pay higher entrance fees to fund conservation programs (a survey found that 80 percent of visitors would support this), the actual revenue from these fees is only around 20 percent of the park's operating budget.[5]

Furthermore, because the regulations were imposed by an outside authority, the people of the community did not feel any sense of involvement, so they sidestepped the rules whenever possible. Development continued largely unplanned and ad hoc, with too many competing facilities in some locations, and none at all in others.

A different approach to tourism was taken in the Annapurna Conservation Area Project (ACAP), started in 1986 by the King Mahendra Trust for Nature Conservation. This program covers an area of 2,600 square kilometers that is the home of about forty thousand people from a number of different ethnic groups. It is believed to be the single most geographically and culturally diverse region in the world.[6]

Rather than create a national park and impose regulations from offices in the capital, the ACAP focused on planned land use, community development, and environmental protection. Local people were involved in planning from the beginning. The project aimed to be financially independent, so it received permission from the government to charge visitors an admission fee (currently twelve dollars) and use the proceeds to fund its programs.

Revenues obtained, more than a half-million dollars annually, were used to fund programs in reforestation, trail and bridge construction, and development of alternative technologies such as solar water heaters and fuel-efficient stoves. Educational programs were developed for schoolchildren, adults, and tourists to raise awareness of conservation. In addition, owners of trekking lodges organized to raise standards and income by setting minimum rates for different types of accommodation. Previously, extreme price competition between lodges had cut profits to virtually nothing.

In general, outside observers have found the bottom-up approach taken by the ACAP to be more successful in improving environmental conditions by involving as many members of the community as possible. Sagarmatha and other national parks had taken a "preservation-oriented" approach, aiming to keep the land in a supposedly pristine condition for visitors by restricting local people's right to use the resources. Needless to say, the community played no part in this decision. Though revenue from tourism has helped bring a higher standard of living to many people in the community, this imposition of restrictions from outside alienated them.

Social Impacts

Once two cultures have come in contact, there is no going back, no matter how benign the contact may be. Given the influx of western tourists, it's not surprising that people in the trekking regions of Nepal have picked up such exotic tastes as cassette players and apple pie. It's not unusual to see a woman bustling around a teahouse kitchen in a traditional skirt of age-old design with a well-worn pair of Nike running shoes peeking out under the hem.

Small-scale changes like this are not necessarily harmful to a culture, but there are many other less visible impacts of culture contact. Western trekkers in Nepal not uncommonly find themselves enchanted by the communities they pass through, fascinated by traditional ways of life that still persist and the openhearted hospitality of the people. Not surprisingly, travelers often respond by trying to "give something back" to the host community—a generosity that can have unanticipated effects.

Some of this is on a very small scale. Trekkers in the Annapurna region often find themselves besieged by mobs of children shrieking "One pen! One rupee!" or "Mithai! Mithai!" (*Mithai* means sweets.) Encounters with previous travelers have taught the kids that such begging brings rewards, and that (despite the scolding of their parents and teachers) foreigners are an inexhaustible source of treats. Needless to say, few foreigners go around handing out the toothbrushes needed to ward off the damage their candy causes.

Interaction with tourists can also result in more serious social divisions. Across Nepal, people who were able to establish personal contacts with foreigners often benefited financially. Foreign partners

It started pouring, in an icy cold wind. . . . All the while we were feeling tremendously sorry for ourselves, the Nepalese were trudging by, wrapped in their blankets and flapping their flip-flops in the mud, with perfect equanimity. I saw one woman with the bearing of a young princess making her stately progress through the rain, wrapped in a bright red sari, baby sleeping on her back, a pink plastic sheet drawn elegantly around her like it was the classiest rainwear in the world.
—Kristin Johannsen, Nepal travel journall

helped families along trekking routes obtain loans to build their own lodges. In some cases, generous foreigners paid school tuition for the children of an exceptionally charismatic guide or lodge owner, helping them to attend boarding schools in the capital. Gifts like these can actually worsen existing inequalities in the villages, as better-educated people with a better command of English are more able to make profitable contacts with foreigners and further increase their income.

Obviously, the increased income brought by tourism has helped to improve the standard of living of many Nepalese families. In addition to those deriving income directly from tourism, including guides and porters, owners of lodges and teahouses, and farmers who rent pack animals to trekkers, many others benefit indirectly. Whole villages have supported themselves selling firewood in strategic locations, while others have prospered growing vegetables to sell to trekking groups.

However, the income from tourism is very unevenly distributed. One village located on a main trekking route may have a dozen lodges and small shops, while a few miles away, an equally scenic village has only one—or none at all. A study in 1991 in the Everest region found one village packed with twenty-four lodges and a number of others with no tourist facilities at all. Overall, by 1985, 65 percent of all families in that region had income from tourism.[7]

Unfortunately, 100 percent of families in the region face the higher prices caused by the influx of money into the local economy. Before the tourism boom, most rural people had very little need for cash, living off their crops and livestock and trading for the goods they could not produce themselves. In Khumbu, the price of rice increased tenfold with the tourism boom, until it cost three times the average price in Kathmandu. The price of potatoes, the local staple, increased by *1800 percent* over time. Other goods used by local people, including kerosene, cooking oil, and milk powder, soared in price, along with tourist goods like candy, beer, and bottled water. Most households also benefited from the much higher income that accompanied tourism, thus offsetting the effect of this inflation to some extent—but those cut off from the cash economy, such as households consisting of only elderly people, were in a difficult situation.

Needless to say, not all the revenue from tourism goes to the rural communities. Many travelers book their trips through agencies in

Kathmandu, or even in their home countries, which retain the lion's share of the proceeds. Much of the cost of building even a local-style tourist lodge goes outside the community for materials such as window glass and sheet metal for roofs. In a subsistence farming area, porters must haul in much of the food and drink a tourist consumes—everything from crates of beer to pancake mix. One study found that the leakage rate for tourist spending in the town of Ghorepani in the Annapurna region to be around 45 percent.[8] Another researcher determined that of the average three dollars a day spent by a trekker, only twenty cents of that remained in the village.[9]

Several studies have found that, overall, the cultures of different ethnic groups in Nepal have not been harmed by the boom in the tourism industry. The Sherpas, in particular, are often cited as an example of a community that has preserved its culture in the face of the onslaught of foreigners—and, in fact, seen it reinforced by the contact.

From the time they were first hired to work with British mountaineers, Sherpa guides and porters have had a highly positive reputation among foreigners for their courage, strength, and loyalty. This gives them a powerful incentive to maintain and even capitalize on their identity as Sherpas. The overwhelmingly positive image of Sherpas has sometimes led members of other ethnic groups to pretend to be Sherpas in order to work for foreigners.

Sherpas are proud to share aspects of their tradition with visitors. However, it seems likely that this has brought changes to some of their practices, such as religious ceremonies. If visitors find one type of ceremony fascinating to watch and other less picturesque ceremonies boring, which will be performed more frequently? Furthermore, tour-

> I can remember traveling in Haiti on an assignment to help with reforestation and going to a village that was having a procession. Our vehicle did not come directly onto the procession, but we were on a new road that had just been completed and I doubt now that the procession had ever before been distracted by vehicles—and thus we were by our presence weakening the bonds within that community, at least in a small degree. If nothing else, it made me more sensitive to the impacts of touring another's community.
>
> —Al Fritsch

ism is inherently a denial of the value of rootedness, instead valuing mobility. If not properly nuanced, this in itself can weaken the fabric of a host community.

Dependence on Tourism

Though attempts were made to minimize the environmental and cultural impacts of nature tourism in Nepal (with varying degrees of success), there was one type of impact that could not be minimized: a growing economic dependence on tourism. By the end of the 1990s, it had become Nepal's second-largest industry. In a good year, up to a hundred thousand people worked as trekking porters, not to mention countless others who cooked, provided rooms, or sold souvenirs to foreigners.

Like many other so-called "developing" countries, Nepal had pinned its hopes on tourism as the main motor for development. In the mid-1990s, with the annual number of tourists around four hundred thousand, the government was making wildly optimistic projections of up to a million visitors yearly by 2000. The actual number in that year was 463,646. Then the numbers began to slide. In 2001, the total fell by 22 percent, to 362,544. The next year was even worse. While 200,208 tourists visited Nepal in the first eight months of 2001, only 131,359 came in the first eight months of 2002.[10]

This decline in tourism was caused by a series of events from which the industry has yet to recover. In December 1999, an Indian Airlines flight from Kathmandu to Delhi was hijacked, and the government of India, at times a difficult neighbor, suspended all flights to Nepal for months, claiming that Nepal had poor internal security and was overrun by extremists. Indian visitors had previously made up 30 percent of the total.

Then, on June 1, 2001, virtually the entire Nepalese royal family was massacred in an apparent palace coup, which was followed by months of extreme uncertainty throughout the country, and a further decline in the number of foreign visitors. No sooner had the numbers begun to pick up when the September 11, 2001, terrorist attacks in the United States brought the world tourism system to a virtual halt, causing long-lasting changes in people's preferences in travel destinations.

As if this weren't enough, the international press was increasingly focused on a Maoist anti-government insurgency that had been active for years but was recently growing more intense. Despite the rebel leaders' insistence that tourists were not a target and the government's assertions that the situation was firmly under control, reports of rebel bands extorting trekkers further dampened travelers' enthusiasm for exploring the out-of-the-way corners of Nepal.

January 2002 found tourist arrivals down 47 percent from the same month a year before, the effects of which spread throughout the economy. Tourism businesses were hit hard, with many newly built hotels unable to make payments on their loans. Even the director of the Nepal Tourism Board candidly admitted that all sectors of the economy were suffering, down to such indirect participants as the poultry farmers who provide the eggs for all those banana pancakes.

Some areas were hit harder than others. In February 2002, Maoist guerillas set off bombs at Lukla Airport, the main point of access for tourists visiting the Mt. Everest area. All flights were immediately halted, and foreigners stranded at the airport were evacuated by the military. Coming as it did at the beginning of the spring tourist season, this event had a devastating effect on the area's economy.

Nepal's experiences with nature tourism provide some clear lessons for the rest of the world. Though planning and government policy were able to control some of the negative environmental and social impacts of a massive growth in tourism, these proved of no avail when the tourists simply stopped coming. Appalachia's tourism planners need to give careful consideration to the results of a similar situation here.

Suppose our dreams came true, and in the future, visitors thronged here, resulting in a greatly expanded Appalachian economy heavily centered on tourism. What would be the result to the regional economy if

- world events sent U.S. gasoline prices up to four dollars a gallon—now a typical price in Europe?
- nature tourism became untrendy just as quickly as it became the vogue?
- an environmental catastrophe like the failure of a slurry pond in a key location led travelers to perceive the whole region as polluted and undesirable?
- one or more Appalachian states became the target of a politically motivated travel boycott campaign?

These scenarios, and a number of others, are hardly implausible. The case of Nepal highlights not only the importance of careful regulation of tourism growth, but also of the danger of relying on nature tourism as the foundation of a regional economy.

Now we'll turn our attention to the other side of the world—literally.

Belize: Mother Nature's Theme Park?

Armadillos, boa constrictors, crocodiles, deer, howler monkeys, jaguars, manatees, pumas, ocelots, toucans, whale sharks . . . this is not the directory of a big city zoo, but a roster of the wildlife that draws throngs of ecotourists to Belize.

Such natural variety is staggering in a land area of only 8,867 square miles, a bit smaller than Massachusetts. Located on the east coast of Central America, the ecosystems of this country, once known as British Honduras, stretch from rainforests to mangrove swamps to the world's second-longest barrier reef and include three of the Caribbean's four coral atolls.

Belize has always been something of a backwater. It's the second-smallest country in the Americas and has the smallest population—only 249,183 people, fewer than Lexington, Kentucky. It was originally part of the Mayan empire, and it contains a number of important Mayan temples and other ruins. In the sixteenth century, the Spanish arrived and attempted to convert the inhabitants to Christianity, with little success.

Then in the seventeenth century, British buccaneers arrived and settled there and started logging the forests, using African slaves as laborers. In 1798, the British forced the Spanish out entirely, and the area became a colony called British Honduras in 1862. This explains why Belize is the only Central American country where English is the official language (though in reality the linguistic situation is far more complex than that). Due to a territorial dispute with neighboring Guatemala, the country did not gain full independence until 1981. Unlike the rest of Central America, its atmosphere and culture are Caribbean.

This complex history has left Belize with an intriguing mix of inhabitants. Today, the biggest segment of the population (44 percent) is mestizos, people of mixed Mayan and European ancestry who speak

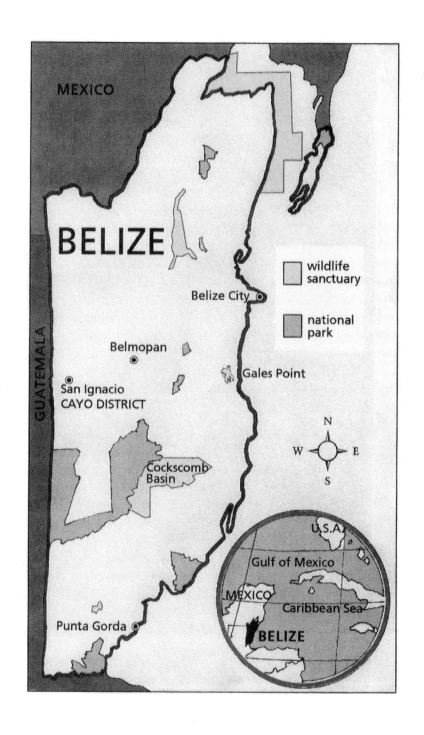

MEXICO

BELIZE

wildlife
sanctuary

national
park

Belize City

Belmopan

Gales Point

San Ignacio
CAYO DISTRICT

Cockscomb
Basin

N

W   E

S

GUATEMALA

U.S.A.

Gulf of Mexico

MEXICO

Caribbean Sea

BELIZE

Punta Gorda

Spanish. The next largest group is the Creoles (30 percent), people of mixed African and European descent who speak English. Maya Indians, who make up 11 percent of the population, speak several different Mayan languages. Seven per cent of Belizeans are Garifuna, people of mixed Arawak Indian and African origin, whose ancestors were exiled from islands in the eastern Caribbean during the eighteenth century. They speak their own Garifuna language and have very distinctive music and folk customs. The remaining 8 percent of the population is like an atlas of the world's peoples: Chinese, Arabs, South Asians, even colonies of conservative, German-speaking Mennonites who fled persecution in Mexico to take up dairy farming on the fringes of the rainforest.

Partly due to the very small population, little of the land is cultivated—only around 5 percent of the country's area is used for farming. This has made it possible to set aside a large proportion of the land as nature preserves. Forty percent of Belize's territory now has protected status—the highest proportion of any country in the world—and over 70 percent of the country's original forest cover still remains.

But the small population has also held back economic development. Agriculture is still mostly at the subsistence level, apart from a few large plantations that produce citrus for export, and industry is also undeveloped. In 1998, the annual per capita income was roughly $3,000 (as compared with $6,700 in Costa Rica). Many Belizeans still manage by doing a bit of hunting or fishing, growing a few vegetables, and working at seasonal odd jobs when cash is needed. The largest city, Belize City, has fewer than fifty thousand people. The national

Traveling by bus in Belize is never boring. Even though it's pretty uncomfortable, bouncing along an unpaved road in an ancient American school bus (really—half of them still have the names of some little town in Iowa painted on the side) just looking at the passengers is so entertaining. You'll see a Mennonite farm boy in straw hat and suspenders stuffed in next to a black guy with huge dreadlocks, and a tiny Maya woman with a baby in her shawl sitting with a haughty old Chinese lady. Everybody gets good and cozy because of course the seats were designed for eight-year-olds . . .

—Kristin Johannsen

capital, Belmopan, has a population of only 6,785, and many of the towns marked on maps are just handfuls of houses on the side of the road. "Sleepy" is a word that appears frequently in foreign visitors' descriptions of Belize—even the official tourist literature calls the country "relaxed."

Despite the low incomes, the cost of living in Belize is significantly higher than in other Central American countries. Several years ago, a look around the largest "department store" in Belize City turned up a wide array of familiar American brand names, while the only Belizean products visible were beer, jam, and a (delicious) local hot sauce made from carrots. Virtually all processed foods and other consumer goods are imported; since Belize is a small market far from major transport routes, shipping costs are high. Travel guidebooks warn budget travelers to expect their daily expenses to jump when arriving from other Central American countries. In fact, many Belizeans take long bus trips to do their shopping in Chetumal, Mexico, where shops are better stocked and prices are lower.

One thing that isn't undeveloped in Belize is its tourism industry. Its diverse natural beauty and peaceful atmosphere draw streams of tourists of every description, around 50 percent of them from the U.S. in a typical year. The fact that the country is accessible by land (many buses cross from Mexico) makes it attractive to young American budget travelers, and its reputation as an unspoiled haven for nature lovers (as well as its off-the-beaten-track status) draws the more affluent. In 2000, Belize received 326,642 foreign visitors—half again the population of the country.

Since tourism began developing around the time of independence, nature has always been the main drawing card. Probably the first nature tourists to discover Belize were scuba divers, who are generally more willing than most other well-heeled travelers to put up with uncomfortable travel and "Third World" uncertainties in order to explore undiscovered dive sites. The clear warm water, healthy coral formations, and staggering variety of marine life (over four hundred species of fish and seventy types of hard coral) made Belize legendary among divers. With reefs paralleling the entire 185-mile-long coast, there was plenty of room to spread out, and the Blue Hole, a collapsed underwater cave four hundred feet deep, is unique in the world.

Later, in the early 1990s, the Belizean government and tourism

developers began to focus heavily on the country's inland attractions—
its tropical forests, wildlife, archaeological ruins, and the lifeways of
its traditional villages. Both Belizean and international NGOs began
promoting ecotourism, for all the familiar reasons—to protect the environment, to pay for conservation programs, and to generate much-
needed income for rural people.

However, not all the people who have benefited from the subsequent boom in nature tourism are Belizeans. As a sparsely populated
country eager for outside investment, for years Belize has made it as
easy as possible for (well-off) foreigners to settle there permanently,
offering generous tax breaks and easy access to residence permits. Provided they can prove an independent income of at least $24,000 a year,
people as young as forty-five are allowed to "retire" there, and to
import personal effects, cars, boats, and even airplanes tax-free. Many
North Americans have retired in Belize, drawn by the exquisite natural
environment, the lower cost of living, and the (mostly) peaceable, En-
glish-speaking society. And many younger expats have settled there to
take advantage of lucrative business opportunities—particularly in
tourism.

According to the Worldwatch Institute, roughly 65 percent of the
membership of the Belize Tourism Industry Association is made up of
expatriates, and an estimated 90 percent of the country's coastal development is being carried out by foreigners.[11] Even such official-sounding
organizations as the Belize Zoo and the Monkey Bay Wildlife Sanctuary
are actually expatriate-controlled. Of the largest and most profitable
nature tourism businesses, very few are owned by native Belizeans.

In the Lap of Luxury

What kind of enterprises have these foreigners built? One of the most
celebrated "nature tourism" resorts in Belize is The Lodge at Chaa
Creek, in the western Cayo District of Belize, near the Guatemalan
border. Built by two expatriates, Mick and Lucy Fleming, it started out
in 1977 as a vegetable farm out in the jungle, accessible only by dugout
canoe. When backpackers began trekking out there to visit, the
Flemings decided to build their first guest cottage out of materials
found on the property.

Today, the scene is rather different. In 2002, Chaa Creek's promotional materials boast of "an airy restaurant with its own temperature-controlled wine cellar," "fine antiques gathered from Mexico and Guatemala," and their spa, "an oasis of luxury" where guests can "rejuvenate and invigorate with massage, aromatherapy, and detoxifying treatments," providing "a tranquil and extraordinary sensory experience that promotes harmony between the inner and outer self." (Apparently, spending a couple of weeks out in the rainforest is no longer sufficient to induce relaxation.) Chaa Creek even has a brand-new conference center with state-of-the-art audiovisual equipment and facilities for PowerPoint presentations—irresistible, doubtless, to organizers of ecotourism industry talkfests.

And the plaudits keep rolling in. *Travel Weekly, Spa Magazine, The Times* of London, Fodor's travel guides, and other upscale publications have all written glowingly of Chaa Creek. In 1998, American Express named it the "Green Hotel of the Year."

Overall, many observers have noted a trend towards increasingly "soft" ecotourism, with visitors less willing to exert themselves, less interested in learning about nature, and more eager to part with large sums of cash for a fashionable taste of an exotic environment—in the most comfortable setting possible. Increasingly, new resorts are targeting this market.

A short item in the Sunday travel section of U.S. newspapers in June 2002 touted the opening of "a small, exclusive beachside eco-resort" in Belize, near Cockscomb Basin National Park. Kanantik Reef and Jungle Resort, it announced, features twenty-five air-conditioned, thatch-roofed cabanas, with a daily rate of $300 per person (double occupancy).

Kanantik's website gives full details, in between photos of toucans and coral heads. "Luxuriate in solitude," it purrs, at this "eco-sensitive resort." "Surround yourself . . . in 300 acres of natural and untouched land, full of wildlife." Dine on "Creole-Mediterranean cuisine," and don't worry—there's an "authentic firewood Italian pizza oven, pasta maker, gelato machine . . ." The usual roster of jungle tours and snorkeling trips are on offer—along with visits to Maya ruins.[12]

"The cause of the Maya vanishing remains a mystery," says the website's description of archaeological excursions. "Who are the Maya? Where did they come from? Where did the millions go that once lived there?" Guests could answer these questions quite easily, if they felt so inclined, by heading a few miles inland from the resort to the not-so-picturesque villages where thousands of Maya still live in Belize, struggling to make a living. Or, possibly, answers could be found even closer at hand in the kitchen and laundry of the resort, where local women will undoubtedly fill the lowest-paying jobs.

Who, exactly, is behind this "eco-sensitive" enterprise? According to the article, clearly a lightly rewritten press release, "The resort is owned by a private investment group whose principals include Italians Roberto Fabbri, a former custom yacht salesman, and financier Francesco Moscatelli." Any environmental credentials were not recorded.

It's difficult to see how resorts such as this can make any legitimate claim to the "eco" brand. Clearly, these large-scale luxury lodges do not fit even the generous definition of ecotourism that we have been using: though they involve travel to natural areas, they neither provide serious environmental education nor bring very many economic benefits to the community. Employment is low-paid and seasonal, and given expatriate ownership and heavy reliance on imports, most of the revenue generated leaks back out of the community.

In a report for Environmental News Network, Linda Baker quotes a Belizean rainforest guide for an Australian owned deluxe eco resort who works from five in the morning until ten at night, seven days a week, and says he must rely on tips from clients for survival.[13] For a single night at Kanantik, guests pay more than most Belizeans get by on for a month.

Obviously, if this kind of commercialized luxury nature resort is springing up all over, it's because demand for such facilities is growing. Many observers have noted a shift away from "hard-core" ecotourism, where the focus is on education, conservation, and benefits to the community, towards what researcher Martha Honey calls "ecotourism lite." Summarizing her interviews with ecotourism operators and tour guides in several countries, she notes: "In recent years, there has been a gradual trend for many ecotourists to be less intellectually curious, socially responsible, environmentally concerned, and politically aware than in the past. Increasing numbers of older, wealthier, and "softer" travelers have begun opting for comfort over conservation."[14]

A spate of articles in such publications as U.S. News and the New York Times carried titles like "Ecotour, Hold the Eco" and "Confes-

sions of a Reluctant Eco-Tourist," featuring anecdotes about the unpleasant insects to be found in rainforests and the joys of lolling about
at the resort's pool.[15] When natural environments become one more
luxury good for the well-heeled to buy and consume, obviously every
little detail must be just what the customer ordered. If the most affluent
consumers want just the palest tint of green on their tropical vacation,
the market will be only too happy to oblige.

Bungle in the Jungle

Have smaller ecotourism projects proven more beneficial? Because the
country is one of the world's premier ecotourism destinations, facilities
and programs of all sizes and descriptions have sprung up across Belize
like, well, mushrooms in the rainforest. And as the Worldwatch Institute
points out in their report *Traveling Light*, "Homegrown ecotourism initiatives generally require less infrastructure and overhead than larger
tourism projects and rely more heavily on goods, materials, and staff
from the surrounding area."[16]

But with its small population and dearth of local scientists and
consultants (the only institution of higher learning in the country, the
University of Belize, is tiny), even the most "homegrown" community-
based project tends to be the brainchild of outside experts. Their lack
of familiarity with the realities of Belizean rural life and their cookie-
cutter solutions have made too many projects ineffectual or even
harmful.

Jill M. Belsky, a sociologist at the University of Montana, carried
out an in-depth study of one "community-based" ecotourism project
in Gales Point, Belize, and found that despite the best of intentions,
outsiders' imposition of their own agendas meant that the project,
rather than strengthening the community and improving its standard
of living, worsened inequality and divisiveness.[17] She and her students
made six visits to the village between 1992 and 1998, staying in family
B & Bs and carrying out interviews, while observing the goings-on of
everyday life.

Gales Point is a small village of about eighty households located
about thirty miles south of Belize City. Its mangrove swamps, lagoons,
and forests are home to a number of endangered species, in particular
hawksbill sea turtles and Caribbean manatees. Until the 1990s, the

area was fairly remote, accessible only by boat and only to locals familiar with the route—to an outsider, the network of low, mangrove-covered islets and shallow lagoons along the coast of Belize is a baffling maze.

The Creole people of Gales Point are descendants of Africans enslaved by the British colonialists and forced to work as logcutters. Since the time their ancestors were freed, most people in the area have relied on fishing and hunting for subsistence along with some farming, and many did seasonal work in Belize City to earn cash. Though some aspects of their traditional way of life may not fit our conceptions of "sustainability"—for example, sea turtles, manatees, and "bush meat" were important sources of food for them—the small population in an inaccessible area probably did little harm to natural systems.

In 1991, a group of foreign consultants presented the Belizean government with a proposal to establish a biosphere reserve of 170,000 acres around Gales Point called the Manatee Special Development Area. The "Manatee Advisory Team" was made up of U.S. Peace Corps volunteers, a Fulbright scholar, a U.S. Forest Service biologist, and an American wildlife biologist. They adhered to the orthodox ecotourism philosophy, which holds that income from foreign ecotourists would provide the incentive necessary for local people to begin protecting their fragile environment.

The program began by setting up a series of associations for farmers, craft makers, B & B owners, and tour guides, to be coordinated by an umbrella organization. But problems occurred almost immediately, largely because the program's founders ignored the political realities of the community and country, seeing it instead as some kind of idealized case study. Though the founders claimed that over 50 percent of the adult population of the community became involved in the program, in fact membership in the associations overlapped considerably, and Belsky found that in fact only ten of the eighty households were represented.

Needless to say, these were some of the better-off families in the community. In order to take tourists to see the manatees, a guide needed a motorboat with a large engine, life jackets, a license, and money up front for fuel. To operate a B & B, a family needed comfortable furniture, mosquito nets, fans—and a house big enough to have a spare bedroom. Loans were made available to purchase some of these things, but there were accusations of favoritism, and when after several years there was a drop in the number of visitors, families who had borrowed money to get involved in tourism were hard-pressed to make their payments. Belsky reports that some people turned to hunting wild game to sell for cash in Belize City—an ironic consequence of a conservation program.

Furthermore, a lot of the program's funding depended on the Belizean government, and the party then in power, the People's United Party. Gales Point traditionally had supported the PUP, but when its rival, the United Democratic Party, was voted into office in national elections, financial support for projects in Gales Point, such as a cooperative hotel then under construction, dried up. Some people in the community responded by switching their allegiance to the UDP, but in general, participation in ecotourism projects declined. One woman told Belsky, "Politics is bringing us down, the whole village."

Later, some of the most affluent members of the community were able to get outside funding for tourism projects they supported. One man who had lived for twenty years in the U.S. (and earned a U.S.-level income) became chairman of the village council, and obtained a $40,000 grant from a World Bank environmental program. However, none of the money received was used to pay off debts or to help more families gain income from ecotourism, and the projects the grant did fund alienated many people in the community. For instance, a beautification program offered to pay people to clean up their own yards, actually offending many residents.

In the end, some people in Gales Point ended up actively sabotaging ecotourism efforts. One resident vowed to let his garbage pile up all over the beach to show that local people and not foreign tourists should decide what the town looks like. Other people dismantled the signs that were put up to mark the water routes to the village and to the manatee breeding grounds so that tourists would need to hire locals in order to find them rather than coming in on tourist boats from Belize City.

It's interesting to note that another team of academics did a "one-off" survey in Gales Point in 1994 and concluded that ecotourism was a success there. Asking each household whether they had benefited economically from tourism, a team headed by Kreg Lindberg found that 24 percent of the households had some income from tourism and that 56 percent of households said they supported having a protected area around the village. The authors state that "impacts on others, not just on the individual and his or her household, may be important factors contributing to attitudes"—a somewhat patronizing view of rural people as "noble savages," in contrast with the small-town politics that Belsky describes in such painful detail.[18]

Lindberg and his colleagues also offer no comment on the fact that benefits from (and support for) ecotourism are far lower in Gales Point than in any of the other Belizean communities they studied. In the village of Maya Center, in contrast, 67 percent of households reported income from ecotourism, and ninety-two percent said that they were in favor of the neighboring protected area.

In the end, these ecotourism efforts seem to have benefited Gales Point very little. During the 1990s, the government built a road allowing easier access to the town but ended up repossessing land that had been traditionally (though unofficially) used for farming. Some of that land has since been clear-cut and then sold for citrus plantations in an effort to promote export production and tackle the national debt. One resident told an interviewer, "We don't have land to farm in Gales Point, we're never going to get ahead. Food is so expensive and now the government won't let us hunt any more. What are our kids going to eat?"[19]

Belsky concludes that outsiders saw Gales Point as "wantonly despoiling nature because of material and cultural deprivations; foreign tourists and consultants with 'good' conservation values and surplus income could demonstrate for residents how maintaining the landscape and wildlife for the benefit of ecotourists is in their best interests."[20]

In a study of ecotourism in South Africa, Frank Brennan and Garth Allen found that ten years of community-based tourism development under the post-apartheid government had brought little benefit to poor black communities. They maintained that "despite the arguments of many environmentalists . . . conservation involves power over the distribution of resources. It is a political issue. Agencies that mediate access to natural resources continue to hold the power to set agendas," concluding that, in South Africa, "Ecotourism is essentially an ideal, promoted by well-fed whites."[21]

Given the thorny realities of local politics and social inequality, it can be difficult for even the best-intentioned ecotourism projects to direct income to the people who need it most. When the impetus and planning come from outsiders who are unfamiliar with the intricate web of history and relationships in the community, it's not surprising that the results can be far removed from what the designers expected— or intended.

And even relatively successful community-based ecotourism projects are more vulnerable to outside events than a commercial resort with deep-pockets financing from overseas. The Toledo Ecotourism Association, a group of thirteen community-owned guesthouses in Maya and Garifuna villages in the far south of Belize, was hit hard when Hurricane Iris roared through the region in October 2001, a month after the terrorist attacks in the U.S. sent the world tourism industry into a slide. With foreign visitors staying away in droves, the TEA hoped to rent out sleeping quarters at rock-bottom rates to relief workers, but in order to do that they were forced to appeal on their website for donations to repair the damaged guesthouses.

Future Prospects

The economy of Belize is heavily dependent on tourism. According to the Belize Tourism Board, spending by international tourists makes up 19.3 percent of the country's GDP (as compared with 3 percent in Nepal) and 67 percent of the total service sector. It is currently the country's single largest employer, providing one in four jobs.

Until now, the large-scale commercial operations have received the lion's share of nature travelers to Belize. A survey in 2000 of foreign tourists using the country's only airport found that 75 percent stayed at a hotel or resort, 22 percent chose an ecolodge or guesthouse, while only 7 percent of visitors stayed at a community guesthouse. However, of travelers planning a return visit to Belize, 23 percent said they would like to try a community guest house. The researchers concluded that as travelers become more familiar with Belize, they will become more willing to branch out from the beaten path and seek out smaller, locally owned tourist facilities.[22]

There were other surprises in the survey, which covered a broader base of travelers than previous research that looked only at travelers who had made reservations through tour operators. For one thing, there were more young visitors than previously thought—57 percent were under forty years old. Almost 50 percent were traveling independently and had made their own reservations. And an overwhelming 87 percent used the Internet in researching and planning their trip—a plus for Belize, where English is widely spoken and the telephone system works reasonably well.

Despite the push towards upscale resorts and the palest of green tourism, it seems that there still is a sizable minority of travelers who want to learn about the environments they visit and do some good for the people who live there. But as these younger travelers age and move up the economic scale, will they, too, begin to demand more creature comforts and pay less attention to the educational components of their nature vacations? Investors are clearly betting that the answer is "yes."

What Can Appalachia Learn?

Nepal and Belize are worlds away from the Appalachian states, both geographically and socially. But there are important lessons we can learn from their experiences in developing and promoting nature tourism. The clear message of both of these case studies, despite their remoteness from Appalachia, is that ecotourism cannot possibly be a cure-all for the economic ills of any region for several reasons:

1. Unless it is carefully restricted, nature tourism can lead to more environmental damage, undermining the attractiveness of the very resources on which it depends. In looking at Nepal, we saw how an influx of trekkers caused extensive environmental damage to the "pristine" area that they had come to enjoy. Trails were eroded under the tramping feet of hikers. Mounds of garbage piled up in remote areas. The ever-growing demand for tourist lodges built in the traditional style, for exotic meals, and for hot water for washing led to vastly increased consumption of wood and even to severe deforestation in certain areas. Similarly, in Belize, unscrupulous scuba diving operators have damaged coral reefs with the anchors of their boats and disturbed turtles and other marine life.

And given the widespread tendency in Appalachia for people to wish to go about their business undisturbed by government regulations and "interference," it's all too easy to see how similar scenes could occur there. In areas where garbage collection systems are inadequate, the refuse left by the increasing numbers of tourists could pile up and deface the landscape. Large groups of nature lovers could do severe damage by tramping through the most sensitive mountain ecosystems on foot.

2. Even well-intentioned ecotourism can actually worsen social and economic inequalities in a destination area. In Nepal, Sherpa communities located near heavily used trekking routes were able to prosper from providing facilities like lodges and tea shops for tourists, while other villages only a few miles away received no tourist income at all. And even within the villages that hosted tourists, not everyone benefited. Well-off families who could spare a member from other work to cater to the tourists and better-educated people with knowledge of English or another foreign language were obviously in a better position to cash in on the tourism boom.

In Belize, we saw that starting even the simplest business like a B & B or a guide service requires an outlay of money that the families most in need of income can hardly afford. And where there's no guarantee that a tourist business will succeed, even an interest-free loan can be a big risk for a family—even assuming that the loans are provided fairly and equitably, which is also problematic.

In the words of the old saying, "Them as has, gets." Is Appalachia likely to be any different from these two countries? Given that road access is still not easy in some parts of the region, it's clear that geographical location can be an important factor in determining which tourism businesses will flourish and which will quickly fade. Towns near already established tourist routes will find it much easier to lure visitors. If travelers perceive that it takes an unreasonable amount of time to get to an attraction, they will opt for something closer at hand.

Furthermore, given the vehemence of local political battles in some mountain communities, it's not unlikely that disputes will arise like those that occurred in the Gales Point community in Belize. In developing local tourism programs, "objective" outsiders may be unfamiliar with the dynamics and the personalities in the community—while insiders can easily be accused of favoritism.

To be successful, a tourism development program will have to walk a very fine line, making opportunities available for everyone who wants to participate without ignoring the existing social network of the community.

3. Becoming dependent on tourism makes an economy highly vulnerable to disturbances from outside factors. Both Belize and Nepal have experienced the social and economic dislocation that occurs when tourists simply stop coming—whether because of a civil war or a natural disaster in the area, world events, or just a change in tourism trends.

A lopsided economy based overwhelmingly on one industry can never provide a secure, high standard of living to the majority of its people. For part or all of Appalachia to become heavily centered on tourism is no healthier than dependence on any other single industry— like coal or logging. Any shock that disrupts the central industry is magnified through the regional economy, causing slumps in even the most indirectly related businesses, and spreading widening rings of unemployment. If tourism is to play a positive role in improving the environment and way of life of Appalachia's people, it must be as one component in a sustainable and diverse economy.

There are other lessons that can be learned closer to home. The next chapter looks at the experiences of two of the prime nature tourism destinations in the U.S.—Hawai'i and Alaska.

CHAPTER 6

Lessons for Appalachia 2

Nature Tourism in the U.S.

Ask Americans about their idea of a dream vacation and many of them have the same response—Hawai'i, the "tropical paradise," or Alaska, "the last frontier." In a nation filled with natural wonders and landscapes of great beauty, these two faraway places capture the imagination. The mystique of a lush rainforest climbing the slopes of a fiery volcano, or a glacier tumbling down to the icy sea, is an image that resonates, drawing travelers from great distances, sometimes at great expense.

In both Hawai'i and Alaska, nature tourism has been extensively developed over the past decades in very different environments and situations. But in both states, local residents have found themselves in conflict with the desires of tourists and tourism developers. What are the sources of conflict, and what has been the outcome?

Trouble in Paradise?

"That's the nature of Hawai'i's overwhelming beauty and almost perfect climate: It makes people feel fulfilled and restored. Those who live here have an inherent sense of well-being and personal connection, which they readily share with strangers through their famous form of hospitality, known as 'Aloha!'" So says a top-selling travel guidebook to Hawai'i, *Frommer's Hawaii* (32nd edition). Considering some of the facts and statistics about the state, however, one begins to wonder how many and who exactly of these residents glory in this inherent well-being.

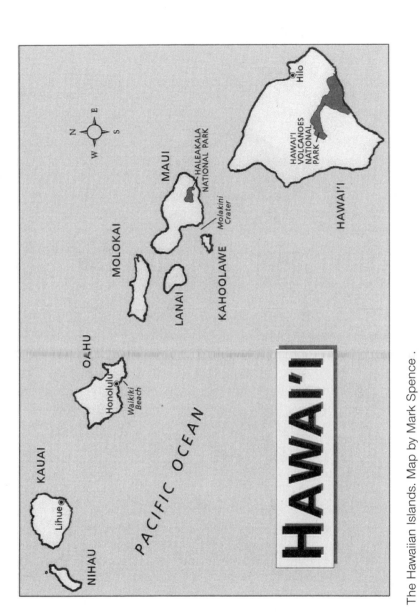

The Hawaiian Islands. Map by Mark Spence .

In their "island paradise," residents of Hawai'i face some of the highest costs of living in the entire U.S.—though personal income per capita is below the U.S. national average. Driven by the boom in construction of resorts, condominiums, and other tourist facilities, real estate prices have headed for the stratosphere, leaving the Great American Dream of home ownership far out of the reach of the middle class. By 1981, the price of a single-family home in Hawai'i was already three times the national average for the U.S. Very little is produced on the islands, and virtually all the daily necessities must be shipped in from the mainland U.S., resulting in a cost of living much higher than in other U.S. states. Many of these economic realities are due, directly or indirectly, to tourism and the economic structure set up to benefit from it.

Hawai'i is one of America's premier tourist destinations. With its population of about 1.2 million people, the state attracts almost seven million tourists in a given year, and it ranks fourth among the states in the number of international tourists. Though visitor totals plummeted in the wake of the 2001 terrorist attacks on the U.S., the industry recovered much more quickly in Hawai'i than in other destinations worldwide, in part because Americans consider it a domestic destination and Japanese travelers, who make up a sizable proportion of visitors, perceive it as a safe place for an exotic vacation.

It's not hard to understand why people flock there. The islands have some of the most spectacular natural attractions anywhere, including active volcanoes, thundering waterfalls, teeming coral reefs, and miles of palm-lined beach. Isolated by more than two thousand sea miles from any continent, they have developed ecosystems unlike any others in the world. Over 90 percent of the birds and plants in Hawai'i are found nowhere else. The landscape varies from lush tropical greenery to frosty mountains, and half of the land area is over two thousand feet in elevation. And to people in most parts of the U.S., the Hawai'ian climate sounds close to ideal: the coldest temperature on record at the Honolulu airport is 54 degrees Fahrenheit, while the hottest is 94.

But there are plenty of places in the world where tourists can partake of glorious tropical scenery and a pleasing climate. One of the key ingredients in Hawai'i's popularity is its culture—the "aloha spirit" mentioned above is shorthand for that. Though only about 20 percent of residents in today's Hawai'i are ethnically Native Hawai'ian (partly or entirely), aspects of their culture feature prominently in tourism promotion: *hula* performances, traditional foods, Hawai'ian music, and of course the flower *lei* used to welcome visitors. Examining the experience of this state, where culture is heavily emphasized in tourism, can give some valuable insights for Appalachia, where a similar emphasis is often proposed.

The History of the "Fiftieth State"

The majority of American tourists in Waikiki would probably be shocked to hear that plenty of those smiling brown natives consider themselves to be citizens of an occupied country. The story of how the Hawai'ians' government was overthrown and their nation wiped off the map, has been glossed over in travel guidebooks—and in our school textbooks.

The first human inhabitants reached Hawai'i relatively recently. Polynesian people from the Marquesas Islands in the South Pacific first settled in Hawai'i about fifteen hundred years ago, bringing with them a way of life based on cultivating taro and fishing in lagoons. Their society had a complex organization, with a hierarchy of kings and chiefs. To maintain this aristocratic system, the land had to be intensively cultivated, and food plants from other islands, such as coconut and breadfruit trees, were brought in and established.

Captain James Cook "discovered" the Hawai'ian Islands in 1778; this was their first contact with the world outside Polynesia. Within a few years, the islands were serving as a provisioning station for western ships trading with China. It was not until 1795 that Hawai'i became a unified nation, when King Kamehameha the Great united the entire archipelago under his rule, using weapons obtained from the British to help consolidate his power.

It didn't take long for the British to discover valuable resources on the islands. Their tropical forests were filled with sandalwood trees, which brought high profits when traded for tea in China. Sandalwood that cost a penny a pound in Hawai'i brought thirty-four cents in China. In order to obtain British guns, many chiefs forced their people to cut and haul sandalwood, and the forests were quickly stripped.

But just as the last sandalwood trees were being hauled away,

Hawai'i found a new role in the western economy. In the 1840s, it began serving as a wintering place for American whaling ships, and Hawai'i quickly became tied to the U.S. economy. In 1848, foreign businessmen pressured the Hawai'ian king into a land "reform" program, which carved up land that had been held by the crown, and divided it among the king, the 208 chiefs, and some commoners (who ended up with less than 1 percent of the total). For the first time, foreigners could own land. Massive sugar plantations were quickly established, and when the Civil War tripled the price of sugar in the U.S., the planters became vastly wealthy.

These planters and their descendants controlled Hawai'i's economy and politics for decades, a circumstance that changed the face of its population forever. When they decided that Native Hawai'ians were unsatisfactory as plantation laborers, they began to ship in tens of thousands of Chinese and later Japanese workers. Today the state's population is roughly 9.5 percent Native Hawai'ian in ancestry, 41.5 percent Asian, 24 percent Caucasian, and 25 percent people of other groups or mixed ancestry. No ethnic group is in the majority, and for many visitors the multiethnic character of the islands is in itself an attraction.

The early planters faced one major threat to their profits. As long as Hawai'i was an independent country, the price of sugar in the U.S. was subject to the whims of the U.S. Congress, which set the tariff rate on imports. Though the landowners were able to manipulate the Hawai'ian government—in 1887, they forced King Kalakaua to sign a new constitution that made the monarch a figurehead and allowed U.S. citizens to vote—they couldn't always get Congress to cater to their wishes.

Finally, in 1893, opportunity knocked. When the new queen of Hawai'i, Liliuokalani, declared a new constitution taking back her powers, the landowners formed a Committee on Public Order, which used this "crisis" as a pretext to call in the U.S. Marines to maintain order. The queen was forced to abdicate, and American businessmen set up their own Republic of Hawai'i. Five years later, the once-independent nation of Hawai'i was formally annexed as a territory of the United States.

The big landowners were now free to operate unimpeded. As the population of Native Hawai'ians continued to decline through disease and poverty, planters went ever further afield in their search for labor, bringing in Filipinos to work the fields. When sugar beets started undercutting the price of cane sugar in the U.S., the planters moved into growing pineapples. And when countries in Asia and the Caribbean started producing pineapples more cheaply than Hawai'i, the giant agricultural companies began diversifying into banking—and tourism.

By Leaps and Bounds

People have been visiting Hawai'i on pleasure trips since the days of steamships. Mark Twain called them "the loveliest fleet of islands that lies anchored in any ocean," and an 1875 guidebook gushed, "The earth's paradise! Don't you want to go to it?" Hawai'i got its first hotel in 1872, and air service began in 1929. But until air transport became commonplace, Hawai'i was a very remote destination that only the wealthiest could afford. Even in the 1950s, the average length of a tourist's stay there was a month (now, it's ten days).

Americans became more aware of Hawai'i in the 1940s after the bombing of Pearl Harbor, and the islands played an important role in World War II, as a forward base and refueling station in the Pacific Theater of Operations. In the 1950s, airlines were looking for destinations they could use to lure pleasure travelers to fill up the excess capacity resulting from the development of larger planes. They hit upon Hawai'i.

At first there was a bottleneck in the flow of visitors—there were too few hotel rooms to accommodate an increase in tourism. Seeing an opportunity, the large Hawai'ian conglomerates expanded into the construction and operation of resorts. Hotel construction accelerated, the destination was heavily promoted, and by 1963 one of the competing airlines (Pan Am) was providing ten thousand seats a week to Hawai'i by itself. Price wars between the airlines combined with widebody planes finally brought the price of a Hawai'ian vacation within reach of middle-class families by the late 1960s. The number of visitors skyrocketed, from fifteen thousand in 1946 to four million in 1979.

Today, the state's economy is overwhelmingly based on tourism, which brings in $11 billion annually—a third of the state's total revenue. It also accounts for a third of all jobs and 64 percent of the state's exports. And, just as with the other destinations we've looked at, this predominance of the tourism industry makes the economy very vulnerable to outside factors. The state reached its peak of seven million tourist arrivals in 1990, and since then visitor totals have declined slightly. This started with the 1991 Gulf War, and was worsened by the decade-long recession in Japan (which provides about one in four of Hawai'i's visitors) and also by competition from destinations in the Caribbean.

Reacting defensively, Hawai'i's tourism industry has spent a lot of money studying the precise nature of the problem and possible remedies. The state spends $60 million every year on tourism promotion and research. One recent state-funded study earnestly measured Hawai'i's attractions and facilities against those of the Caribbean, Thailand, Mexico, and other destinations, and found the islands wanting in comparison.[1] Among the proposed solutions are the construction of still more hotels and the formation of "strong working relationships" with airlines.

A sizable percentage of the research effort goes into monitoring local attitudes towards tourism and persuading locals, through advertising campaigns, to keep supporting tourism with their taxes and to show the proper "aloha spirit" to the throngs of tourists. Trying to look on the bright side, an industry association interpreted survey results indicating that 52 percent of citizens favored limited growth of tourism to mean that these respondents supported "growth."[2]

Tourism promotion efforts like these generally highlight data on the sizable role of tourism in Hawai'i's economy, the number of jobs it creates, and the tax revenues it produces. But according to the industry's own research, all this propaganda does not seem terribly effective. In a 1999 statewide survey, they found that 49 percent of residents believe that "their island is being run for tourists."[3] The same survey also noted that many residents discourage young people from pursuing careers in tourism, believing (accurately) that it doesn't pay well and provides little job security.

Nature As Commodity

In Hawai'i, nature has been comprehensively packaged for sale to tourists of every sort, from Japanese golfers to beach lovers to bird watchers on a quest for obscure species for their life lists. Even the most mainstream resort tourism is dependent on nature, since the environment and pleasant climate are the prime attractions. And this mass tourism brings with it the usual catalog of environmental woes: visual pollution, wasteful use of resources, production of garbage, air pollution due to traffic congestion, and so on.

Resort tourism on a massive scale has, not surprisingly, caused environmental damage on a massive scale. Sewage, chemicals from golf courses, and construction runoff have blanketed and killed coral reefs throughout the islands. Development has chewed up countless acres of wild land. Garbage is a serious problem in a state with a limited land area and few recycling facilities. In localities where tourists can at times outnumber locals by more than four to one, natural systems are often stressed beyond their capacity to recover. Water resources are stretched dangerously thin by the massive demand from golf courses, hotel laundries, and tourists' personal use; they are predicted to reach a crisis point in the next few years.

What about new forms of tourism that claim to be environmentally sensitive? As everywhere else, "ecotourism" has become a buzzword in Hawai'i, and a tremendous range of tours and activities are on offer, ranging from harmless (and unsexy) guided nature walks to some appalling travesties of nature tourism. There are small-scale operators running low-impact excursions like kayaking tours and guided bike trips on paved roads, but the "eco" tag is too often nothing but bait for tourists.

Some of the most dubious tourist activities in Hawai'i wrap themselves in the trendy mantle of green, such as "ecotours" that penetrate remote areas with four-wheel drive vehicles. Even ORV tour operators have tried to stake a claim to the green designation—one company's website featured a photo of a driver racing an ATV through a field with the heading "Kauai ATV Ecosport" and the slogan "Got mud?"

Among the most horrifying examples are the pricey helicopter tours that fly tourists over inaccessible areas like the interior of Kauai. "A helicopter tour is the most ecologically friendly way to show our visitors the islands without destroying their natural beauty," claims a brochure produced by Island Helicopters of Lihue, Hawai'i. It takes a remarkably vivid imagination to apply the term "ecologically friendly" to an activity that is so diabolically noisy that participants must wear "avionic headsets" (are these also supplied to the wildlife they fly over?) and that consumes staggering amounts of fossil fuels for the benefit of a handful of thrill-seekers.

Think of the noise and disturbance caused on the rare occasions that an isolated helicopter might fly over your house, whether it be a military flight or an emergency airlift to a nearby hospital. Then consider that the small island of Kauai, just thirty-three miles long, has nine different companies offering helicopter sightseeing for tourists which can take only a handful of people on each flight.

Many nature tours have caused damage to the very environments that people came to enjoy. Whale-watching tours became so numerous and invasive that they threatened to disrupt the life cycle of the creatures that the visitors came out to see. An underwater crater off Maui called Molokini drew so many snorkelers that observers found the surface of the water coated with a film of suntan lotion. The entire north shore of the island of Kauai was finally, belatedly, closed off to speedboat trips, which were harming marine life.[4]

In Hawai'i, too, we see the term ecotourism so broadly applied as to be meaningless—or even harmful. Members of the Hawai'i Ecotourism Association range from one-man nature guide services to major resort hotel chains. Its membership roster includes a helicopter tour company (which claims to have quieter helicopters than other operators), the Kona Historical Society, cruise ship operators, an insurance company, mountainside B & Bs with three rooms, and at least one company that will help you to tear up the Hawai'ian landscape on one of their ATVs. All of these disparate enterprises feel the need, and the right, to claim the ecotourism label.

Tourism Out of Control

Given the choice, few people would allow forms of tourism that harm their homeland or their culture. But when Native Hawai'ians lost control of their islands, they also lost control of how their economy, including tourism, would develop. Most other Hawai'ian citizens who descended from later immigrants similarly have no voice, as their only role in tourism is as poorly paid service employees. But while Native Hawai'ian culture serves as one of the major attractions for tourists, it is the Native Hawai'ians who have paid the highest price.

The tourism industry claims that it brings all Hawai'ians a higher standard of living while helping to preserve the islands' unique culture. The standard argument is that by providing jobs for residents and raising outsiders' appreciation for their cultures, tourism benefits everyone in the islands.

University of Hawai'i professor and native rights activist Haunani-Kay Trask outlines a very different view of what tourism brings to the islands:

> What Hawai'ians get is population densities as high as Hong Kong in some areas, a housing shortage owing to staggering numbers of migrants from Asia and the continental United States, a soaring crime rate as impoverished locals prey on ostentatiously rich tourists, and environmental crises, including water depletion, that threaten the entire archipelago. Rather than stop the flood, the state is projecting a tidal wave of twelve million tourists by the year 2010. Today, we Hawai'ians exist in an occupied country. We are a hostage people, forced to witness and participate in our own collective humiliation as tourist artifacts for the First World.[5]

Too many tourism developments have proceeded with total disregard for residents and their way of life—particularly Native Hawai'ians. For example, on Kauai, a twenty-two-acre ancient Hawai'ian burial ground was excavated to build a condominium resort at Keoniloa. Faced with community opposition, the developers set aside a single acre to relocate all the graves that were disturbed—and then incorporated it into the resort's grounds as a marketing ploy. In countless places, ancient temples called *heiau*—many of them still in use—have become sights for tourist snapshots.

Less visible but just as devastating are the impacts of tourism on people's traditional sources of livelihood. Chemical pollution from golf courses and sewage from hotels have destroyed age-old fishing grounds. When land is bought up for a resort, farming families and whole communities are forced out of rural areas where they have lived for generations. Many of these people find themselves semi-homeless, living in settlements on remote beaches, where they risk being evicted by developers once again.

The only easily available jobs are in the tourism industry, but service wages are just as low in Hawai'i as they are elsewhere in the U.S., despite the higher cost of living. Many Native Hawai'ians are forced by economic necessity to emigrate to the U.S. mainland to survive.

There is a vigorous, albeit divided, Hawai'ian sovereignty movement, which seeks to regain Native Hawai'ian control over the land that once belonged to them. Different groups have set different goals, ranging from obtaining monetary compensation for the Hawai'ian crown lands that were expropriated until independence as a full-fledged nation. The largest group, Ka Lahui, demands the same rights to self-government as Native American tribes have, along with restitution from the U.S. government for the overthrow of the Hawai'ian monarchy and the return of two million acres of land to Native Hawai'ian control. The government is now administering this land—supposedly for the benefit of Native Hawai'ians, but in reality for U.S. military and commercial interests.

But for the moment, Hawai'i's citizens have little input in shaping the development of tourism as carried out by massive corporations. Native Hawai'ians, as the poorest and least educated, have the least control of all.

Aloha for Sale

But it's the marketing of Hawai'ian culture that should really give us pause.

In Hawai'i, mass tourism was intentionally developed by large landowners as a way to smooth out the economic instability of a plantation economy based on sugar and pineapples. As we've seen, nature is an important selling point for Hawai'ian travel, but the key product packaged and sold to tourists is the culture. There are other places Americans can go to enjoy palm trees and pretty beaches without having to worry about passport checks or boiled drinking water—California, Florida, and the whole Gulf Coast have a lot to offer. What these destinations lack is a safe sense of foreignness, the "exotic" allure of Hawai'i, purveyed in tourist staples such as hula shows, luau dinners, and the tour company representative who puts a *lei* around your neck at Honolulu airport.

One of the main selling points for Hawai'i is its so-called "aloha spirit," the warm hospitality of the native culture. At the same time that Hawai'i is presented as thrillingly exotic, a paradise far removed from the workaday world, tourists are assured that (unlike in foreign countries) these brown natives are not threatening—they are Americans, they love to have visitors and are pleased to share their island with the world. They work in the tourism industry not out of a need for money and a lack of other options, but out of sheer warmth and friendliness and a desire to welcome unfortunate souls from colder climes.

Once Hawai'i had been targeted for tourist development by powerful corporations, the traditional culture of Native Hawai'ians became one more resource available for exploitation. Customs, ceremonies, and artifacts were torn from their context and repackaged as products for the tourist market. Sacred symbols became decorations for hotel rooms, ancient temples became tourist attractions, and religious stories became quaint "folklore" for evening entertainment.

"Enjoy the history and legends of the ancient civilizations that once inhabited these verdant valleys," says the brochure of a purveyor of luxury catamaran tours—never mind that these "ancient civilizations" are alive but not well, in settlements of homeless people around the islands. A "Garden Luau" offered by another operator features as entertainment an "International Pageant" that "depicts dances and songs from Tahiti, Hawai'i, China, Japan, the Philippines, New Zealand, and Samoa," a showcase of "the lively ethnic groups that have come to call Hawai'i home."

An example of culture artifact turned into commodity that particularly angers Haunani-Kay Trask and other activists is the hula, the traditional Hawai'ian dance so often performed as entertainment for tourists. How many visitors realize that, far from being provocative entertainment in sexy costumes, the hula is actually an age-old religious ritual? Trask writes, "Thus hula dancers wear clown-like makeup, don costumes from a mix of Polynesian cultures, and behave in a manner that is smutty and salacious rather than powerfully erotic. In the hotel version of the hula, the sacredness of the dance has completely evaporated while the athleticism and sexual expression have been packaged like ornaments. The purpose is entertainment for profit rather than a joyful and truly Hawai'ian celebration of human and divine nature."[6]

In addition, the people themselves became something for sale—subservient brown natives to cater to your wishes. Only a tiny percentage of Americans actually have servants in their homes, but at a top-end resort, suddenly every guest has an army of smiling staff members to gratify his or her every whim. The image of Hawai'ian hospitality particularly trades on this stereotype of native people as submissive servants, a commodity to be purchased.

Rev. Kaleo Patterson, a tourism activist on Maui, sums up: "Tourism has meant an invasion of all that is sacred to our people. Our culture has been turned into a 'Hula marketing' campaign. We are romanticized, to appeal to the fantasies of world travelers. Popular images show smiling, flower-adorned girls and hula dancers, exotic moonlit feasts with natives serving hand and foot. This kind of marketing and promotion perpetuates racist and sexist stereotypes that are culturally inappropriate and demeaning. It sells an artificial cultural image with complete disregard for the truth."[7]

Despite the key role of Native Hawai'ians in the marketing of Hawai'i, they have benefited the least from tourism of any ethnic group in the islands. Charges Rev. Patterson, "While local elites and transnational corporations benefit from tourism, Native Hawai'ians remain the poorest, sickest and least educated of all peoples in Hawai'i."

The facts back him up. Infant mortality rates, educational attainment, and other measures of well-being are dismal for these natives of a supposed "earthly paradise." Native Hawai'ians have the poorest health of any ethnic group in the U.S., including an incidence of heart disease 44 percent above the national average. Of their teenagers, 32 percent drop out of high school, while only 5 percent go on to earn a college degree (compared with 16 percent of other Hawai'ians). Though they make up less than 20 percent of the state's population, they are 38 percent of its prison inmates.[8]

It's not a coincidence that, in many places around the world, environments and cultures come under threat at the same time. Many of the earth's most stunning natural environments are located in remote areas, inhabited by people who have not been integrated into the global economy and have been able to retain many aspects of their traditional cultures. This explains why so much of what is called "ecotourism" mingles natural and cultural attractions. Because these environments exist far from urban centers, and were thought, until recently, to have no economic value, their native inhabitants were left alone and their cultures more or less allowed to remain undisturbed.

Such areas are marginal, peripheral in both a physical and a political sense. Native Hawai'ians lived in beach communities and fished undisturbed until their land became desirable for sugar plantations—or for vacation condominiums. No one really cared what Central American peasants were doing until fast-food companies wanted huge amounts of cheap beef for their burgers. Appalachian families lived and farmed in peace for generations, until it was found that they were sitting on top of thick seams of coal or surrounded by economically valuable timber.

Now that groups such as these are under threat, they are often advised that the way to preserve their homelands is by sharing their natural environments and cultures with visitors. But if outsiders motivated only by profit control the course of this development, the "culture" that is shared can too easily become a collection of demeaning stereotypes, a caricature that is easy to package and sell, rather than a living treasure and a source of pride to the community.

Questions for Appalachia

Appalachia, like Hawai'i, has a unique combination of natural and cultural attractions. Living in an inaccessible region, mountain people developed ways of living and thinking distinct from mainstream America, and they have managed to preserve something of their uniqueness well into this homogenized era. But as we've seen, the people of a region need to be very cautious in using their culture as a tourist attraction. Who gets to decide what components of a culture are "for sale"? Local people? Promoters? Visitors? As Ian McIntosh asks in *Cultural Survival Quarterly,* "Are indigenous people another 'resource' to be mined by ecotourism?"[9]

If "culture" becomes a draw for tourists, what would prevent situations like these, which would be all too familiar to Native Hawai'ians, from occurring?

- A busload of tourists pulls up and starts snapping pictures at an outdoor revival meeting or at one of the enormous family reunions that are an Appalachian specialty.
- Gift shops refuse to stock the work of craftspeople who don't adhere to the customers' concept of what "traditional" art should look like.

- A developer decides that an untended family cemetery would make a picturesque component of the grounds of a resort hotel.
- A "hillbilly" theme restaurant dresses its waitresses in skimpy, patched dresses and straw hats.

Thousands of miles north of Hawai'i, there is another state where indigenous culture lives on in a setting filled with natural wonders. Alaska has had a somewhat different experience with nature tourism. Here, too, are some valuable lessons for Appalachia and other communities confronting the growth of tourism.

Way Up North

It's hard to wrap your mind around Alaska. The list of superlatives seems endless: it's the biggest, the coldest, the emptiest, the wildest of the states. With plenty of time on their hands during the long dark winter, Alaskans seem to enjoy dreaming up new and ever more startling factoids about their state. A few examples: The 45,000-mile coastline of Alaska is as long as that of all other forty-nine states combined. If Manhattan had the same population density as Alaska, only seventeen people would live there. If you superimposed Alaska on the "lower forty-eight," it would stretch from the Georgia coast out past Los Angeles into the Pacific.

The state is another of America's premier tourism destinations, a daydream, trip-of-a-lifetime place. Around a million awestruck visitors come every year to cruise the fjords of the Inside Passage in southeastern Alaska; view the slopes of Denali (Mt. McKinley), the highest peak in North America; fish for salmon in Arctic rivers; even venture north to the shores of the Arctic Ocean. All around them is a wildness almost inconceivable elsewhere in the United States.

Only 626,932 people (2000 census) share a state as large as a quarter of the "lower forty-eight." Of these, 16.2 percent are Native Americans, the highest proportion in any state (the U.S. government does not officially recognize Native Hawai'ians as a distinct ethnic group). These Alaska Natives are members of quite different cultures: Yupik and Inupiat Eskimos, Aleuts, and Tlingit, Haida, Athapascan and Tsimshian Indians. Ninety-three percent of these Natives live in small

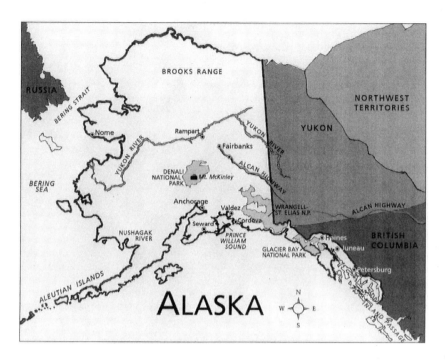

Alaska, Map by Mark Spencer.

In Denali National Park, we camped with absolutely no other people around in this vast park, bigger than some states, in a vast state. We pitched the tent near a sign telling us to be on the lookout for grizzly bears. We joked about it and tried to sleep, in the late summer night chill. Afterwards, the locals asked, "Didn't you take guns along?" "What would I do if I confronted a grizzly with a gun?" I retorted. "About the same thing I'd do without a gun—crap in my pants." Apparently our ignorance made for sounder sleeping at the time.

—Al Fritsch

rural communities, and many still lead some version of a traditional subsistence lifestyle.

Many of Alaska's non-Native residents have arrived relatively recently, drawn by the oil boom and the economic expansion that surrounded it. When Alaska became a state in 1959, its population was only a quarter of a million. Only a third of Alaskan residents were actually born there—the second-lowest proportion of any state. Most of these people are concentrated in just a few areas, with the city of Anchorage accounting for almost half the state's total population.

With all that nature and so few people, it would seem that nature tourism could flourish unhindered. But the experience of Alaska—especially issues of control over tourism—has important lessons for communities elsewhere.

The Last Frontier

The United States took control of Alaska in 1867, when it purchased the land from Russia. That date is very significant in a way that's not so obvious. At the time when Alaska was acquired just after the end of the Civil War, the U.S. Army was caught up in violently suppressing the Native American nations of the frontier west, and Congress was preoccupied with the political battles of Reconstruction. Little thought was given to the Native peoples in the distant new territory. They were never militarily conquered, and since no one could see any immediate economic value in their remote homeland, the U.S. government accepted Natives' claim to the land in principle. Unlike so many other indigenous peoples, they were able to continue their traditional lifestyle undisturbed for decades after they fell under outside control.

The discovery of oil in Alaska in 1957 changed all that. Besides producing the final push for statehood, it also made establishment of a clear-cut system of land ownership urgent. Native Alaskans were the most successful of all Native Americans in having their territorial rights officially recognized. The Alaska Native Claims Settlement Act, finally signed into law by President Nixon in 1971, created twelve Native corporations and gave them the right to choose a total of forty-four million acres of land. Alaskans of at least one-fourth Native ancestry would receive shares in these corporations. The state of Alaska was also allowed to select land, while other areas were designated as wildlife refuges and national parks.

Alaska's fifty-two thousand Natives received joint control of 846 acres and $18,548 in assets per person. Unfortunately, not all of the Native corporations that were established made environmentally sound decisions. While some have been very conscious of their stewardship of resources for the future, others put sole emphasis on quick financial benefit for their members. Some of the corporations have engaged in such dubious activities as clear-cutting large stretches of their forestland to take advantage of favorable timber prices.

Tourism developed slowly in Alaska. Visitors began trickling in even before statehood, though access was difficult and expensive. The Alcan Highway, built during World War II to give the military overland access to Alaska, was opened to the public in 1948, but it was still an arduous drive over pitted gravel roads. Psychologically (if not in reality) Alaska remains, for many people, the "Last Frontier," as its state motto proclaims—a remote, untouched place where resources could never be exhausted and every person is free to act without restriction. Legendary hunting and fishing were among the attractions that first drew visitors to the state.

One early, and appalling, form of nature tourism in Alaska was aerial hunting of polar bears. During the 1950s, wealthy sport hunters from the "lower forty-eight" began hiring pairs of planes in the Arctic. Upon sighting a polar bear, one plane would land the hunter on the ice while the other herded the bear towards the hunter, who could then easily shoot it. The bear was immediately skinned, and hunter and trophy flown back out again. No skill was required, and no danger was involved. Over two hundred bears annually were slaughtered this way between 1960 and 1972, when the practice was finally banned. It was "about as sporting as machine-gunning a cow," the *New York Times* editorialized.[10]

Other environmentally unsound schemes managed to escape such public criticism. Because Alaska was so remote and so thinly populated, it was often viewed as a handy site for projects that would provoke a furor if attempted anywhere else. For instance, in Project Chariot in 1959, the U.S. Atomic Energy Commission planned to use nuclear explosions to blast out a new harbor in the Arctic, thirty miles from an Inupiat Eskimo village. Though the AEC pushed the idea for years, it was never carried out; later studies found the scheme could have released as much radioactivity into the atmosphere as 675 Chernobyl disasters. Similarly, the Rampart Dam Project would have turned the Yukon River into a reservoir the size of Lake Erie, destroying staggering amounts of wildlife habitat, to produce hydropower in the vague hope of developing an aluminum industry up on the tundra.

One scheme that did become a reality was the Alaska Oil Pipeline. Despite concerted opposition from a spectrum of environmental groups, the massive pipeline was completed in 1977. In 2001 it carried 362 million barrels of oil across 789 miles of wilderness from the North Slope oil fields on the Arctic Ocean to the tanker port of Valdez on the Pacific. In the years since the pipeline opened, a number of accidents have released toxic crude oil onto the fragile land within the Arctic Circle. One of the most devastating environmental disasters of all time occurred on Good Friday of 1989, when the tanker *Exxon Valdez* ran aground in Alaska's Prince William Sound, spewing out 10.9 million gallons of crude oil and poisoning thousands of miles of coastline.

Despite these environmental assaults, Alaska's sheer size means that it has preserved some of the most untouched natural landscapes in the nation and the world. The state is a magnet for nature-loving tourists, and many of the state's most visited attractions are nature-based: the fjords of the Inside Passage, the Mendenhall Glacier and Glacier Bay, Denali National Park. In common with the general profile of ecotourists, typical visitors to Alaska are older (around fifty), better educated, and more affluent (with a household income of $60,000) than the average American.

Who Owns Nature?

As in many other parts of the world, tourism in Alaska is increasingly controlled by large outside corporations. According to the state government, nearly two-thirds of all tourists arrive on package tours, arranged and paid for outside the state. Although the state government asserts that 90 percent of the visitor industry is composed of small businesses, the fact is that many of these businesses are exceedingly small and have little economic impact, while a disproportionate influence is exercised by a few massive companies.

Tourism commercializes the social relationship between host and guest. At the market in Luxor, Egypt, a boy looks suspiciously at a group of foreign tourists on a Nile cruise. Photo by Kevin Millham.

(Above) Many of Appalachia's drawing cards for tourists are natural wonders. Cumberland Falls, near Corbin, Kentucky, is famed for the "moonbow" formed in its mist by the light of the full moon. Photo by Kevin Millham. (Below) Appalachia's heritage of fine craftwork is one of the region's attractions for visitors. In her studio in McKee, Kentucky, Carolyn Carroll sews both traditional and modern quilts. Photo by Kevin Millham.

Some Appalachian tourist attractions combine historic and scenic elements. One such site is the Cumberland Gap National Historical Park, located where Virginia, Tennessee, and Kentucky meet.

Many all-terrain vehicle (ATV) enthusiasts seek out the most beautiful scenery to pursue their favorite recreation, such as the area around Kentucky's Red River Gorge. The environmental destruction they cause in fragile areas can be irreparable. Photo by Kevin Millham.

One of ecotourism's attractions is the possibility of more meaningful interactions with local people. This Hindu holy man in Kathmandu, Nepal, is happy to meet foreign visitors. Photo by Kevin Millham.

(Above) Some villages in Nepal have benefited economically from the influx of adventure tourists in their country. This teahouse along a popular trekking route in the Annapurna region serves western-style food to trekkers—including spaghetti bolognese. Photo by Kevin Millham. (Below) True ecotourists can contribute to improving the environment they visit. In Belize, a group of volunteer scuba divers prepares to carry out an underwater survey and fish-count along the world's second longest barrier reef. Photo by Kevin Millham.

(Above) True ecotourists must show sensitivity to the communities they visit. This riverside funeral in rural Nepal was interrupted by the arrival of a group of trekkers. Photo by Kevin Millham. *(Below)* Even small amounts of income from ecotourism can make a difference to rural families. This Shan man in Burma guides visitors around the waterways near Inle Lake in Burma. Photo by Kevin Millham.

(Above) Tourism can provide an incentive to preserve and maintain local traditions. Rail fences like these are a part of Appalachia's scenic heritage. Photo by Kevin Millham. *(Below)* Future Appalachian tourism should encourage the development of small rural businesses. Sarah Culbreth throws a vessel on her potter's wheel at Tater Knob Pottery near Berea, Kentucky. Photo by Kevin Millham.

(Above) Tourist attractions along the Blue Ridge Parkway educate while entertaining. Mabry Mill, in Virginia, depicts pioneer life in the region. Photo by Kevin Millham. *(Below)* True ecotourists have a responsibility to share what they've learned with others at home. The Burmese military dictatorship forcibly relocated all villagers who were living near the ruined city of Pagan to prevent them from having contact with tourists. Photo by Kevin Millham.

(Above) Knowing the history makes all the difference in what you see. A cannon at Antietam National Battlefield in western Maryland reminds visitors that this seemingly peaceful farmland is the bloodiest site in American history. Photo by Kevin Millham. *(Below)* Appalachia's white-water rivers are a magnet for adventure sports enthusiasts. Here, a kayaker takes on the Monongahela River near Morgantown, West Virginia. Photo used with permission of the West Virginia Division of Tourism

Costumed interpreters make Appalachian history come alive at Pricketts Fort State Park in Fairmont, West Virginia. Photo used with permission of the West Virginia Division of Tourism

(Above) Appalachia's mining heritage can play a part in future tourism development. At the Beckley Exhibition Coal Mine in West Virginia, visitors descend into an actual mine. Photo used with permission of the West Virginia Division of Tourism. (Below) An aerial view of downtown Gatlinburg. In recent decades, the town has grown almost beyond recognition. Photo used by permission of the Gatlinburg Department of Tourism.

Hiking at Haleakala, Hawai'i. Hawai'i's diverse environments are a magnet for nature tourists. Photo by Ron Dahlquist. Photo courtesy of the Hawaii Visitors and Convention Bureau.

(Above) Keiki Hula dancers. Native Hawai'ian culture is often seen as a "tourist attraction." Photo by Joe Solem. Photo courtesy of the Hawaii Visitors and Convention Bureau. (Below) Eskimo Ice Fishing. Alaskan natives' subsistence rights complicate tourism decision making. Photo courtesy of the Alaska Division of Tourism. Copyright Alaska Division of Tourism.

Eskimo Couple with Dog Sled Team. Many Native Alaskans still follow traditional lifeways. Photo courtesy of the Alaska Division of Tourism. Copyright Alaska Division of Tourism.

Camping on the Ruth Glacier of Mount McKinley in the 1980s. Many Americans view Alaska as the nation's last unspoiled wilderness. Photo courtesy of the Alaska Division of Tourism. Copyright Alaska Division of Tourism.

Chief among these are the cruise ship lines. Alaska is one of the fastest-growing cruise destinations in the world, with ten different cruise lines operating twenty-two ships there in 2000. Most of these ships follow a standard route along the Inside Passage, the dramatic waterway through the "panhandle" of southeastern Alaska. To this day, the area is only accessible by water, as the landscape of fjords and glaciers is too impossibly rugged for roads. Everyday transportation between towns is provided by the Alaska Marine Highway, a long-distance ferry network.

The cruise lines discovered the region in the 1970s, and the glaciers, forests, and Gold Rush towns were an instant hit with visitors—besides providing a handy alternate destination for cruise ships during the summer low season in the Caribbean. Cruise traffic has grown in Alaska almost uninterruptedly. Between 1995 and 1999, the number of cruise passengers there increased by an average of 15.3 percent per year. Today, around 70 percent of the state's tourists visit the Inside Passage, and 60 percent of these travelers come by cruise ship.

As in many other places, the influx of visitors threatens the very environment they come to enjoy. The city of Juneau, with a population of only 30,000, receives 700,000 cruise passengers every summer, and towns of only a few thousand people receive almost as many. Small-town residents complain bitterly about the narrow streets blocked by sightseeing hordes, the "Disneyland atmosphere," the incessant noise, and the pollution from the ships.

Many small independent tourism businesses in Alaska are actually satellites of the cruise industry, relying on them for the vast majority of their customers. For example, in Juneau, a number of helicopter services take cruise passengers for quickie "flightseeing" tours over nearby glaciers during the few hours their customers spend ashore there. For the tourists, it's an unforgettable view of one of nature's wonders. For local people, it's an almost unbearable sonic assault. In 2000, helicopters made a total of 16,583 flights. Because of the long northern daylight, the helicopters take off as early as seven in the morning, and as late as ten at night. Residents speak of being "pounded" by the noise.

The cruise ships themselves have dismal environmental records. The Bluewater Network calls them "floating cities that produce enormous volumes of waste." Each day, the average cruise passenger produces 3.5 pounds of garbage—up to six times as much as a person on shore. A single ship can generate eleven million gallons of wastewater per day. And too much of this waste goes straight into the sea. Cruise lines have repeatedly been fined for dumping raw sewage in Alaska and elsewhere. Royal Caribbean admitted to routinely dumping waste oil, photo-processing chemicals, dry-cleaning fluid, and other highly toxic substances into U.S. harbors, and paid $18 million in criminal fines.

Communities that try to regulate cruise tourism have found themselves in deep trouble. When the little town of Haines, Alaska (population: 2,000) protested against pollution caused by cruise ships and imposed a head-tax on passengers, they were dropped from the itineraries of all major cruise lines in 2000. This devastated the town's economy, which was so heavily centered on cruise tourism that they had funded a new dock for the ships. Company executives insisted that the itinerary changes were due to cost factors alone.

The big cruise corporations have tried to augment their control over Alaska tourism by branching out into land operations. For example, P&O Princess Cruises now operates a chain of luxury wilderness lodges across the state for their passengers, including one at the entrance to Wrangell-St. Elias National Park, the largest in the U.S. Royal Caribbean has formed a subsidiary called Royal Celebrity Tours for land-based operations. Needless to say, these companies cater to high-end tourists, and their offerings are hardly low-impact—excursions by helicopter, bush plane, and jet boat to remote areas, and hunting and fishing trips to sites traditionally used by natives for subsistence.

By owning and operating as many aspects of the tourism industry as possible, these large corporations aim to minimize the risks they face from community opposition in settled areas. In building luxury hotels far from towns, they can further boost their profits while avoiding any outside interference at all. In many rural areas of Alaska, local governments do not exist. However, this does not mean there are no people there—the majority of Alaska Natives live in over two hundred small villages scattered across the vast territory.

Around the world, people have found that buying into tourism as a motor for growth means that their local economy is increasingly affected by decisions made in corporate boardrooms on some other continent. The people of Haines, Alaska, found themselves jobless almost overnight as a result of discussions in corporate headquarters in London's financial district. And when the lion's share of the revenue goes to outside owners, local people find that, though they bear most of the damage caused by tourism, they receive very few of the benefits.

Balancing Demands—Hunters, Ecotourists, and Subsistence

Alaska has a unique "wildcard" factor not present in other tourism destinations, which makes the situation both more complicated and more promising. This is the Native peoples' traditional right of subsistence, which has been recognized both in law and in custom.

With a growing season measured in weeks, all but a very small fraction of Alaska's land is useless for agriculture. Traditionally, the people of Alaska—both Natives and others who have settled in wilderness areas—have lived by hunting, fishing, and gathering wild plants. As activist Gabriel Scott writes, "While it appears incomprehensible to people living in some of the world's scoured-over regions, the land here provides. Subsistence hunting and fishing support, to varying degrees, a vast majority of Alaskan rural residents. Subsistence provides an economic base independent of the global cash economy. And getting one's living directly off the land you inhabit is a critical part of Alaska Native culture."[11]

To this day, Eskimo villagers hunt whales in the Bering Strait for meat, while inland Indians catch and preserve large stocks of salmon and other fish. In the far north, Athapaskan Indians rely on the huge herds of caribou as a source of food. The Alaska National Interest Lands Conservation Act, enacted in 1980, guarantees a priority for "nonwasteful subsistence use" of wildlife by such rural residents.

A group of us once went south to the wild and wooded Seward area. We camped by a glacier, and the ice was the bluest I had ever seen—but it just added to the chill of Alaska. I had already had to buy an extra heavy shirt—and this was in late summer. There was absolutely no one else around. We saw the salmon struggling mightily coming up the ice-melt stream—the bear sure loved them. We were tempted to try a little fishing, but no one wanted to do the cooking.

—Al Fritsch

As an indicator of the significance of wild foods in rural Alaska, a 1994 study by the Alaska Department of Fish and Game found that while urban Alaskans ate an average of 22 pounds of wild foods per year, rural residents averaged 376 pounds per person. This figure was highest in remote western Alaska, where mainly Eskimo residents consumed 767 pounds of wild foods per person—clearly the bulk of their diet.[12]

But subsistence hunting has led to heated conflict in Alaska. For example, in some prime tourist spots, such as Glacier Bay, numerous cruise ships are permitted but subsistence hunting by traditional users is banned. Sport fishers who spend large sums of money to fish for salmon in Arctic streams do not want to see the stock depleted by Native subsistence fishers. And deep-green ecotourists would be outraged by some of the traditional Native practices. For instance, the law permits some Eskimos in the western Arctic to hunt bowhead whales, now an endangered species, as a part of their traditional diet.

The issues underlying subsistence are thorny. Who should have the right to subsistence hunting and fishing? Only Natives? All rural residents, since supermarkets are hardly plentiful in the wild? People in need, people who customarily live off the land, all Alaskans? How will people granted subsistence rights be identified? And what, exactly, does subsistence mean? Hunting only for food? To make clothing as well? To earn cash? To affirm one's cultural identity? In a statewide survey in 1998, respondents named "subsistence" as the single most pressing issue for Alaska's elected officials to work on, by a three-to-one margin over the runner-up, education.

Although Alaska still has an image of a boundless, bountiful wilderness, the reality is that the arctic climate makes its carrying capacity quite limited, and conflicts between different users are already growing more acute. Tourists want easy access to ever more remote, "pristine" environments. The Native population is growing at a rapid rate, and many Native Alaskans are adamant about their right to continue their traditional lifeways with modern modifications, such as using snowmobiles for winter hunting. And sport hunters and fishers, both residents and visitors, want to continue enjoying their pastimes in remote settings. The low productivity of the land means it cannot support a large population of big game animals, making a clash between wildlife lovers, subsistence hunters, and sport hunters unavoidable.

Taking Control of Tourism

What on earth does this have to do with Appalachia, which is virtually certain never to see a cruise ship or an Eskimo whale hunter? Appalachia has in common with Alaska a tradition of stubborn independence and a wish to be left alone. In both places, people tend to be suspicious of government at all levels and want to make all decisions individually, free from "interference" by others.

But in Alaska, people have found it increasingly necessary to overcome this attitude in order to work together to shape the future of their communities. Tourism is growing throughout the state, and unless communities move first in deciding what form it should take, they find too often that the decision has been made for them, by outsiders with no other criterion than the bottom line.

Alaska has a large number of environmental groups, including active chapters of national organizations such as the Sierra Club, and many of these have taken stands on issues centered on tourism. In addition, local organizations have formed to work on specific issues such as helicopter noise and pollution caused by cruise ships. (One group is called Cruise Control.)

The success of these groups can be gauged from a paragraph in a marketing report commissioned by the State of Alaska. "Resident rebellion against many forms of tourism must be kept to a minimum if the industry is to be appropriately managed and developed," the 2000 "Strategic Market Analysis and Planning for Alaska Tourism" warns, going on to explain that "a number of vocal residents and organizations have aggressively fought significant efforts aimed at improving the state's tourism-related economy."[13]

Some communities have moved beyond merely trying to control the damaging impacts of tourism, seeking instead to shape the future of tourism development in their areas. One innovative program is the Guiding Alaska Tourism (GAT) Initiative, sponsored by the Alaska Wilderness Recreation and Tourism Association (AWRTA), a trade organization of environmentally friendly businesses. The purpose of GAT is to "provide tools and information to assist Alaskans in guiding tourism growth and development in their community." When invited by a community, GAT provides services ranging from simple presentations on tourism issues to helping the community produce a comprehensive local tourism plan.

As AWRTA points out, "Alaska tourism is uniquely based on resources held in common"—public land and waterways, Native-owned
land, public facilities, and fish and wildlife. Because of this, all Alaskans have a stake in deciding the future of tourism in their state. Their
community workbook *Guiding Alaska Tourism: Strategies for Success*
describes two examples of the type of proactive planning it supports.[14]

In remote, roadless southwestern Alaska, a group of Native Corporations cooperated to plan tourism development along the Nushagak
River, an area that attracts affluent sport fishers who fly in for vacations. They decided to issue sport fishing permits and concentrate
sport fishing lodges and camps along the river's West Branch, while
leaving the East Branch undeveloped and available for local subsistence fishers. In this way, otherwise conflicting needs were reconciled.

A different strategy was used in input given by the AWRTA for
the Chugach Forest Management plan in Prince William Sound.
Along with Appalachians, Alaskans have a strong dislike for government regulation. When the United States Forest Service was planning
tourist development along the sound, rather than banning access to
one bay, steps were taken to attract users to another, less fragile bay
nearby. These measures included providing docks, cabins, and moor-
ing buoys to encourage use and marketing the preferred bay to visitors. Local guides and outfitters made voluntary agreements about
use of the two bays.

GAT has been involved in several different types of communities in
varying capacities, drawing lessons from the planning process in each.
The communities faced different situations. For example, the isolated
seaside town of Cordova wanted to lessen its dependence on fishing,
the primary industry, without becoming equally centered on tourism.
Among the areas they needed to consider were the types of tourists to
invite, the number of visitors that was desirable, the existing attractions to market, new attractions that needed to be developed, which
areas were in need of protection, and how to capture the maximum
benefits of tourism for local businesses and residents. In Denali Bor-
ough, along the highway to Denali National Park, residents wanted to
avoid ugly roadside sprawl without imposing a lot of regulations, and
decided to use incentives and education to promote development that
fit the local environment.

The GAT Initiative has collected a number of concepts that communities have found useful in working to plan the future of tourism. Among them are:

- A "Right-Now" Product—Communities begin the planning process with a simple, low-risk project that brings people together and builds credibility. For instance, one community worked together on a marketing brochure for local attractions.
- "Micro-Brewed Tourism"—Rather than marketing a high-volume, lower-value product to a mass audience, communities, like micro-breweries, can choose instead to sell smaller "batches" of a high-quality, high-value product. This means targeting a particular kind of visitor and developing tourist attractions that will appeal to them, based on the unique qualities of a particular place.
- Intensity of Use Districts—The community designates a range of recreational areas for different degrees of tourism. Some sites that can handle many visitors are designated for heavier development, while others receive few facilities, and the most fragile areas remain undeveloped.
- Increasing Shoulder Season Tourism—In many destinations, the bulk of tourists are concentrated at particular times of the year, while other months see very few visitors. Scheduling events before or after the main "season" and developing new types of attractions can help ease the seasonal disruption caused by tourism and spread income more evenly throughout the year.
- "Telling Better Stories"—The way a place describes itself is a key factor in the type of tourism it develops. GAT gives the example of describing a hike through a meadow as "beautiful, grassy, and peaceful," as opposed to describing the same hike as the setting of a Civil War battle. The two stories will attract different types of visitors and give them different types of experiences. Teaching tourists about the places they visit not only gives them an experience they will willingly pay more for but can increase support for community and environmental causes.

From Alaska to Appalachia

Communities around the world that have become involved with tourism find themselves confronting the globalization of the economy in a very real sense. In Alaska, residents in small towns and rural areas have seen their quality of life, and even their livelihood itself, devastated by decisions made in corporate boardrooms on the other side of the world. A change in the itinerary of a major tour company can soon transform a quiet village into a swarming tourist trap—or suddenly leave half its residents unemployed. Construction of a new wilderness lodge can close off access to the river that provides a family's main supply of food.

Until now, Appalachia has seen relatively little of this "remote-controlled" tourism development. But corporations of every sort face the imperative to expand or die—and Appalachia is ripe for development. As was pointed out earlier, most parts of the region are less than a day's drive from the major U.S. cities of the East Coast and Midwest, making the area attractive to potential developers of golf courses, resorts, theme parks, and any number of other possible tourist attractions. Which types of development would actually improve the quality of life in your town? Unless people and communities take the initiative and reach an agreement on what kind of tourism they want (if any), they may find that faceless corporate executives far away have already made the decision for them.

On the last page of their *Strategies for Success* workbook, the GAT Initiative summarizes their recommendations for communities considering tourism in a few brief sentences: "Be inclusive. Tourism is based on public resources, so get everybody involved. Define what's unique about your place, your town. Start with something easy, something everybody can agree on. Do a plan. First define a common vision, then find locally acceptable ways to get there. Partner to get the job done. Work with agencies, nonprofits, local governments, businesses. Be realistic, be patient. Success takes persistence, sustained work. Not every community will be a destination overnight."

These points are every bit as relevant to people in the towns and quiet hollows of the mountain South as they are to Eskimos on the shores of the Arctic Ocean.

Learning from the Wider World

In the case studies of the last two chapters, we've looked at many forms of tourism in natural settings. Some of them label themselves as ecotourism, while others make no such claim. But several common themes have emerged in looking at these places so widely scattered around the globe.

Nature tourism is not uniformly a good thing. The "eco" label is at times nothing but greenwash—a trendy marketing ploy for the same old destructive tourism. But even environmentally benign activities can cause damage when they get too large. It's vital to look beyond labels and examine the true impact, both negative and positive, of any tourism program or activity, no matter what it calls itself. Marketing culture as a tourist attraction can open a Pandora's box of conflict. Who decides what aspects of culture to share with tourists? Who sets the limits? And who will be allowed to define what that culture really is— the visitors and the outside "experts" and consultants? Or the people who embody that culture in their daily lives and their worldview?

Benefits from tourism don't necessarily go to the people who most need them. Communities are not undifferentiated abstractions but diverse groups of individuals and families. Each person and family in the community has a different background, different assets, and a different outlook, and they are not all equally placed to take advantage of economic opportunities that may arise from tourism.

Communities need to be proactive in planning for tourism. Unless citizens take decision-making about tourism into their own hands, the decisions are likely to be made for them by entities far away and not for the benefit of local people.

For people and places that are contemplating tourism development, it's important to examine the overall picture and not get carried away by wishful thinking or the trend of the moment. In the next chapter, we'll outline and weigh the positive and negative effects of ecotourism as it has developed to this point.

CHAPTER 7

The Bottom Line

Ecotourism's Balance Sheet

So far, we've looked at the development of ecotourism and considered some of the problems with nature-based tourism in specific locations. It's time to consider the overall picture, weighing the pluses and minuses of ecotourism in order to assess its potential for Appalachia.

The existing literature on ecotourism is overwhelmingly positive. Ecotourism supporters and developers have written the bulk of it, ever since the concept first appeared. It is only in recent years that a few observers have cast a critical eye on the principle and on specific ecotourism projects. Since so much has been written on the benefits and promise of ecotourism, we will cover that side of the balance sheet in less detail, and devote more space to some concerns that haven't received as much attention.

It's important to note that we are talking here about ecotourism as it has actually been developed and applied until now. Proponents spend a lot of time talking about ecotourism's *potential*—about what it could accomplish if the conditions were right: given unlimited funding, an environmentally aware public, an ever-expanding travel market. Even E—*The Environmental Magazine*, in its January/February 2001 special issue on ecotourism, hedges: "Can ecotourism help connect us with the rest of the world, and by doing so, actively make it a better place? There are many who believe it can."

Ecotourism has many vocal supporters. Among them are governments of both industrialized and Third World nations, a number of large non-governmental organizations, environmental groups of differing shades of green, tourism industry organizations large and small,

162

and many individual environmentalists and travelers. Ecotourism, they proclaim, will harness the world's largest industry to benefit the world's most endangered places and the people who live in them. Travelers can help save the world while having fun. For all concerned, it's a win-win proposition.

Less often heard are the voices of those who believe that ecotourism has often failed to deliver what it promises. Among those who are skeptical or outright critical are supporters of indigenous people's rights, grassroots activists in Third World countries, and some environmentalists.

Indigenous rights activists charge that too many ecotourism projects have harmed native peoples. Though many projects make a lot of noise about community input in ecotourism development and "stakeholder involvement" in planning, in fact there are a number of cases in which indigenous peoples have been displaced from their land and impoverished by programs calling themselves ecotourism. In the UK *Guardian Weekly,* Sue Wheat reports on a number of tragic situations.[1] In the Moulvibazar District in Bangladesh, Khasi and Garo people staged a hunger strike to protest the eviction of more than one thousand families from their tribes' ancestral lands in order to set up an "ecopark." In Brazil, a village near the colonial city of Fortaleza went to court to try to save their land from illegal private development into an "ecological resort" for fifteen hundred tourists.

Even governments have trampled on the rights of their own citizens in the quest for ecotourist dollars. Wheat quotes a Khwe Bushman from Botswana who told her, "We were about to start community ecotourism on our lands, as Bushmen in Namibia have done. But then the intimidation, torture, and evictions started again. The government did not want to lose tourism business to us." Though representatives of more principled organizations protest that they do not tolerate such abuses, much less promote them, the fact remains that the massive imbalance of power weighs heavily against those who actually live in the "pristine" environment—and in favor of outsiders with lucrative development plans.

Fundamentally, indigenous rights activists argue, ecotourism is a top-down strategy that marginalizes those who actually live in the destination. According to the Rethinking Tourism Project, "The idea is that ecotourism will work only if managerial specialists—ecologists, business administrators, construction engineers . . . etc.—and their universalistic forms of knowledge are in control of the development process. But managers are usually empowered at the expense of local communities: they speak for them at higher levels of government and international conferences, control relationships with funders and corporate profiteers, and commonly devalue local knowledge and authority as ignorance or superstition."[2] Too often, they charge, ecotourism is the work of outside experts who "know what's best" for poor communities, which are shut out and silenced.

A number of grassroots activists in the Third World have taken a similar position, charging that ecotourism consultants and advocates place their own agendas ahead of the interests of the community or the environment. In response to the U.N. proclaiming 2002 the International Year of Ecotourism, a coalition of thirty activist groups and individuals from both industrialized nations and the Third World established a website calling for an "International Year of Reviewing Ecotourism," and posted critical articles and essays with case studies from a number of countries.[3] Their fundamental criticism is that advocates of ecotourism pretend that the travel industry, development agencies, NGOs, governments, and poor rural communities all have similar (and compatible) aims in developing ecotourism—when in fact this is not the case.

The travel industry, obviously, is interested in profits; development agencies in getting foreign debts repaid and budgets balanced; NGOs in showing off successful outcomes for their own projects; governments in boosting the national economy (and the personal economy of the national elite); and people in local communities in things such as higher income, self-determination, and a better future for their kids. It's easy to see how these aims can come into conflict—and hard, in fact, to think of a venture that could successfully and permanently reconcile all of them.

Finally, some environmentalists charge that, despite its pretense of political neutrality, ecotourism is actually closely linked to the push for free-market "liberalization" by global capitalist interests. Rather than protecting the environment as a matter of the public good, ecotourism attempts to tie environmental protection to the individual's desire to consume—and makes it possible to earn a profit from people's desire for a cleaner world.

Researcher Rosaleen Duffy summarizes this critique: "Ecotourism operates within current norms and, crucially, within existing business or market logic. Ecotourism also relies on the individual exercising power through choices about consumption, rather than acting as a citizen engaged in collective and organized protest. In this way ecotourism, as a subset of the global tourism industry, is firmly embedded in green capitalism, where the individual bears responsibility for environmental conservation or degradation rather than governments or private industry."[4]

These environmentalist critics say the basic premise of ecotourism is flawed: the environment cannot be protected simply by putting a price tag on it, nor can real environmental awareness be raised by manipulating people to "consume" exotic places. Counteracting the environmental damage caused by the existing economic system requires citizen activism to reshape that system.

Clearly, ecotourism has had a very mixed track record, with existing projects ranging from beneficial to devastating to local environments and communities. In this chapter, we will draw up a balance sheet, listing both the accomplishments and the pitfalls and what they might mean for Appalachia.

On the Plus Side: Benefits to the Tourist

If experience is the best teacher, then a firsthand experience in nature can obviously teach far more than any book or course. There can be no doubt that countless existing nature tourism programs have given travelers worthwhile contact with the earth's wonders and diverse ecosystems. Scuba divers hovering over a teeming coral reef, photographers snapping away at a family of elephants in Kenya, hikers examining the astonishing plant life of the rainforest—all are gaining insight and appreciation.

Nearly every child has at one time or another gone on a school excursion to the local park, and fieldwork has been an integral part of advanced study in geology, botany, zoology, and ecology for decades. There are crucial lessons that only a personal encounter can teach. Die-hard birders and wildlife watchers have long spent their vacations traveling on quests to come eye-to-eye with new species, and now a broader sector of the public is being drawn to learn firsthand in nature.

For many nature travelers, this personal contact will increase their commitment to protecting the natural environment. Scuba divers, for instance, are deeply concerned about global warming, which now threatens to destroy their beloved coral reefs by warming the oceans past the narrow temperature band in which corals thrive. Scuba diving magazines, in between their articles about gadgets and gizmos, often carry features about developments that threaten harm to the oceans and recruit volunteer divers to count fish species or clear away underwater trash.

Megan Epler Wood of The International Ecotourism Society points out that many people are actually more receptive to new ideas and new information when they are in an unfamiliar place on vacation. "Travelers can be more open to new ideas related to sustainability when presented to them as part of their away-from-home experience," she says.[5]

Visitors can also serve as on-the-spot investigators of the environmental realities in other parts of the world. Many think of tourists as naïve and apt to make silly comments. However, inquisitive travelers can also rise to the occasion and ask some insightful questions. They can penetrate the wall erected by tourism promoters and reach out to local people who can fill them in on the truth. This takes effort, for the more one knows about the culture and environment, the more can be uncovered. In this regard, the ecotourist who follows the crowd taking notes all the while has an ultimate motivation that is broader than personal recreation and education. In fact, it can redeem an otherwise self-indulgent trip, outweighing some of the drawbacks that we will discuss.

Economic Benefits to the Destination

There can be no doubt that a number of countries and regions have obtained considerable revenue from the influx of tourists that have come to see their natural wonders.

Prior to the 2001 terrorist attacks in the U.S., many observers believed that ecotourism was the fastest-growing section of the travel industry, accounting for 7 percent of the world tourism market. Though there was a sharp downturn in travel to "exotic" destinations afterward, many industry insiders were confident that this market would rebound. According to Jonathan Nash, a policy analyst at the Population Reference Bureau, ecotourists spend between $93 billion and $233 billion a year in developing countries.[6] That's a lot of income for small, struggling economies.

One of the first large-scale nature tourism destinations was Kenya, to which many visitors have come on safaris since the British colonial days—armed then with rifles, today with cameras. After it won independence in 1963, tourism expanded dramatically, growing by more than 300 percent between 1960 and 1972. By 1990, wildlife tourism was bringing in $480 million per year, amounting to 43 percent of the country's total foreign exchange. In 1997, the country received over 750,000 visitors, nearly all of them drawn by the opportunity to view elephants, lions, cheetahs, giraffes, zebras, hippos, and dozens of other animals.[7]

Likewise, Costa Rica has received increasing numbers of nature tourists and has taken in an increasing stream of revenue. During the 1980s, it began making a name for itself as a destination with superlative natural attractions, a tiny slice of land covering 0.035 percent of the earth's surface that contained 5 percent of the planet's biodiversity. Between 1990 and 1999, the number of visitors to nature-based destinations increased by 136 percent. By 1995, tourism was bringing in more dollars than coffee and bananas, the previous economic mainstays.[8]

On a local level as well, many nature travel destinations—and ecotourism programs—have brought considerable income into communities. Martha Honey of the Institute for Policy Studies cites Costa Rica as a destination where a sizable number of local people have benefited from the ecotourism boom by opening small businesses, such as craft shops, small restaurants, white-water rafting companies, and tourist cabins. Costa Ricans have also found employment as guides, park rangers, and hotel workers—from maids to managers.

The income from ecotourism can make a real difference to rural families with few other opportunities to earn cash. For example, the Worldwatch Institute cites two programs that have brought meaningful benefits to rainforest tribes in the Ecuadorian Amazon.[9] The Cofan people have established cabins and a craft shop that bring in $500 annually for each person in the community, while a project in the Huaorani community distributes the earnings from tourists equally

among all families, producing twice the income they would earn working for an oil company. It's hard to argue with results like that.

Environmental Benefits

The first great argument in favor of developing nature tourism was
made when someone sat down to calculate the number of tourists who
would come to see an African elephant in the wild and the amount of
money that each would probably spend. African villagers who had
never given much thought to the value of elephants, who considered
elephants at best a target for hunters and at worst a menace to agriculture, suddenly began to realize that they could be a valuable resource.
Since then, a number of economists have run the numbers on the
amount of income that different types of wildlife could generate. One
recent study calculated the value of a single lion in a game park at
$575,000.[10]

Though people in remote communities around the world may be
at a loss to understand why wealthy foreigners would pay a lot of
money to come and see their "backyard," national governments and
economic elites were not slow to realize that, in many cases, there was
more money to be made by keeping a beautiful environment intact to
draw streams of future visitors than by mining it, building on it, or
plowing it up.

Foreign tourism has been a factor in the establishment of national
parks and other protected areas around the world. In Costa Rica, more
than 25 percent of the country's land is now under some form of protection (compared with the worldwide average of 3 percent). Beginning in 1945, Kenya gradually set aside 12 percent of its total territory
in fifty-four different parks and preserves. A number of nations in
Southeast Asia, including Indonesia, Thailand, and Malaysia, have
developed national parks to preserve their natural wonders for the
enjoyment of foreign visitors (and the most affluent locals).

Theoretically, the admission charge for ecotourists should bring in
enough revenue to pay for protection of the endangered ecosystems.
Whether this actually is the case depends largely on whether funding is
available in the first place to set up and staff facilities like ranger stations and visitor centers. There have been success stories, such as in the
Galapagos Islands of Ecuador, where a sharp increase in admission

charges for foreign visitors to the national park has raised considerable sums for government conservation programs.

An article in the *Irish Times* reported on two highly productive arrangements in Africa. In Madagascar, park authorities turn 50 percent of the entrance fees over to local communities for use in sustainable development projects. In Rwanda's Parc des Volcans, where well-heeled tourists fork over $170 apiece to see the gorillas for an hour, these fees generate $1 million annually to support the management of all protected areas in the country.[11]

On the other hand, where there are few facilities or staff to enforce regulations, the revenue will be totally inadequate to meet operating costs for that protected area, let alone to fund new conservation efforts. Studies in Komodo Island National Park in Indonesia (habitat of the Komodo dragons, the largest lizards in the world) and Khao Yai National Park in Thailand found that only meager sums were being collected from foreign visitors, not even enough to pay for the few facilities that do exist.

The Downside: Flaws in the Current Practice of Ecotourism

Despite the obvious benefits obtained from some programs, there are negative effects in ecotourism as it now exists—as well as some inherent problems that can't be resolved within the current paradigm of tourism. We'll discuss those in the next section.

Environmental Impacts

Ecotourists may be less inclined than other visitors to litter and emit waste into the environment, but the services associated with their presence may be just as damaging as in any other form of tourism. A case in point is the recent oil spill in the Pacific, near the sensitive Galapagos Islands belonging to Ecuador. The ship that caused the spill was not carrying ecotourists, but its business customers served and fueled the total ecotourism industry, just as the rapid population growth of the islands (from five to twenty thousand in a mere decade) has been touched off by the jobs associated with the tourism industry.

Even the most carefully planned tourism causes environmental impacts, and the more "pristine" the area, the more it will be affected. Areas visited by tourists suffer from the sheer impact of people, even the careful visitor who inadvertently tramples trails and occasionally slips a tidbit to the wildlife, who takes a tiny piece of coral for a souvenir and leaves a plastic bag behind on the beach. The danger is greater where rare plants or animals are especially sensitive to human impact. For instance, certain African wildlife such as the leopard are known to be highly disturbed by nearby human sightseers. In fact, these animals are disturbed to the point of leaving their native habitats to escape the tourists. The government of Nepal has restricted tours in certain areas of the Himalayas because the carrying capacity of the fragile region cannot sustain the impact of the increasing number of tourists.

Furthermore, these small groups of ecotourists may be the "thin entering wedge" for future development of mass tourism, as in Valene Smith's model of the stages of tourism. Brian Wheeller points out, "The sensitive traveler is the perpetrator of the global spread, the vanguard of the package tour—where he or she goes, others will, in ever-increasing numbers, eventually follow. Who, in the long term, is responsible for the most damage—the mass tourist to the Mediterranean, or the sensitive traveler to the Amazon, the Himalayas, or the Sahara?"[12]

There have been a number of cases in which projects that were labeled "ecotourism" in fact caused serious damage to the environment. Though ecotourism purists protest that these were not "real" ecotourism, the fact that there are no generally accepted standards or definitions makes that argument meaningless. Who gets to decide what qualifies?

Meanwhile, governments, developers, and travelers have accepted some extremely dubious projects as ecotourism. For example, in Costa Rica a project called "Ecodevelopment Papagayo" set out to build a gargantuan resort complex along a string of seventeen beaches, including vacation homes, hotels, two golf courses, marinas, and shopping centers, a total of over twenty-five thousand rooms in all—compared with the national total of thirteen thousand hotel rooms in 1994. The overall impact on previously undeveloped beaches is horrifying to contemplate. The project was controversial from the start, but despite opposition, the first phase was completed in 1993, and several massive "ecological" beach hotels now house mobs of guests.

A truly fragile environment is too sensitive to tolerate even a hand-

ful of visitors. Hikers on Alaska's tundra leave footprints that can remain for decades. Even less remote places can be harmed by a small
number of visitors.

With no universally accepted standards for what constitutes
ecotourism and little regulation by governments eager to cash in on the
"world's largest industry," the only thing standing between fragile environments and damage from ecotourists is the expertise and, ultimately, the consciences of the developers—not something that can
necessarily be relied upon.

> I have done very little "ecotourism" but did get an opportunity when
> in Colorado to descend into the Black Canyon of the Gunnison River.
> We were told by a hiker to insist on going down to the bottom. This
> thousand-foot descent by the aid of steel cable was so steep that
> each footstep on the gravel surface results in pushing loose gravel
> further down-slope. While going down it seemed quite inappropriate
> to open this cable route to large numbers. If everyone were doing it
> the canyon slopes would be heavily damaged. As the two of us came
> out I regretted our visit even though it was a thrilling experience, which
> taught us much and was certainly memorable. The U.S. Park Service
> had tried to dissuade us but we insisted.
>
> —Al Fritsch

Economic Leakage

Because ecotourism generally takes place in less developed areas, there
is a higher need for goods and services from outside—leading to a
higher leakage rate from the local economy. Despite the high cost of
many ecotours (in their 2002 "Ecotourism Trips and Lodging Packages" brochure, TIES listed a $2,598 "Desert Ecosafari" in Egypt,
$2,870 for a week of snorkeling in the Bahamas, and a $6,080 cruise
in Vietnam), very little of that money actually goes to the people of the
destination community.

One major difficulty involves transportation. Nearly all overseas
ecotourism destinations (and most domestic ones) are reached by air,
meaning that a large chunk of the travelers' total spending goes directly to the airlines. Given Americans' mistrust of foreign air carriers,
much of this money never even leaves the U.S. Furthermore, when
traveling on a package tour, a large proportion of the remaining expen-

diture goes to the travel industry, never reaching the community to be visited. Further leakage occurs for imported goods, foreign staff, and tax breaks to foreign companies. According to the World Bank, 55 percent of every tourist dollar leaks back out of the national economy in Third World countries.

After subtracting the portion of expenditure that goes to large companies in the urban centers of the destination, very little is left for the local community. This includes payments for such things as locally owned hotels, restaurants, souvenirs, and guides. According to Martha Honey, a 1991 study found that of the total spending by tourists in the Galapagos Islands, a prime ecotourism destination, 85 percent went to airlines and cruise ships, which spend very little locally, and only 3 percent each went to hotels and park entrance fees. Only about 15 percent of tourist spending actually entered the local economy.[13]

The Clearinghouse for Reexamining Ecotourism cites a 1997 study conducted by forestry expert Bernd Sticker on an ecotourism project in Taman Negara National Park in western Malaysia. Sticker concluded that only a tiny proportion of the money spent by ecotourists actually reaches the destination communities in Third World countries. He found that about two-thirds of the expenditures of European and North American ecotourists went to foreign airlines and travel agencies. A large proportion of the in-country expenditure was spent before and after the ecotour itself, in the large cities and well-established tourist centers of the destination country.[14]

Many ecotourism proponents are very conscious of this and have tried to design programs that will capture more tourism income for the people who need it most. But the fact remains that as long as the firms that receive the lion's share of a vacation's price—the airlines and tour companies—are outside the target community, ecotourism is not a very efficient way to give money to people in need. If ecotourists were truly interested first and foremost in helping poor communities, they could provide more assistance by making a $500 donation to an effective development charity than by taking a $2000 tour.

As we have previously pointed out, Appalachia may be able to avoid some of the pitfalls of leakage if local planners pay close attention to where tourism income goes. In developing nature tourism, or any other form of tourism, a focus on building up locally owned businesses (rather than incentives to lure outside businesses into the region) would bring far greater benefits to communities.

Ecotourism—An Elitist Trend

Ecotourism, as it has been practiced until now, is a form of travel largely targeted to the well-heeled and well-educated. If one reads between the lines, this is clearly an important factor in the travel industry's enthusiasm for the concept. As noted earlier, surveys have found the typical participant in an ecotour to be older, better educated (82 percent have college degrees, according to one study—compared with 23 percent of the U.S. population as a whole), and more willing to pay a premium price than travelers in general.[15] It's hard to imagine an average, working-class family forking out several hundred dollars a day to stay in cabins with no electricity and take lukewarm solar-heated showers—though they may occasionally save up for a blowout trip to Disney World costing that much.

Even certain well-intentioned attempts to regulate tourism and control its cultural and environmental impacts have worsened this elitism. For example, the Himalayan nation of Bhutan has taken a diametrically opposite approach to its neighbor Nepal. Where Nepal has always been a magnet to travelers searching for adventure on the cheap, Bhutan strictly controls the number of tourists (only 7,500 in 2000) and enforces a mandatory minimum expenditure of $250 per visitor per day. (The more impecunious of Nepal's 400,000 annual tourists can easily get by on as little as ten dollars a day.) This puts Bhutan out of reach as a destination for all but the wealthiest travelers and gives a Bhutanese visa stamp in one's passport the cachet of a rare collector's item.

On a global scale, we need to remember that, despite tourism's claims as the "world's largest industry," pleasure travel is almost exclusively reserved for the top tiers of the most affluent countries in the world—with ecotourism an even smaller subset. Only 22 percent of Americans currently hold a valid passport. Anita Pleumarom of Thailand charges, "What has often been overlooked is the fact that ecotourism is a highly consumer-centered activity, mostly catering to the 'alternative lifestyles' of the new middle classes of urbanized societies."[16]

But why should a firsthand learning experience in a natural environment be reserved only for young professionals and affluent empty-nesters? It can be argued that, in America, those who could learn the most from ecotourism are precisely those who have the least access to it now—families with young children, lower-income urbanites with little chance for getaways in natural settings, rural people hindered from seeing other places by geographical isolation, disability, or lack of money. People such as these, who may have little experience or understanding of natural environments, can derive a lot of enjoyment and learning from nature without traveling far.

An excellent example of a program aimed at the needs of people who have little opportunity for contact with nature is the Sierra Club's national Inner City Outings Program. In Kentucky, the program takes youths from Louisville on camping and backpacking trips in places such as Red River Gorge. Transportation and all equipment are provided for participants. According to the group's website, "The goal of the Inner City Outings program is to help people discover the beauty and challenges of the wild lands we treasure, acquire the skills necessary to enjoy them safely, and learn that human activity and the natural world are interrelated. This means trust and communication are necessary, as are physical safety and respect for limits, and recognizing the fragility of nature (environmental education). The program's success helps to increase the environmental awareness, interpersonal skills, and self-esteem of the participants through active involvement with nature."[17] What more could any ecotour hope to accomplish?

To truly promote broad-based environmental education and awareness, ecotourism needs to be accessible to the family with a carload of kids and a cooler full of sandwiches—not just the double-income couple with frequent flyer miles to burn. The current elitist view of ecotourism as something confined to exotic, "pristine" environments can never aspire to be more than a niche market—and indeed, that's all the travel industry wants it to be. No one, least of all big corporations, is likely to get rich offering budget-priced, family-friendly environmental experiences close to home—but that's exactly what we need to do.

Inescapable Contradictions

As we have seen, the ecotourism model as it has developed until now has had some serious failings, which could possibly be remedied in future development. But the concept itself has important, inherent flaws, which point to the need for a broader rethinking and transformation of tourism—which we will outline in our final chapter.

1. Ecotourism, like all present-day forms of tourism, depends heavily on the petroleum economy.

Few current supporters of ecotourism would question an "ecotour" that takes North Americans to the southern reaches of South America by commercial jet, flies them to Antarctica, sails them around on a diesel-powered research ship, and zips them to the shore in inflatable Zodiac speedboats—as long as all trash is hauled out and no wildlife traumatized. Such tours exist, with a 2002 price tag starting at around $4,000—plus airfare. The amount of fossil fuel consumed by a single traveler on such a trip may be more than a Third World resident uses in a year—or over many years.

Every current type of tourism, no matter how bright green, broadly educational, or locally beneficial, depends on nonrenewable resources that we are now depleting. Airplanes, cruise ships, and surface transportation are inextricably tied to the oil-based economy of which we are part. Though there is considerable debate over the amount of petroleum that remains, the inescapable fact is that given a finite supply of oil, all tourism is inherently unsustainable—and the more it centers on travel to faraway, "exotic" environments, the less justifiable it is, from a perspective of true environmental awareness.

Jet air transport, unavoidable for most present-day ecotourism, is one of humankind's most environmentally damaging activities. It produces more pollution per passenger-mile than any other form of transportation, producing 3 percent of the world's total CO_2 emissions —which is equivalent to the entire output of all industry in Great Britain. It is also responsible for the production of four million tons of nitrogen oxides, which could be responsible for exacerbating future global warming.[18]

But that's not the only environmental damage caused by ecotourism. Consider also that in many land destinations for ecotourism, the only transportation option for those unwilling to walk is the four-wheel-drive vehicle—the SUV. Despite the fact that few of them ever see more challenging terrain than a middle school parking lot, they are capable of traversing extremely rough ground, such as the mountainous sand dunes of Arabia. Their deplorable gas mileage has made them a target of countless environmental campaigns—and yet SUVs are a common feature of land-based ecotourism.

There is evidence that our era of plentiful and cheap oil may be reaching its close. An article by Bruce Thomson in 2001 reported a global decline in oil discoveries, which peaked in 1962. Annual new discoveries have returned to 1920 levels and continue to decline. Thomson asserts that evidence from the oil industry shows that oil extraction from wells will be physically unable to meet global demand by 2010, causing shortages of fuel for transportation and industrial machinery not geared for use of alternative fuels. One serious difficulty is that airplanes cannot run on natural gas, nuclear energy, or coal, more plentiful nonrenewables. Consider further that petroleum is used in an estimated five hundred thousand other products, from plastics and medicines to inks and asphalt.[19]

The popular belief is that in the future we will find ourselves using slightly harder to extract, but still plentiful, oil sources. Petroleum companies insist that we will discover more as-yet-unknown deposits. But much of the earth's geology has already been thoroughly studied. Some claim there are 210 billion barrels left to be discovered, and 1,000 billion left to extract. There are a half million oil wells in the world, but many of these are very small. In the U.S., 80 percent of wells produce fewer than three barrels a day. Some pessimists say that alternatives to replace the 40 percent of total energy that oil currently supplies are grossly inadequate and cannot be substituted easily.

In the short term, it will be difficult to find alternative energy sources for our current transportation system. Natural gas (20 percent of global energy supply) is not suited for existing jet aircraft, ships, vehicles, or other equipment. Hydropower (2.3 percent of supply) is clearly unsuitable for aircraft, which also cannot run on coal (24 percent of supply). Solar, wind, and hydrogen are not yet major players, and hydrogen is more an energy "carrier" than a source, because it takes more fuel to produce the gas than it provides. The same is true of alcohol as a fuel, for it is now derived through agricultural methods and industrial processing from oil-based sources. The use of shale, tar, sand, coal bed methane, and biomass derived from vegetation will all require huge investment in research and infrastructure to exploit them.

None of these could quickly be substituted to meet the current global demand for oil.

It is likely that the future price of oil will rise, and the cost of long-distance travel with it. Any form of tourism based on traveling to "exotic" environments far from one's home, whether the two-week beach holiday or the ecofriendly educational tour, is not sustainable over the long term.

However, at the same time, the projected rise in energy costs and the de-emphasis on long-distance travel could prove beneficial for tourism in Appalachia—and a powerful argument for ecotourism closer to home. As we have previously pointed out, much of Central Appalachia lies within a day's drive for half of the population of the U.S. (not to mention a comfortable trip on a hypothetical passenger rail system). And the environment of the mixed mesophytic forest, the most diverse forest in North America, provides tremendous opportunities for learning and enjoyment. Though long-distance ecotourism in the era of the petroleum economy is inherently unsustainable, an argument can be made that for many residents of the U.S. travel to Appalachia is an environmentally sound choice.

2. Ecotourism reduces nature to a commodity with a price tag.

One of the main claims made by ecotourism's supporters is that by providing economic incentives for maintaining an environment in its unspoiled form, ecotourism automatically protects the environment. Underlying this claim, however, is the view that nature is just another product (valuable though it may be) to be bought and sold on the marketplace. A gorgeous overlook, a rare form of wetland, one of those $575,000 lions—all of these can be valued and traded, if the price is right.

And once these things acquire a price tag, they can be bought, sold, and exchanged on the marketplace. What if gold is discovered on a reserve inhabited by those expensive lions? What if trends change and tourists suddenly prefer to stay in lodges built from rare tropical hardwoods rather than enjoy them as living trees? If prices suddenly shift, will the economic calculus then be refigured?

Besides the global effect of commodification of the environment, additional consideration needs to be given to the effects on individual tourists. For too many ecotourists, the world's most unusual environments become status symbols to acquire and consume—what one observer calls the "This year the Galapagos, next year Antarctica" syndrome. For them, exotic destinations are nothing more than a series of stamps in the passport or stories to impress one's friends at home. The environment is one more alluring product available for them to consume, a symbol of one's membership in a particular (and lofty) category on the social ladder—and tourism marketers have lost no time in catering to this impulse, with advertising campaigns highlighting the remoteness, exclusivity, and luxury of their properties.

A number of articles in the popular press have documented an increasing de-emphasis on environmental aspects by ecotourists. In a *U.S. News* investigative report, twenty-seven out of thirty-four ecotourism operators admitted they did not give environmental concerns high priority.[20] Travel writer Mary-Lou Weisman contributed an article to the *New York Times* about her experience at a luxury "beach and jungle hideaway" in Costa Rica. Bored after three hours of walking in the rainforest, she decided to spend the rest of her vacation lounging around the pool and the beach "with the other eco-flops."[21]

She's got plenty of company. A number of industry observers have noted the trend towards increasingly "soft" ecotourism experiences, with minimal effort expended and maximum comforts supplied. At an international trade show in 2002, Kurt Kutay, president of Wildland Adventures, Inc., stated, "Our soft-adventure clients are not interested in a 'reality tour'—after all, they're on vacation." David Kagan, president of an ecolodge development company called Wilderness Gate, admitted, "If we have to add air conditioning or drive every guest to the lodge to stay open, that's what we'll do. And we'll still call ourselves an ecolodge."[22]

With the environmental learning component downplayed, many "soft ecotours" are nothing more than mainstream tourism in unusual destinations. While claiming to be appreciating pristine environments, these travelers seem to be motivated primarily by one-upping their friends. In legitimizing their globetrotting as an environmental exercise, they fail to come to terms with their own gluttonous, mindless consumption and lack of awareness.

In response, operators are on a quest for new "authentic experiences" to peddle. At a panel discussion at an ecotourism trade show, operators spoke of the endless need to come up with new products—

"We have to keep finding new ways to distinguish ourselves by the experiences we sell," said Kurt Kutay. Carol Patterson of Kalahari Management, an ecotourism consulting firm, said that many "eco-travelers" were somewhat jaded, feeling they'd "done it all"—which resulted in greater difficulty for tour companies seeking to create "a new travel experience, something that is unique or different."[23] She pointed to this as the force behind the interest in space tourism—and wondered whether "urban ghetto tours" might be in the offing.

Though ecotourists are thoroughly rooted in the dominant consumer culture, they pretend to be educating themselves about global issues—when that is not the issue at all. Affluence makes us insensitive to real needs, leading us to confuse our luxurious self-seeking with something essential for us at this time. An ecotour may in fact deepen one's selfishness and remove one further from the social justice actions that could truly bring awareness and education. And ecotourism is just one more gaudy temptation for those of us who truly desire to live gently on the earth.

3. Ecotourism binds sensitive local economies more tightly to the global market.

By extending the reach of tourism into isolated areas and small communities where it previously has not penetrated, ecotourism ties ever more remote places into the global tourism economy, thus making them susceptible to the boom-bust cycle of tourism. It also pits them against each other as competitors for the tourist dollar.

Dismayed by the uncritical enthusiasm with which ecotourism is promoted by governments and NGOs, the Campaign on the International Year of Ecotourism coalition asks, "Who will take responsibility, when ecotourism initiatives make investments based on miscalculated demand and later face decline, local businesses go bankrupt and entire communities are pushed into crisis?"[24]

Many nations, cities, and regions scramble for tourist spending, and a few succeed quite well. Others do not, but continue striving (and investing) in the hopes that an influx of tourists is just around the corner. The expansion of tourism by residents of western Europe and the Pacific Rim countries has added millions of people per year to the Americans and Canadians who travel long distances by air—this all leads to ever increasing competition for visitors. Many small communities around the world that climb on the tourism bandwagon with the highest of hopes have little idea what they are opening themselves up to.

A charming little Appalachian town that decides to make its first bid for visitors will in fact be competing not only with the charming little town down the road and the one on the other side of the state, but also with similar destinations around the world. A rainforest guesthouse in Belize hopes to lure visitors away from the guesthouse down the river—and from the rainforest ecotourism program in Costa Rica. Though this view may seem exaggerated, modern communication has made it possible for even the most isolated operation to reach out to potential customers worldwide. "The Internet has allowed even the smallest mom-and-pop company the opportunity to look as good, and offer the same online facilities, as the largest international company," says Steven Venter, "Africa For Visitors" guide at about.com.[25]

Some places definitely rank higher on the tourism pecking order: Orlando over Omaha; Mexico over Haiti; Hong Kong over Bangladesh. This competition can create resentment on the part of the forgotten or overlooked places, which may actually be far more authentic and worth seeing than the congested and bustling places that have all the "tourist appeal." Tourists' perceptions of the worth of a destination are based more on its popularity than on its actual features, natural or man-made.

Once a small economy has thrown in its lot with the tourism industry, it becomes far more vulnerable to the repercussions of events and trends in faraway places. We have seen how glassblowers in Ireland and Nepalese egg farmers were devastated when the World Trade Center attack of 2001 caused vacationers to stay home in droves. Anything that negatively affects people's desire to travel will have a disruptive effect.

Another factor not often considered is that the demand for tourism is what economists call "price-elastic." This means that a small increase in the price will cause many people to stop buying the product and switch to a substitute. (The opposite situation, price inelasticity, means that few or no people stop buying when the price goes up—which is the case with products such as insulin for diabetics.)

No matter what we Americans have been conditioned to believe, in terms of economics, vacation travel is a luxury, not one of life's necessities. If the price of one destination gets too high, people will simply switch to another destination. (For example, when the exchange rate for the pound sterling makes trips to London too expensive, American vacationers decide to go to Rome instead.) And if all travel gets more costly—if, for example, scarcity causes the price of oil to increase steadily—people will travel less frequently and find substitute ways to spend their vacations, such as visits to relatives or a week of fishing at a nearby lake. Becoming dependent on tourism makes a community sensitive to anything that affects the price of travel, as well as to factors affecting other things that people might do with their disposable income.

A further negative economic factor is the "life cycle" of a particular destination. When a place becomes a cog in the world tourist machine, it becomes susceptible to a particular pattern of development. Tourism researchers have observed a predictable progression in tourist resorts of all sizes and types. First, a vacation place is "undiscovered," known to only a few connoisseurs and adventure travelers. Facilities for tourists are few and possibly primitive, and tourism is as yet not a major factor in the local economy. As more tourists come, the infrastructure is developed and the destination becomes more mainstream, attracting less adventurous travelers. Visitors now have a choice of places to stay and eat, and there are more activities for them to participate in.

But as long as there is a hope of attracting still more customers, development will continue, until the place is so built-up that it actually begins to repel many types of travelers. People may be put off by the endless miles of hotels and elbowing crowds of visitors at places like Acapulco, Myrtle Beach, Pattaya in Thailand, or any number of beach towns in Spain. These euphemistically labeled "mature destinations" are a subject of great concern for tourism academics, who devote many hours and journal issues every year to dreaming up ways to repackage them for further sale to a different type of audience.

As a luxury and not a necessity, spending for tourism is one of the first things to be cut back in an economic downturn. And when the visitors and the host community are both part of the same national economy—as is the case with domestic nature tourists in Appalachia—the impact is even more severe. The boom-and-bust cycle in tourism can be every bit as devastating to people's livelihoods and a region's economy as in such other industries as mining and logging—two examples that are all too familiar.

4. The most successful ecotourism project is a failure as an ecotourism project.

By definition, a successful business is one that brings in as much money as possible by serving as many customers as it can. As activist Anita Pleumarom summarizes it, "To generate substantial revenue—whether for foreign exchange, tourism businesses, local communities, or conservation—the number of tourists has to be large, and that inevitably implies greater pressures on ecosystems."[26]

Essentially, ecotourism is founded on two conflicting definitions of success. A business is successful when it makes as much money as possible, and an environmental project is successful when it preserves the environment. This is the inescapable contradiction of ecotourism: the more money a project brings in and the more visitors it attracts, the more impact it will have on the environment that it is supposedly trying to preserve.

A prime example of a destination that is being destroyed by its own success is Machu Picchu, the massive Inca ruins in Peru. A unique combination of cultural, historic, and ecological attractions, it is one of the prime travel destinations in South America—and the world. Hundreds of thousands of tourists every year make the arduous journey to this remote location to view the astonishing structures built of granite chiseled from the Andean mountainside.

Archeologists still aren't sure exactly when Machu Picchu was built, but most agree it is at least five hundred years old. It appears to have been the home of around a thousand people, perhaps the Inca elite, who may have stayed there while conducting religious ceremonies. Abandoned about the time of the Spanish conquest, it was forgotten until an American explorer stumbled across it in 1911. Almost immediately, it began to draw a few intrepid visitors, a trickle that in recent years has turned into a tidal wave.

It's a long trip, no matter how it's undertaken. Most foreign travelers fly first to Lima, then catch a one-hour flight to Cuzco, the Inca capital, where they spend a day getting acclimated to the 11,000-foot altitude. They then go on to the town of Aguas Calientes, either by an expensive thirty-minute helicopter flight or a three-hour train ride through the mountains. From there, they take shuttle buses up a rutted road with fourteen switchbacks up the mountain face. Other visitors take a four-day hike along the Inca Trail, winding through several other ruins before descending to Machu Picchu.

All of these modes of travel have their impact on the area, and the tremendous growth of tourism has wreaked havoc. In Aguas Calientes, three tons of garbage is burned or thrown into the river every day. In one recent year, some seventy-six thousand tourists hiked through the nature preserve surrounding the Inca Trail, home to 372 species of birds and many species of rare orchids. Tourists were horrified by the amount of toilet paper and mineral water bottles that has been dumped along the trail—but they continue to add to them.

For a number of years, plans were underway to build a cable car up the mountain, under the pretext of avoiding the environmental impact of fleets of buses hauling tourists up the mountainside. The upper station of the cable car would have been within the ruin itself, and the entire project was to be built in a geologically unstable area. After UNESCO threatened to remove Machu Picchu from the World Heritage list if the project went ahead, the Peruvian government finally suspended plans for the cable car indefinitely. A UNESCO team found that the area, which is visited by some 350,000 tourists a year, has already exceeded its carrying capacity and will not withstand any increase in tourist traffic. According to their recommendations, no new construction should be allowed, and tourist services should be reduced from their current levels to save the site.

Many visitors continue to trek the thirty-mile section of the Inca Trail that leads to the ruins. In 2001, new restrictions were imposed that allow a maximum of five hundred visitors per day to use the trail and increased the charge from seventeen to fifty dollars. But because the trail is not very long, even that number is enough to cause crowding, and the locals still complain about pollution and trash.

It's easy to say that this is not "real ecotourism" and that many of the tourists make no pretense of trying to preserve the environment. But the fact remains that hundreds of thousands of tourists will generate large amounts of bodily waste, trash, and pollution, no matter how conscientious they are.

It is easy to conceive of small-scale ecotourism projects that bring in modest amounts of income and cause modest environmental impacts. But the larger they grow and the more money they bring in, the more environmental damage they cause—and as businesses operating under the imperatives of a capitalist economy, there are no built-in brakes on growth, nothing except falling profits to tell them when they are not meeting their goals. Would 350,000 visitors be a good thing for Machu Picchu if they all used ecofriendly, locally owned tour operators? That's doubtful, to say the least. But there is nothing in the current model of ecotourism that even argues for a theoretical cap on its growth, and little or no attention is given to the overall carrying capacity of locations or regions for different types of activities. Richard Butler points out, "It is extremely difficult to reduce numbers [of visitors] in a free market situation without prejudicing the viability of the industry."[27]

Furthermore, a successful ecotourism project will generate other types of development that make no claim at all to environmental soundness. According to Anita Pleumarom, "An incredible amount of money is spent to promote ecotourism. Big loans have come from the World Bank Social Investment Program and Japanese agencies to develop national parks, in the name of ecotourism. This leads to road construction, accommodation, power stations, reservoirs—all environmentally damaging. Khao Yai National Park, for example, looks like a building site as areas are developed for campsites and buildings."[28]

Granted, it's hardly likely that hundreds of thousands of visitors will descend on a single Appalachian eco-attraction—or even a town full of them. But taking the example to an extreme makes this contradiction plain—and if current trends continue, real-life examples are not too far in the future.

The Bottom Line

All told, the bottom line of our balance sheet for ecotourism is not totally negative—but not as endlessly promising as its many cheerleaders would have us believe.

There is no doubt that there are successful, well-planned, well-run ecotourism projects in locations around the world and that they have made a difference on a micro scale, preserving threatened environments while giving income to communities that need it. For example, in Guatemala, the Eco-Escuela de Español has helped foreign visitors learn about the ecology of the rainforest and improve their Spanish. It has also brought meaningful income to the host families who provide housing for the guests. In Costa Rica, Honduras, and Mexico, the RARE Center for Tropical Conservation has trained more than two hundred people to work as rainforest guides for tourists, giving them employment and an incentive to protect rare species.

But on a global scale, ecotourism is not going to "save the planet"—or even a meaningful chunk of it. It is a trendy activity pursued by only a small fraction of the population of the wealthiest nations on earth, in only a handful of locations that are viewed (rightly or not) as pristine, exotic, and desirable. Its inherent contradictions limit its effectiveness as a tool for environmental conservation. And as discretionary spending, ecotourism, as in all tourism, produces an income flow that can dry up literally overnight—as we witnessed on September 12, 2001.

People in Appalachia who pin their hopes on tourism (in any form) as the region's economic salvation are as shortsighted as those who favor any other kind of single-industry economy. However, we do not mean to say that environmentally sound tourism has no role to play in healthy economic development for the region. Tourism, like all other economic activities, needs to be carried out in a manner that conserves our resources and our unique environment for the future. And we believe that well-planned, community-based tourism can play an important role as one component in a more diversified Appalachian economy.

To see what this might look like, in the next chapter we'll contrast two very different trips through Appalachia, ten years from now.

CHAPTER 8

2020 Visions

Two Alternative Futures for Appalachian Tourism

As we have seen, tourism in Appalachia now stands at a crossroads. Travel in the United States is growing tremendously, and the region is well placed to benefit from the recent trends towards nature tourism, travel as a family, and the preference for destinations closer to home. The issue that faces us is: what kind of tourism do we want to develop? The choices we make now, whether consciously or unconsciously, will have a major impact on the region's future, and we need to consider in detail what the results will be. What kind of Appalachia will they shape?

Further Down the Road

Let's take a fantasy vacation to a place called Redbud County, some-where in the heart of Appalachia, some years in the future. . . .
Redbud County, summer, some years from now
The Smith family rolls into town for their long-awaited vacation. "Ooh, look at all the garbage!" says eight-year-old Kaitlyn. "Ugh, don't look at that," her father says, "some people are just ignorant." Arriving at Motel 99, they are signed in by Mrs. Owens, a weary-looking woman who works nights and weekends for minimum wage. She's too tired to do much beyond wish them a good evening and point the way to their room. The room is identical to any other room at any other motel in the chain, and, with the curtains closed and shutting out the glorious view of the mountains, Mr. Smith finds himself wondering why they bothered driving all that way—they could be in any state of

the union. There's no restaurant at the motel, so the Smith family piles back into the car and drives around the sprawl at the highway exit, finally settling on fried chicken at a fast-food joint. "I thought we might find some local food here," Mrs. Smith says, "but I guess that's a thing of the past."

The next morning, after a fast-food breakfast, Mrs. Smith goes shopping at the row of souvenir stands that line the main street, while Mr. Smith and the kids check out a theme park called Hillbilly Land. A satire on an old-time farm, it has fallen-down cabins to pose next to and barefoot actors in patched clothes sipping from jugs of "moonshine." As Mrs. Smith looks in vain for souvenirs that were made locally, Mr. Smith and the kids go for a jeep ride through the hills. "It's the newest sport here—mountain bashing!" their driver says. "We look for the steepest slopes we can find, and then make these trucks show their stuff!" Ten-year-old Nathan is enthralled with the ride around the forest. "Let's go straight up that hill!" he shrieks to their driver. "Sure, we can do that," the driver says, though he's secretly a little worried. But he just graduated from Redbud County High School, and he's relieved he actually got a full-time job—if he doesn't keep the tourists happy, he might not have it very long. Fortunately, they make it up the hill without an accident, though mud and branches are flying everywhere.

That afternoon, after lunch at another fast-food place (they've asked around, but that's all there is), the Smiths decide to get out of town and go for a walk. They drive a short distance away from town, then head off down a gentle trail through the forest, following a nature walk in a guidebook they bought. "Now this is more like what I—" But Mrs. Smith doesn't even get a chance to finish her sentence. Her words are drowned out by the roar of seven ATVs rocketing down the trail (even though it's signposted for use by hikers only), and the family flees up the hillside to get out of the way. "It's not like I imagined it," says Nathan. Their father laughs, a bit uneasily. "Well, did you really expect it would look like it did in the old days?"

"Can we stay at the motel tomorrow?" Kaitlyn says anxiously. "And eat pizza and swim in the pool? And. . . ."

"It sounded like such a good idea," says Mr. Smith to his wife that evening as they watch TV in their motel room. "I thought it would be different," she says. "Those brochures we got made it look so peaceful and pretty. . . . Well, I guess we made a big mistake. Let's go somewhere else next year." "Fine with me," says Mr. Smith.

How did this happen? Ten factors have led to this depressing scene.

1. All tourism is unregulated.

Tourist programs have been in sharp decline in recent years because of congestion, overdevelopment, loss of interest by outside visitors, and a decline in civic pride and professionalism on the part of the tourism industry itself. The businesses that remain are mostly chain operations that seek to lure visitors through massive seasonal promotion, cut-throat price competition, huge and environmentally destructive projects that are not tolerated elsewhere in the country, gambling and cheap forms of popular entertainment, and a variety of questionable advertising gimmicks. Tourist facilities are located in accordance with the dictates of profit, with no concern for the needs or wishes of community residents. As a result, some areas are plagued with intensive tourist development, placing a huge strain on local services such as roads, water supply, and police departments—while other localities that would welcome moderate amounts of tourism are bypassed entirely by developers.

2. The landscape is devastated.

Continued buildup of litter, especially a veritable carpet of empty beverage containers and food wrappers, lend an air of complete neglect to the region. Complaints go unnoticed. Pristine areas have been progressively denuded and overdeveloped, and what has not been clear-cut and stripped has been built over with signs and theme park operations—a "Gatlinburgization" of the whole region. Only narrow borders of white pine stand near the highways, since most of the other varieties of trees have died out. Tourism is in sharp decline, except for a few music-related attractions, that feature aging groups of musicians.

3. There are no restrictions on recreational activity.

Tourists and locals are able to do exactly what they want, where they want, when they want, and with whom they want. Motorboats, ATVs, and snowmobiles have been permitted to rampage anywhere they please. No one is allowed to interfere with this freedom, or else the activity will not be enjoyable—after all, unlimited enjoyment is an inalienable right. Tossing garbage out of boats or cars is by now such an ingrained habit that no one even cares if they're seen doing it. ("So what—the place is a mess already.") For people of this mindset, any restriction on their leisure is beyond the bounds of legitimate government. The best government is no government, and hardly anyone even discusses the matter any more. The opponents of noise and congestion have long been run off, and good riddance to them. Putting regulations on the individual infringes on the God-given right to do whatever we please.

4. Ecologically fragile areas are left unguarded.

To designate government or private land as too fragile to traverse goes against many things mountain folks stand for: the ability to roam the countryside unimpeded, freedom from governmental interference in use of land and the idea that land is tough and resilient, never fragile. ORV-disturbed areas that had twenty-foot-deep gullies in 2000 have still deeper ones now. Trashed land is considered just that—a dumping ground for more trash. Recreational tourists think the trees will just grow back in time or regard them as so unimportant that it doesn't really matter if they grow back again. Motorized recreation enthusiasts (on land, water, or air) are convinced that this is "wasteland" and only deserving to be demolished still further—which they are happy to do, using more powerful engines every year. History is on their side, with a surge in both the horsepower and the number of these vehicles. ATV enthusiasts use the Internet to spread the word about "undiscovered" creek beds and forest tracts. For them, freedom means carrying wire cutters to snip through fences and travel where they will. They are the true elite—and to hell with the private landholders, who are too intimidated to say anything anyway.

5. The forest continues to disappear.

The current, third wave of deforestation is far more serious than the first two, in the 1800s and the early 1900s. In both of those, oxen, horses, river rafts and crosscut saws were used to a great extent. In the current epidemic, heavy machinery enters and disturbs the forest floor by destroying undergrowth and by compacting the soil so severely that new growth of quality trees is quite difficult. The resiliency of the land has been damaged, and the possible regrowth of a quality forest is impaired. The scars will remain longer, and the devastation will be an eyesore for generations to come. The spongelike ability of a good forest to hold rainfall in the mulch and leaves has been destroyed through overharvesting. This has led to increasingly severe floods because of the steep slopes of the land. People living in the narrow constricted hollows and valleys continue to lose homes, barns, and bridges, and find less and less assistance available for rebuilding. Even their will to fight back is beginning to disappear.

6. Tourist businesses are outside-owned, employing badly paid seasonal workers.

Few, if any, of the tourism businesses are locally owned. Most hotels, restaurants, and attractions are owned and operated by big corporations headquartered outside the region; they hire local people on a seasonal basis and pay them minimum wage without any benefits. This harkens back to the era of day labor, when people were happy just to get a few days' work. There are no benefits, no medical insurance, no guarantee of work tomorrow, and no unions or other worker support system. Workers are on their own, and they try to be grateful for whatever work comes along. Because of these conditions, there is immense out-migration, especially among the young high school and community college graduates. The work force is gradually becoming older and less educated, and there is an erosion of the sense of community. More and more professionals and recently educated young people leave in search of worthwhile employment. Many of them would have stayed if the people in their communities could afford to buy anything beyond the barest necessities of life. For the most part, the seasonal workers must make do with a flea-market economy.

7. Social and political capital continues in steep decline.

The breakdown of community is speeding up throughout the region, in part because of the decline of the tourism industry. People are going elsewhere for work, and so there is a steady erosion of the community, making people less inclined to join organizations and volunteer. Membership in civic groups such as the Lions Club, the Rotary Club, the PTA, Masonic lodges, Veterans of Foreign Wars, and churches is in decline throughout the region. The discouragement is partly due to the broken promise of a few decades ago that tourism would revitalize the region. Due to the lack of environmental awareness, along with the expansion of extractive industries (coal, timber, rock and minerals, and natural gas), the countryside is looking ragged and the will to clean the place up no longer exists.

8. Tour guides are untrained.

Though at first volunteer guides did a credible job, with the decline in tourism and dissatisfaction over the deteriorating environment, the more lucrative tourist trade has gone elsewhere. Few professional tour guides are left, and volunteers find it more and more difficult to muster enthusiasm for a declining trade where few people require their services.

9. Artists, musicians, and storytellers are paid a pittance.

Biases against mountain residents continue to exist, with "hillbillies" expected to entertain for pennies, because they are seen as a virtually worthless group who have an obscure talent for dancing jigs and singing quaint tunes. Mountain crafts and arts fare little better. The art is primitive and the crafts somewhat crude, with designs specified by the wholesale buyers who ship the junk out to big city knickknack stores. A few dollars with a generous quarter tip is sufficient to keep these whittlers and banjo-pickers in beer money. Besides—if they were any good, they'd take off to the big city, wouldn't they?

10. Tourism goes elsewhere.

Move in, trash it up, move on. That is the story of Florida beaches, unpoliced state parks, polluted seashores, and overdeveloped theme park areas. The trashing process goes way back in American history. There are still a few undiscovered areas of Appalachia to be found, trampled over, and abandoned, as the touring herd moves on in undisciplined fashion to the few remaining pristine areas of this tired old Earth.

A Gloomy Scenario

We hate to introduce our discussion of the future on such a pessimistic note, but there is a real possibility, if the people of Appalachia do not take a proactive approach and work to guide future development, that tourism could become just another rip-off of the region's resources, trashing the land to profit some outsiders while bringing little real benefit to the mountains. We do not maintain that this pessimistic scenario is inevitable, but if there are no modifications of today's status quo, complacency and silence will usher in a gradual deterioration of the region through lack of regulation and a sharp decline in the quality in tourism facilities.

All the components necessary to produce this pessimistic scene are already in place: a desperate need for business in the region, a large population of un- and underemployed people eager for any type of job, a widespread belief that the land is already trashed, a bias against poor people's needs for environmental and lifestyle improvement, a disdain for law enforcement by both residents and visitors, tolerance for petty illegal acts such as growing marijuana or raising gamecocks, a greedy tourism industry that lacks a sense of environmental concern and generates extremely high leakage rates, and the lack of a multistate master plan with a green tourism component. Extrapolating from these factors, a dismal outcome is a strong possibility.

An Alternative Appalachian Vision

But it doesn't need to be like that. Here is an alternative vision of the future of Appalachian tourism. Let's take another imaginary trip to rural Redbud County, somewhere in the mountains, some years in the future. . . .

Redbud County, summer, some years from now
The Smith family rolls into town for their family vacation. "Ooh, look at all the wildflowers!" says eight-year-old Kaitlyn. "We'll take a look later," her father promises, "after we check in and get unpacked." Arriving at Mountain View Bed-and-Breakfast, they are welcomed by Mrs. Owens, a lifelong resident of Redbud County who started her business after the last of her children went off to college. She's a fount of information about the area, telling her guests about the local artists who made every last one of the quilts and handmade dolls that decorate the three rooms she rents out to visitors. Mrs. Smith admires a beautiful woven coverlet and says she's always wanted to learn how to weave. "My friend Lucy made that," Mrs. Owens tells her. "She gives lessons. If you like, I can take you over to her studio tomorrow and introduce you." There's no dinner served at the B & B, so the Smith

family strolls down the town's main street for fried chicken at Mamaw's Kitchen, which really is run by a grandmother and three of her younger relatives. The Smiths really enjoy the music that's playing in the background, and it turns out that the singers are two more of Mamaw's relatives—and she has CDs for sale!

The next morning, after a breakfast of freshly laid eggs with home-made biscuits and honey from a local farmer, Mrs. Smith takes off with the innkeeper to visit the weaving studio, while Mr. Smith and the kids visit a farm. At Mountain Home, a living replica of an old-time farm, they pet the goats and sheep, pick and eat berries, and try their hands at tasks such as churning butter and carding wool. Kaitlyn is en-thralled with the short pony ride around the pasture, saying to their guide, "Let's take the horses into the woods!" "Sorry, but we can't do that," the guide tells her. "There are too many endangered plants and flowers in there, and you wouldn't want to hurt them, would you? But if you want to know more about the woods, you should go on one of Uncle Bill's Nature Walks. He knows all about the plants and animals in the forest, and he can teach you all kinds of interesting things."

That afternoon, after lunch at Mamaw's (there are two other small restaurants in town, but the Smiths just can't bring themselves to dine anywhere else) they meet up with Uncle Bill for his daily nature walk. He drives them a short distance away from town, then leads them on a long gentle hike through the forest, along a trail that a class at Red-bud County High School developed and provided signage for. As they walk along, he points out dozens of kinds of trees and plants, explain-ing how they were used as food and medicines. He tells them how the plants and animals live together in one big connected ecosystem. "It's so quiet out here," says Nathan. "It's just like in Daniel Boone's time!" Their guide laughs. "Well, that's not quite true. But we've been work-ing hard to restore the forest to its natural state."

"Can we go canoeing tomorrow?" Nathan says eagerly. "And go on that cave walk, and swim in the river? And. . . ."

"This was a great idea," says Mr. Smith to his wife that evening, as they watch the sunset from the porch of the B & B. "I knew it would be," she says. "Those brochures we got made it look so peaceful and pretty. . . . I'm so glad we heard about this place. Let's come back again next year." "Fine with me," says Mr. Smith.

The picture is one of responsible tourism in a healthy environment. Frantic competition for outside tourist dollars is a thing of the past. Through coordinated efforts on the part of all the states in the region, a more satisfying approach to tourism has been established, one that serves more happy visitors, who in turn tell more and more of their friends about their good experiences. Thus, interstate cooperation in joint promotional ventures has led to growth in tourism throughout the Appalachian region. The proximity of the region to over half of America, the natural beauty of its well-preserved landscape, the friendliness of the native people, and the ease of travel to and around the region have all helped to boost its popularity.

The following ten points were the key to making this a reality by 2020:

1. Appalachian tourism is green.

State and regional policies have promoted environmentally sound tourism as the only type that is acceptable. Tourism development has taken place on a moderate scale across the region, with the fundamental decision-making taking part on a local level. Citizen groups at the county level held extensive "town meetings" to discuss and debate what types of tourism to allow in their community, and where. Careful consideration was given to carrying capacity and the potential number of visitors, with some communities on major roads planning for larger-scale tourism, others choosing to allow only small-scale enterprises, and a few opting out entirely.

State tourism and environmental agencies coordinated their efforts. What became evident early on in the attempt to attract more tourists was that the environment is such a key factor that the two agencies could not work independently. Promoting a healthy environment draws more tourism, and the revenue from increased tourism funds further environmental preservation. Promoting a tourist destination requires much more than just pictures of a clean environment for the covers of brochures. Pleasant and unspoiled surroundings are indispensable to a satisfying vacation. State tourist and environmental agencies now cooperate so closely that in some states they have been merged.

The tourism industry has made a commitment to honesty in advertising, sweeping nothing under the rug. The industry believes that the consumer's right to know extends to all Appalachian tourist promotion literature. This includes not only the prices for accommodations and attractions, but the actual condition of the place to be visited—is it reclaimed mined land? How much has the landscape been affected by human activities? All Appalachian states have hotlines where tourists can make complaints, report litter, and praise the scenery or the services. This openness gives the tourist a sense of confidence in making vacation decisions. Neither the tourist nor the host is always right. Mission statements hang on the walls of every tourist business, explaining that this place honors both the people who visit and those who work here. This people-oriented mission statement is posted in a location that is visible to both guests and employees.

A standardized "Green Star" rating system has been established by the region's state governments to measure and compare the environmental soundness of tourism establishments. A detailed system of standards incorporates criteria for such businesses as hotels, tourist attractions, and guide services, comparing such factors as energy and other resource use; impact on the land, plants, and animals; quality of the experience from the tourist's point of view; and promotion of environmental and cultural awareness. Each business is awarded a ranking from zero to five green stars, which they may freely use in their promotional materials, and all businesses are evaluated annually by outside assessors. A publicity campaign has raised visitors' awareness of the system, and studies show that many prospective tourists now compare ratings when making arrangements for their vacation.

2. The landscape is tidy, thanks to local cleanup programs.

A prosperous tourist program requires a tidy landscape. The satisfaction of the tourists and other visitors to the region has improved thanks to greater attention to picking up trash and litter. Untidy conditions have been known to depress entire populations and lead to even more untidiness and neglect. In the past, outsiders were often horrified by the amounts of trash deposited along the roadside and in illegal dumps—a consequence of the lack of facilities for proper disposal. A concerted effort on the part of interstate task forces and subregional teams has cleaned up illegal dumps, prosecuted litterers, and supported people's efforts to clean up their own community.

In the past, Kentucky's director of tourism received many letters from out-of-state visitors complaining about the littered roadsides and recreation areas in an otherwise incredibly beautiful state. A "Keep Appalachia Clean" program has finally put an end to this. The rise in quality tourism, as opposed to a tourism that tolerates junk, has been pronounced. With this rise more money has come into the region to lodging, food, and entertainment establishments and to the local service people. Appalachian tourist agencies are now working hand-in-hand with adopt-a-road and adopt-a-stream groups—a vital effort, since the number-one tourist activity has always been sightseeing. Many residents were surprised that this cleanup program required no new major legislation, only the will on the part of the state and local governments to take measures to save their tourist areas.

States have established recycling centers in every county. It seemed rather expensive at first to provide the financial incentives and loans to get it started, but most of the centers are now paying for themselves, and more and more materials are being recycled—two types of plastics (#1 and #2), newsprint, cardboard, mixed metals, office white paper, colored paper, telephone books, high grade computer printing paper, slick paper, mixed paper, old clothing, and green, brown and clear glass. Income from recycling of materials has become a major incentive to clean up trash.

While volunteer workers continue to clean up roadsides and streams, the major source of workers for public cleanup programs is prisoners serving in county and minimum-security state and federal prisons. People convicted of littering no longer pay fines, but rather must perform days of community service—one week for the first offense. The ignominy of being required to work has become a major incentive in reducing littering. Movable hidden cameras placed at problem dumpsites serve to bring litterers to justice.

States have greatly reduced litter by requiring deposits on all beverage cans and bottles. Gradually, the Appalachian states have overcome the resistance from beverage manufacturers and proceeded to enact effective legislation. Disposal fees on plastic and paper fast-food packaging have reduced the amount of litter from these sources and have collected about $10 million a year in the region. These deposit fees have helped fund the region's start-up recycling programs and dump-removal programs.

3. Regulation of recreational activities is now an accepted practice.

At long last, there is general acceptance of the principle that some restriction on personal behavior is necessary for the benefit of all. Visitors and hosts alike realize that regulations improve the health and safety of all—now, tots have swimming areas protected from the intrusions of speedboaters; bird watchers don't have to see birds scared away by noisemakers. The loss of those visitors who now stay away because of increased regulation is more than offset by an increase in appreciative visitors—and in the quality of life for residents.

One of the most noticeable problems was that public recreational lands had been underpoliced. Starting with the increased drive for national security following the 2001 terrorist attacks, new measures have been implemented. Efforts have been made to set up police helicopter and light airplane surveillance programs, which are coordinated with police ground forces. This enforcement program has involved photographing people who harm the environment through their activities and punishing offenders with mandatory work service programs in lieu of fines. All motorized vehicles (snowmobiles, ATVs, motorboats, and other internal-combustion vehicles) are registered in the respective states of the region. These registered vehicles must be insured and may be driven only on public roads or specially designated off-road areas by licensed drivers sixteen years of age or older. No one is allowed to take motorized vehicles on private property without the explicit permission of the landowner—the state laws in effect for many years are finally being enforced.

Unsafe and environmentally harmful recreation has been banned. Some rules, such as the banning of drugs in recreational areas, have been in effect for a long time, while others have more recent origins, such as the banning of ORVs from wilderness areas and national forests, except on public roads. Restrictions such as limits on horseback riding at certain times of the year help to maintain the pristine condition of sensitive trails. Rock climbing using permanent spikes is forbidden on all public lands, as is digging up wild native plants. No one is allowed to participate in harmful traditional practices such as handling rattlesnakes (even for religious ceremonies), wrestling black bears, or holding cockfights. While some may see these as noble expressions of tradition, the fact remains that they are dangerous. And insurance rates are high these days!

Hikers and campers are now required to pack out all garbage, camp only in designated areas, refrain from gathering firewood, and build campfires only in designated places at specific times. Whitewater rafting is carefully regulated for safety and minimal environmental impact. Most outdoor experiences involve the use of commercial motels, hotels, campgrounds, or bed-and-breakfast establishments—not wilderness camping. Bird and wildlife watchers have been allotted designated areas free from disturbances of other recreational activities.

Regulations have finally been imposed to limit the emissions from internal-combustion recreational vehicles, including snowmobiles, ATVs, and dirt bikes. Noise pollution from motorized sources has also drawn the attention of regulators, because of disturbance of wildlife, hearing loss to riders, and noise in neighboring communities. Manufacturers are working to reduce noise considerably on new motorized vehicles.

4. New forms of tourism safeguard the most fragile areas.

The general public, and especially schoolchildren, are now much more aware of the natural treasures of Appalachia: mountains, rock formations, caves, creeks and rivers, wildlife, forests, and plant life. The perception that the region and people were of little worth, once widespread, is vanishing. The growing view is that the region is a fragile and priceless treasure and that its people have a unique and valuable culture. Part of this awareness came through expanded environmental education programs; part has been due to setting aside lands as wilderness areas. Though these wilderness areas are designated off-limits to damaging recreational or economic activities, creative programs have been implemented to allow these fragile areas to be enjoyed by a larger component of the population. Careful attention has been given to assessing the carrying capacity of specific types of environments, and to each destination as a whole.

Environmental education is widespread. Programs were first started within individual school districts and then expanded to entire states, and finally to the Appalachian region. Now, all children have a firsthand nature encounter experience three times during their school years: grade four, grade eight, and the junior year of high school. Fourth graders attend slide shows and take day trips during this highly impressionable period of education and begin to learn about the treasure of Appalachia. At grade eight students attend publicly supported nature camps (near, but not in, fragile areas), either within their state or in other parts of Appalachia. This has been modeled after a program employed by the Society for the Protection of Nature in Israel (SPNI), which operated over two dozen youth camps throughout Israel. High-school students take part in more vigorous activities including over-night hiking/camping, rappelling, and whitewater rafting. The three-part educational program teaches appreciation and respect for the eco-logical resources in Appalachia.

Owners of property adjacent to fragile areas have been encouraged to jointly declare their land to be off-limits, and to designate their property as wildlife conservation areas or bird sanctuaries. This is done through the assistance of state wildlife conservation agencies. Local citizens, deputized local magistrates, and police patrol the desig-nated wildlands or sanctuary areas. This keeps out unauthorized people such as hunters. Communities have designed and posted signs of a uniform size and shape to make the status of the land immediately obvious.

When access to certain wilderness and wetland areas was barred to visitors, observation platforms were built nearby. These are permanent walkways and viewing stands constructed such that interested natural-ists can have a proximate experience of the flora and fauna of the no-entry regions. These platforms have proven quite successful from an educational perspective, providing information, maps, audiotapes ac-tivated by the visitor, brochures, and mounted viewing instruments. All wetland areas and some forested areas have been furnished with viewing platforms for the use of nature-loving tourists.

Low-capacity small aircraft touring is not encouraged because of the heavy fuel consumption. However, per passenger consumption is reduced considerably when more sightseers are able to share a single aerial observation tour. Furthermore, the trips may be combined with other worthwhile purposes such as aerial photography of land distur-bance. The impact of flying over a fragile area is far less damaging to the total environment than ground travel to and from the same site. The aerial view is, in fact, a far better approach to seeing remote rug-ged terrain and rock formations.

Some people insist on a firsthand experience of fragile environ-ments, which can threaten the very land they want to enjoy. For that reason, virtual and proximate experiences have been encouraged by the Appalachian states. The documentation of fragile areas through photography is done by professionals for two types of audiences. Basic videos are produced for general science classes at lower and higher elementary school levels, while more sophisticated videotapes are made available through the ecological/tourist agencies for high schools, home use, and public television channels. Virtual tourism is considered both a learning component of every school curriculum and an opportunity for those who are unable to travel easily. Tourism to the most fragile places (once a form of so-called ecotourism) is off-limits at any price. Instead of actual visits, all have access to virtual tourism.

Visiting a site oneself is always the most satisfying. However, some people are not able to do so because they lack the time or financial resources, or have disabilities that make travel difficult. TV travelogues, along with virtual touring, have been produced with such people in mind. High-quality documentaries can give many people access to experiences and knowledge that would otherwise be unavailable to them.

5. The forest continues to improve.

The environment is not a static thing; it can be harmed, or it can improve. Through good preservation techniques, an effort is made to halt environmental decline, and through restoration projects, previously damaged environments are healed. Preservation and restoration procedures apply all the more to forested areas. Much has been made of the increase in Appalachia's forested land today as compared to a century ago, but simply covering former corn fields and pastures with trees has not been sufficient. Some of the forest cover is of poorer quality trees. Efforts have been undertaken to bring the American chestnut back, to replant oak, and to remove kudzu and exotic species, which once infested the Appalachian region and many fragmented forest areas in America.

The natural Central Appalachian forest, a narrow band of vegetation stretching from southwestern Pennsylvania to northeastern Alabama, is what noted biologist Lucy Braun called the Mixed Mesophytic Forest. Now every schoolchild in the region knows that this is the oldest and most varied hardwood forest in the world. At least a hundred species of trees and woody plants are found on the slopes, hilltops, and coves of the region, a unique phenomenon among temperate climate biosystems. Through educational programs, more Appalachians, especially youth, have come to appreciate this treasure. In turn, the growing awareness has led to understanding both publicly and privately owned forests as "commons," for the benefit of all the people, not just some owner or manager. Visitors are drawn to the forest's beautiful scenic views, the most important non-timber resource of them all. This and other non-timber forest products (NTFPs) have helped make tourism, not extractive industry, the most significant portion of the Appalachian economy in forested areas.

A "Forest Commons" zoning policy has been established. The region's people have come to see the land as more than just a patchwork of private plots. There is a wholeness to this region when all stakeholders are able to decide how the forest will be used. Older laissez-faire traditions have disappeared. With the advent of forest land-use planning, the landscape has begun to improve. Scenic viewscapes (that is, the landscapes that can be seen directly from public highways) have been preserved along all the area's primary and key secondary roads. These zoned areas are now off-limits to major timber and chip mill harvesting. Selective logging may only be done under very strict guidelines so that the logging does not mar the beauty of the landscape. Housing and commercial development are also restricted in such zoned viewscape regions. In many ways, this was the most difficult policy change to enact in Appalachia, because so many rural people resist zoning restrictions. The ultimate benefit to all the people in the region is just now being appreciated.

Proper timber management policies have been instituted. The Menominee Nation of Native Americans in central Wisconsin has been logging their tribal land for a century and a half, and it still has beautiful wooded areas. The same types of sustainable forest harvest methods have now been applied to all hardwood areas of mountainous Appalachia. Tree farming has been relegated to other areas of the nation, and chip mills and pulp factories have been closed within the region. The salutary effect has been a vast improvement in the quality and general appearance of Appalachia's wooded areas. Together with the end of surface mining, this has reduced the severe flooding that once occurred in counties with steep slopes and heavy disturbances.

Irresponsible surface mining practices have been curbed. After half a century of surface mining of coal and national reclamation efforts, people in the region know that permanent scars remain in about one-fifth of Central Appalachia's surface area. Mountaintop removal has been halted after considerable debate, and all newly mined lands must be returned to their natural contour, as was first mandated in 1977 federal legislation.

Non-timber forest products have been encouraged. To help improve the most valuable product of the Appalachian forest—namely, its scenic view—alternative steps have been taken for the economic welfare of the landowners and others who derive a living from forestland. Extra cash has been generated by protecting and growing ginseng, goldenseal, black and blue cohosh, and other medicinal herbs with billions of dollars of potential market both in this county and, especially, in Asia. These medicinal crops have proved, when properly managed, more profitable than harvesting timber. The forest is needed as a natural canopy to grow the expanding cash crops of medicinal herbs. Through careful reseeding and protection, these native herbs again flourish in the forested areas. A federal system of marketing cards has been enacted as required documentation, thus halting the traditional practice of poaching (or stealing) the crops of others. Since intruders do not have marketing cards, they are unable to sell any stolen ginseng, making theft pointless. Likewise, a federal grading system has been put into practice; this verifies the quality of the harvested plants, thus bringing better prices for the grower. Sellers of NTFPs now have protection against unscrupulous marketers.

6. Local businesses thrive, and employees earn a living wage.

The majority of new tourism businesses in the region are small and locally owned. Numerous bed-and-breakfast accommodations, restaurants, campgrounds, gift shops, guiding services, and other enterprises have sprung up, with strong support from the state and federal governments. Plentiful low-interest start-up loans, mentoring from experienced local businesspeople under the auspices of the Small Business Administration, group business insurance programs, and local small business associations have helped many residents start businesses of their own. Joint marketing through websites and other media has brought many customers to networks of B & B owners and associations of craftspeople.

Carrots generally work better than sticks in Appalachia, but sometimes a combination of the two is also highly effective. This has proven true in improving the tourist business and the working conditions in these establishments. The industry became economically healthier when it was transformed from a seasonal to a year-round operation, thus giving service employees longer periods of work. Incentives have been given to businesses through free promotion at the state and regional levels. A regional approach has been put in place to help all thrive together and prevent cost-cutters from attracting visitors at far lower prices, creating a downward spiral in deteriorating labor conditions. The general Appalachian policy is to "keep the beds warm," or work towards high occupancy rates throughout the year.

A major improvement to the Appalachian business situation has been the movement from seasonal to year-round facilities. Hosting conferences for groups who seek less expensive facilities along with fewer distractions away from larger city attractions is one of the features of the year-round type of business. Regional joint attempts have brought international conference attendees from Germany, Japan, and the United Kingdom to Appalachia outside the main tourist season. This has been especially fruitful in the small- to medium-sized cities that are served by nearby regional and major airports (Knoxville, Chattanooga, Tri-Cities, Charleston, Asheville, and Ashland-Huntington). Year-round entertainment is achieved by making use of local musicians and artists, with off-season festivals highly promoted by the governmental agencies. There is a reduction or even remission of motel taxes at certain times of the year in order to attract conventions, since a fully used facility takes less expense to maintain than a seasonal one.

A higher legal minimum wage has proved a major boon for the part-time seasonal service employees in the region. Often, these are the only wages that homemakers and retired people receive throughout the year, and this income goes right back into the community for basic goods and services. Housing in the region remains some of the most affordable in the nation. Many part-time workers also grow gardens to provide a portion of their own food. Thanks to inexpensive housing and this possibility of producing one's own food, it is easier to live in rural Appalachia than elsewhere, though it is still a struggle for the working poor. A booming tourism industry directly assists these minimum-wage earners in a significant manner. Service unions have increased their membership among these workers.

Tourist businesses come in many varieties, from multinational conglomerates to mom-and-pop operations. State and federal governments have been offering incentives to the latter in the form of low-interest loans for some time. There are also consulting services to assist with business plans and the siting of operations. In order to reduce the exit of tourist revenue from the region (leakage), state governments offer a variety of incentives to tourist businesses who agree to purchase goods and services locally. They are rewarded with listings in brochures, guides, subsidized coupon booklets at rest stops and information centers, and pamphlets listing food, lodging, and other entertainment accommodations, plus uniform signage and placement on websites. A regional program has been started to give awards to those communities that show the greatest improvement of the environment and in tourism programs.

7. Social and political capital are building up.

With increased employment in the tourism industry, there is a growing sense of self-respect and pride in the natural treasures of Appalachia. People are more willing to invest in their communities through joining the PTA, civic clubs, political parties, sports groups, and conservation organizations. Even the churches have witnessed increased attendance and participation. People are more willing to volunteer for everything from tutoring children to Meals on Wheels; this is due in part to higher employment and a feeling of well-being in a region that is starting to show progress.

Another Appalachian phenomenon is the return of the retirees to the communities where they grew up, which began some decades earlier in the Ozarks. This return of older people has brought money back to the community, and there is the added dividend of expanding the population without increasing the burden on the school system, as often occurs elsewhere. One need that has increased, however, is the health services. States have addressed this need by giving special attention to designated subregional and multicounty health centers for heart treatment, dentistry, eye care, and psychiatric treatment. This has encouraged those with ailments or anticipated medical needs associated with aging to feel freer to return to less densely populated areas.

Helicopter services are now available to transport emergency cases rapidly to health centers at virtually the same speed as in congested urban areas.

Secondary roads are well maintained. The Eisenhower-era interstate highway system blessed Central Appalachia with Interstates 24, 26, 40, 64, 70, 74, 75, 77, 79, 80, and 81, all of which are interconnected with the rest of the system and with the existing Pennsylvania and West Virginia Turnpikes. More recently, attention has focused on improving and maintaining the secondary roads used by residents and visitors alike to gain access to towns further from the interstate highway system. No longer are schoolchildren forced to miss class during the slightest snowfall because the roads are impassible to school buses. The improved condition of the region's secondary roads has increased residential mobility and encouraged the arrival of more tourists.

Health care has improved. Health facilities went through a crisis as small hospitals were forced to close for lack of ability to specialize, the squeeze on costs, and reduced Medicaid/Medicare appropriations. Now, however, hospitals in the region have united to reduce competition and emphasize specialized services in given subregions. Comprehensive care facilities are now operating in every county through increased tax revenues from the thriving tourist and service industry.

Appalachia no longer suffers the stigma of a "Charity Case." Appalachia has had to fight hard against negative stereotypes and advertising. One high-profile response from a regional standpoint has been the establishment of the Appalachian Anti-Defamation League, which has persuaded establishments to remove the title of "hillbilly" from titles or programs, corrected menu cards, asked festivals to change demeaning names, and led people to regard the Appalachian vocabulary and pronunciation as something to be proud of rather than denigrated. People now refer to the "unmentionable h-word," just as no one would dream of applying the "n-word" to an African American. Do-gooder charity for Appalachia has been reexamined and challenged. Bringing in outsiders to help clean up a littered river or to make minor repairs on housing (which locals could easily fix) has been strongly discouraged, unless reciprocal volunteering occurs with Appalachians going to help the poor in the other location. AmeriCorps, VISTA, and other governmental and private agencies now place volunteers from within Appalachia.

8. Tour guides are trained and competent, and information is plentiful.

Hospitality is a major Appalachian asset, but it can easily deteriorate without constant attention. The interstate tourist commissions have given much consideration to maintaining a welcoming atmosphere for tourists. Standardized tourist-friendly signage has been installed to give directions in any areas where visitors might become confused. Brochures advise tourists where to go and the best time to visit, as some areas prefer seasonal tourism over year-round activities.

The professionalizing of the tourism industry means recruiting service employees who are knowledgeable about the treasures of Appalachia—and are ready and willing to show pride to visitors who come to the region. Gone, to some degree, are the summer volunteers who in former times told farfetched stories about the mountains to those visitors gullible enough to lend an ear.

The success of sightseeing tourism is largely due to the increased professionalism of the tour guides. Certification programs for guides have been established in each of the states in the region. Tour guides now post their certificates, showing that they have received extensive training by experts such as Dr. Gene Wilhelm of Slippery Rock, Pennsylvania, who has conducted educational tours in Appalachia and elsewhere for decades. He and other trainers have years of experience in the region and an in-depth knowledge of the natural biosystems—the flora and fauna of the region. Experts are prominently identified through regional and state websites and other promotional literature. These professionally trained tour guides are capable of setting up and operating customized tours, selecting itineraries and modes of transportation, along with making food and lodging arrangements. Many tourists are willing to pay a small additional fee to go on these personally planned and directed excursions.

Inexperienced students and others serve as tour guide interns, and they learn from the professionals through integrated college service programs in which they acquire credit in recreation management. Many of the major schools have recreation-related programs of studies, including Appalachian State in North Carolina; Morehead State and Eastern Kentucky University in Kentucky; Marshall University in Huntington and the University of West Virginia; the University of Tennessee; Virginia Tech in Blacksburg, Virginia; and Ohio University in

Athens. In response to increased tourism, these schools have strengthened their offerings in recreation management. Besides these larger
universities, a host of smaller Appalachian liberal arts colleges have
moved to fill a niche in their respective areas of Appalachia. Some of
these, such as Berea College in Kentucky, have incorporated recreational management into their internship programs.

9. Artists, musicians, and storytellers are recognized and adequately compensated.

The authentic crafts and artwork of Appalachians have long been appreciated, but an unregulated tourist business can result in larger companies requiring the local artisans to focus on those articles that the
business people judge will sell well. This denigrates the work of the
artisans, whose creativity is a very valuable asset for the region. Supporting this creativity has been a hallmark of successful tourism.

States have instituted programs to certify craft articles that were
designed by their makers, and not made to conform to an established
commercial pattern. This is not a restriction on freedom to be creative,
but rather a guarantee that the creative spirit is preserved in economic
activity, which serves to authenticate the creativity of the craftsperson
or artist. Obviously, the value of the craft object may decrease if the
existence of commercial specifications is made known—as occurs
quite often in Third World countries. These regulations have had a
salutary effect of preserving the authenticity of old-time arts and crafts,
and they have given the master artists and craftspeople an added sense
of pride in their work.

The first highly successful Appalachian Festival has been copied in
cities throughout the area. The festival was started as a way to make
expatriate Appalachians proud of their heritage. The various Appalachian states have funded regional fairs and cooperated in promoting
joint ventures, through public service announcements of upcoming
events, flyers of specific events in tourist information centers, websites
with links to regional events, and "homecomings" to welcome people
of Appalachian origin to the place of their roots. With events taking
place each weekend from May to October, it takes a lot of effort to give
each one the publicity it deserves.

The promotion of traditional crafts is high on the list of activities
that have revitalized Appalachian tourism. These crafts are a proud

heritage of the region, no longer linked with poverty but viewed as an expression of native culture and talent. Guidebooks and websites listing artisans and sales outlets are available for each of the Appalachian states. There has been a renaissance in crafts, which has led to higher standards of quality in products like quilts, rocking chairs, corn shuck dolls, sorghum molasses, stone-ground cornmeal, homemade soap, brooms, dulcimers, old-style farm implements, corn shellers, and the like. An online sales program promotes and sells products nationally and internationally. Fans of authentic Appalachian crafts regard it as a fine vacation to travel through the region looking for further treasures to decorate their homes.

10. Tourism is central to Appalachia's economy and identity.

In the last ten years, tourism has replaced mining, logging, and manufacturing as the number one industry in the region, and Appalachia is now seen as a tranquil haven for visitors. In contrast to earlier industries, the new economy furnishes steady employment to more people, promotes regional pride and self-respect, supports an infrastructure of professional services, encourages retirees to return to the place of their birth, brings in sufficient revenue to improve roads and education, acts as an incentive for policing and maintaining fragile natural areas, and provides recreation to the half of the American population that lives within five hundred miles.

Tourism and ecology departments of state agencies have been meeting for a number of years. Annual regional conferences are held in order to coordinate programs. Agendas include reports on successful publicity campaigns; analyses of the successes and failures of state regulations, interstate parks, and wilderness areas (such as Breaks Interstate Park, between Kentucky and Virginia, established back in the twentieth century); and the exchange of information on new legislative initiatives. All involved are aware that many Appalachian vacations usually include several states, which means that attracting visitors to one site can benefit neighboring states as well.

Features in Sunday travel sections, airline in-flight magazines, TV travel programs, and other forms of media recognition always influence the image of the region to outsiders. Encouraging writers to cover the region is part of these joint efforts.

Finally, the economic and ecological forces are merged and working together, a successful partnership to be imitated in other parts of our nation and the world. *Ecos* means "home" in Greek; the two fields of economics and ecology are far more closely related than most people realize. Good ecology is good economics, and the reverse is true as well. This region can ill afford to have a split here, as cynics seem to believe is inevitable.

Back to the Real World

The reality will probably fall somewhere in between the very pessimistic scenario outlined earlier and the very optimistic one outlined just above. Painting an overly optimistic picture may bring about disappointment and discouragement, leading ultimately to the negative outcome described. Our hope is that readers of this book will become actively involved in designing and working towards a positive form of tourism in Appalachia. We are not just dredging up nostalgia for an Appalachian past. The region is threatened by the tourism industry just as it has been by other exploitative ventures in the past. However, there is still some time before the course of tourism development is irrevocably set here. We fervently hope that our optimistic scenario becomes a reality, and it is well within the realm of possibility—if we put our minds and hearts into it.

We are convinced that this positive vision can become a reality if we abandon our past cynicism about the people and the resources of Appalachia, if we cooperate with each other on regional and local community levels, and if we develop a willingness to face and overcome our collective shortcomings. On the other hand, if we let people continue to do whatever they please, we will attract only opportunists from outside, who will soon abandon us for more lucrative prospects.

The key to moving toward this future vision is proactive, bottom-up planning by local, state, and regional citizens' groups and governmental bodies. This needs to start at the community level. We've seen how the Guiding Alaska Tourism initiative has provided support and a decision-making structure for communities who want to take control of the shape of future tourism in their area. Other regions of the U.S. have produced their own conceptions of a community-centered approach to tourism development. For example, a group of organizations in the western states collaborated to produce the *Community*

Tourism Assessment Handbook, which outlines in detail a nine-step process that communities can use to decide whether to pursue tourism development, and, if so, what form it should take.[1]

The handbook's introduction states that the aim is to "help communities predict both the costs and benefits of tourism and to consider the distribution of the costs and benefits before deciding to proceed. The process also is about local control, leadership and ownership of the change inherent in community development. Community members are 'in the driver's seat.' You will call upon the help of various 'experts' or 'resource persons' along the way, but this is your assessment and decision-making process." The handbook includes worksheets outlining what information that the community will need to collect and lists concrete steps that can be accomplished using local resources or, if the community prefers, with outside assistance.

The first step in the process it to organize a Community Tourism Assessment Action Committee, made up of local volunteers. This committee then draws up current visitor and economic profiles and surveys residents' attitudes towards tourism. Next is a process of visioning and setting goals for the future of the community. The committee inventories existing attractions and studies basic tourism marketing information. (What do we have to sell? What do visitors want to buy?) Following this, it identifies potential projects, carries out initial project scoping, and analyzes the impact of potential projects. This entire process can have three different possible outcomes. First, a community may decide that tourism is not for them. Second, a community may identify tourism projects that they want to proceed with. Finally, they may decide to go ahead with developing tourism but require further investigation to decide what types of projects they want.

A process such as this would be ideal for mountain communities who wish to consider developing tourism. Rather than being the work of outside "experts" or agencies, it begins with the needs and wishes of the residents themselves. Given the diverse people and outlooks within these communities, it may not be an easy process to reach consensus about desired futures, but it is bound to be more democratic and beneficial than letting commercial interests from outside decide their fate.

To build for the future means taking some difficult steps in proactive planning, promotion, regulation, and enforcement. To continue the tradition of mountain hospitality requires a positive view of the region's future. Realism dictates that we address all parties forthrightly and consider both the positive and the negative aspects of Appalachia today, as an incentive to take action.

CHAPTER 9

Our Own Backyard

An Ecotour through Appalachia

> I owe my life to these mountains and I want them preserved that others may profit by them as I have.
>
> —Horace Kephart[1]

No discussion of ecotourism in Appalachia would be complete without considering how existing attractions can be part of such a vision. Can we bring the area's ecology to the forefront in museum displays, tours, naturalist talks, and outdoor exhibits? Can this outlook be spread from public facilities to private businesses as well? And can we make ecotourism accessible to the less active half of the tourist population—the senior citizens, the families with small children, the disabled, the tour bus crowd, and those who would unhesitatingly label themselves couch potatoes? In short, can we make the existing Appalachian tourist experience ecological?

We think this is quite feasible, and that some existing tourist facilities in Appalachia already incorporate many features of ecotourism, providing an excellent basis to build on. Let's attempt to apply our emerging principles of good ecotourism and broaden our conception of ecotourism to include sightseeing forays on beaten paths such as popular overlooks, trails, and visitor centers. Surprising though it may seem, such destinations do fit in well with the definition we have been using. In places like these, nature may be experienced, local people can find meaningful employment, and in the process the environment is enhanced. In a few words: a more accessible version of "ecotourism" can initiate ordinary people into a deeper understanding of the environment.

Ecotouring for Everyone

As an example, we'll outline a sample Appalachian ecotour, one which could easily be taken by average Americans. Many families cannot travel overseas to Belize or Nepal, can't even get to Alaska or Hawai'i, aren't able to find more than a few days for a vacation, and simply don't have a lot of money to spend. Already, many such families travel to Appalachia—or at least contemplate doing so. They come each year by the millions to see the proverbial mountain beauty and to stay at cheap Gatlinburg, Tennessee, motels still advertising rooms at $14.95 (with "and up" in small print). They pack coolers of drinks and peanut butter sandwiches, splurge on one or two meals per day at fast-food restaurants, and treat the little ones to a ride on the miniature trains or a visit to the snake museum. Maybe they can't make it to Disney World this year, but at least Appalachia makes a nice change from a crowded beach or grandma's midwestern suburb.

It's a challenge to plan a tour for a mixture of ages, with each person having a vastly different notion of "fun." Thus besides being scenic, cool, easily accessible, and economical, the destination must have diverse attractions to entertain the entire carload of people. More important from an ecological standpoint, the tour should involve activities with low environmental impact, and it should enhance the quality of life of the residents who may be called on to serve the tourist trade. We'd like to add still other stipulations, where possible. The environmental impacts of human-made activities should not be glossed over but rather pointed out; the ecological cost of constructing and maintaining facilities should be openly discussed; and the cobwebs of the historic displacement of native populations to build facilities should be swept away. Such honesty makes the tour all the more refreshing.

Taking all these factors into consideration, Al Fritsch spent five days as a Central Appalachian tourist during the height of a summer season, frequenting the haunts with the crowd. The focus was on public lands because of their high-profile tourist facilities, as well as to avoid favoritism to any private business. In much of this book, we have

The Blue Ridge Parkway. Map by Mark Spencer.

talked about national and state park systems, but this tour included national, state, and local forests as well as the only Native American reservation in Appalachia. While the tour was necessarily limited in scope, we hasten to add that there are many other excellent public and private tourist facilities along the entire Appalachian range, from Alabama and Georgia to New York and Pennsylvania.

Appalachia already attracts millions of tourists, though many of them travel on a limited budget and for shorter periods of time. Detailed tourist brochures exist for these folks. Using this information, we planned a tour along the 469-mile Blue Ridge Parkway to America's most visited national park, the Great Smoky Mountains, with a side trip to the Cherokee Indian Reservation. Here, travelers will find scenic beauty, an escape from the summer heat, varied attractions, and plenty of memories to take home. The average family needs to keep costs down, and many of the thrills on the Blue Ridge Parkway are cheap—or even free. For example, watching artisans at work in the craft centers on the way is fine free entertainment. The average family is not concerned about the efforts of some to commercialize the very public routes they plan to travel, or about the higher camping fees just around the corner—since everything else is going up in price anyway. Whether Appalachia turns into the new Orlando does not matter to them—at least then they would not have to fly to Florida.

The western Virginia through western North Carolina route was chosen for a number of reasons:

Access. As we have mentioned, interstate highways can bring half of America's population to this area within a single day. Though public transport could be used, currently this is far more difficult than taking the car. Driving is generally far more affordable than airline tickets for a family to visit some faraway place.

Beautiful scenery. Certainly, standing at many of the overlooks on the Parkway and looking out at the unspoiled mountains will make one marvel at the treasure of the Appalachian Mountains. One feels singularly blessed with such views—and one also wonders whether these pristine areas could be "loved to death" by the sheer number of visitors.

Low cost. Travelers on this route pay no entrance fees in most places; sometimes there is a jar for voluntary donations at a museum or cultural center. The motels are some of the most inexpensive anywhere in America, and the bargains are even greater in the off-season. Restaurants of all types are available, ranging from the elegant to lower-priced fast-food places a little off the beaten path.

Noncommercial. Some watchdogs are seriously concerned about the commercialization of public recreation areas, including the Blue Ridge Parkway and surrounding public lands. At present, cultural centers are leased to private groups, but no one is going to make a killing there, and the money is dispersed to numerous struggling local artists and craftspeople. The issue of charging admission fees to public lands, which would restrict usage, is an open debate at this time and beyond the scope of this book. Economic accessibility is worth striving for, and limiting commercial "Disney World" adventures to more distant places is still worth the battle.

Variety. A mixed group of older and younger travelers can find both gentle sight-seeing and vigorous outdoor activities on the route, along with playgrounds for small children. For the energetic, there is hiking, fishing, camping, boating, even white-water rafting on the French Broad River. For the elderly, the physically challenged, and those with less stamina, there is plenty to see from the window of a car or tour bus, making this area a rare treat. There is lodging to meet all needs along these routes as well.

Old-fashioned touring. Traveling the Blue Ridge Parkway can be a reminder of an earlier era of travel. It is not crowded except during the main tourist season.[2] The overall speed restriction to forty-five miles per hour and the absence of commercial vehicles keep roadways uncongested, clean, and scenic, providing an atmosphere that makes older folks reminisce about the highways decades ago. There are more motorcycles now, and on weekends more bicycles, but the curves and tunnels give one a sense of old-fashioned touring, minus the old-time shortage of motel accommodations.

Positive view. Nowhere in the course of this trip is there any disrespect or belittling of Appalachian ways or culture. Where old cabins are exhibited, the accompanying displays and literature give a positive view of the traditional culture, despite people's poverty, and portray an industrious, self-sufficient people with a deep love for family and community—and the ability to live comfortably without relying on the outside world.

Educational potential. Al Fritsch has studied nature all his life, but the trip he made on this route gave him a still better understanding of the bioregion. Plentiful information is available in the numerous bookstores and from the free handouts in the parks. The Cherokee and the staff members at the various facilities are quite patient and enjoy answering sincere questions. He learned firsthand how hominy is made, what materials are used to make slat back chairs, and how clay pots are finished and made ready for the kiln. Other visitors, he observed, were asking questions and making use of the learning opportunities.

Eco-impacts frankly acknowledged. An ecotourist would be moved upon learning from the displays prepared by the National Park Service how and why the air quality has deteriorated. The same is true with the educational presentation on tree dieback prepared by North Carolina state park officials at the Mount Mitchell State Park. The contrast between the low automobile traffic on the parkway and the heavy congestion of the interstate highway is educational in itself. On one segment of the trip, Al Fritsch traveled by interstate and local roads in one direction and by the parkway in the other direction. The eighty vehicles he counted in a single mile of travel on Interstate 40 equaled the number observed in the opposite direction over ninety miles of parkway transit.

Social and historic problems. While this may be a lesser draw, those who tour the Cherokee Museum will gain an understanding of the Trail of Tears and the devastation done to Native American nations. The sad story of the displacement of local people during the building of the parks and parkway is harder to uncover, but information is available on this difficult subject as well.

The Blue Ridge Parkway

Any one of the twenty million people who travel on the 469-mile Blue Ridge Parkway (BRP) as it snakes through the Blue Ridge mountains soon realizes that it is a unique experience. It has rightly been called the "first parkway designed exclusively for leisure travel and recreational use."

A guidebook describing the history of the BRP is quite helpful in planning such a trip.[3] At the start of Franklin Roosevelt's first term in 1933, FDR's advisors suggested expanding the mission of the Civilian

Conservation Corps to give still more jobs to out-of-work laborers. Roosevelt liked the idea of connecting the Shenandoah National Park in Virginia to the Great Smoky Mountains National Park in North Carolina and Tennessee by means of a new parkway. Later that same year, sixteen million dollars was allotted to begin the BRP southward from where the existing Skyline Parkway ended.

The states acquired the right of way, and federal money was used for design, supervision, and construction. The BRP was incorporated into the National Park Service in mid-1936 in order to conserve the scenery and provide recreation. The National Park Service wanted to restore some of the damaged land along the route and taught conservation measures while engaging in construction using 90 percent local laborers. While construction on the BRP dragged on through World War II, by 1966 it was 95 percent complete. However, it would take two more decades for the 7.7-mile section near Grandfather Mountain to be finished. The landowner there objected to proposals that would have hurt the beauty of a large private recreational area. This final section, called the "Linn Cove Viaduct," is regarded as an engineering feat in its effort to do only minimal damage to the rugged terrain of the mountain.

From its beginning at the terminus of the Skyline Drive near Waynesboro, Virginia, to its end at the Great Smoky Mountain National Park and the Cherokee Indian Reservation in North Carolina, the BRP is strikingly different from other American roads. There are no billboards, few entrances and exits, and all trucks and commercial vehicles are banned. What's more, the sides of the parkway are completely lined with greenery during a midsummer trip. There are curves, yes, and a top speed of forty-five miles per hour, and plenty of bicyclists who complicate things by going slower as they labor up the rises and hills. And that double yellow line stretching for miles certainly does complicate any effort to pass. But who's in a hurry, anyway?

The BRP is a federal park, the longest and narrowest in the world. This "snake in the mountains" is maintained by the Department of Interior's National Park Service. Any casual conversation with rangers and other staff quickly makes travelers aware that the Service indeed has dedicated and knowledgeable personnel.

The BRP was conceived in the era between the two world wars, using low-cost (and highly motivated) WPA labor. Its rock walls were built in part by Italian and Spanish workmen. They are landmarks in design and execution, and they add to the elegance of this most scenic of American roads. Even the mile markers are not posted as on other U.S. roads; they are numbered from north to south (the reverse of the norm), and the numerical sequence doesn't start over with every state border.

The BRP was built for people of another era, who took their time when touring and wanted an education along the way. The route has twenty-six artistically built tunnels to keep things interesting and about eighty overlooks and pull-offs from which to savor the view. Along the route, there are thirteen picnic areas, seven fishing areas, and nine campgrounds open from May though early November. All are well maintained. A dozen visitor centers give further directions and information and point to dining and lodging facilities along the way.

Two aspects of the BRP can make it the focus of an eco-experience: the natural beauty already present and the damage produced by human carelessness, both past and potential. There are a host of plants and animals to observe and learn about. One sees wild turkeys and squirrels and hears tales about black bears, elk, and mountain lions. Such spring flowers as the trillium and pink lady's slipper are in the woods, just a short walk from the road. Tourists can have a deeper and more enriching experience by using wildflower and bird guidebooks. They may wish to time their visit to the peak of autumn color, or to the blooming of the rhododendron in spring. The BRP ranges in elevation from 649 to 6,047 feet, and thus one can taste blackberries and raspberries over a six-week span and see spring flowers over a wide time period.

Besides its natural beauty, the BRP can also teach tragic lessons of human damage to the ecosystem, especially at the fragile higher altitudes. The lethal balsam woolly adelgid (*adelges piceae*), a type of insect that kills fir trees, arrived in America a century ago in nursery stock (which is still not fully regulated). It spread from New England to the Appalachians and has devastated the mature Fraser fir, which once flourished in altitudes above 4,500 feet. The destruction of these firs can be seen at places like Mt. Mitchell in North Carolina. Granted, some gaunt dead trees stood on these windswept mountainsides and peaks through the centuries, but what occurred in the mid–twentieth century was a new phenomenon. Having seen earlier photographs, Al Fritsch was pleasantly surprised during the trip to see young firs standing ten or more feet high—but as they approach maturity, are they immune? Experts are uncertain.

And this is not the only threat to the BRP viewscape. The *Parkway Milepost* for the summer of 2002 listed several others. The gypsy moth, a pest that can completely defoliate trees, was introduced in America in 1869, and continues to invade the area. It is most noticeable around milepost 86. The hemlock woolly adelgid, another destructive insect, came to our country from Japan in 1924 and is seen at the Peaks of Otter area of Virginia, as well as the Linville Falls, North Carolina, area. The southern pine beetle has caused some damage, as has the dogwood anthracnose, which is spreading widely on the beautiful dogwood. And of course a modern telltale sign of midsummer is the locust leaf miner, which turns the numerous black locusts along the BRP a rusty brown long before the other leaves turn.

No tour is perfect without a foray on a side road, and this happened to be a festival day at Mt. Mitchell, just two miles from the BRP. The event brought out local craft makers, and so, near the top of eastern America's highest peak, visitors learned how to make hominy by leaching out the lye from wood ashes and cooking the corn until the shells come off. Heavy fog prevented seeing the windswept mountaintop, but, on the other hand, there was so much else to see and there were big crowds in which to mingle. Parents of small children in the Mount Mitchell State Park Museum helped their young ones press the button to make the crow display come alive with loud squawks. Other tiny children ran up to see what the noise was about, and the museum attendant commented, "We try to make our museum child-friendly." These kids are starting their own ecological journey at a very early age.

What about Appalachian culture along the BRP corridor? One begins to wonder where all the people are, after many miles of trees and more trees. The forest is not just a veneer, and one can see from the numerous overlooks on the roadside that there is much unpopulated territory along the Blue Ridge range. There is a substantial exhibit of contemporary cultural artifacts at the Folk Art Center, right on the BRP near Asheville. The building is modern, well designed, and very accessible to those with disabilities, with an exterior ramp to the main floor and a prominent interior ramp to the second gallery floor. The collection of items for sale includes a wide range of pottery, wood-work, jewelry, fabrics of all types, glassware, painting, corn shuck dolls, and on and on. Items on sale and special exhibits are constantly being added and rearranged.[4]

The Parkway Craft Center is located within the 3,516-acre Memo-rial Park, at Mile Marker 294. This property was bequeathed to the National Park Service by Moses and Bertha Cone. Their large mansion contains another tastefully displayed folk art and craft collection. However, for the nature lover, the surrounding woodlands and land-scape are even more of a treat, beginning at the mansion's front porch with a view of a lake surrounded by naturally wooded hills, together with some thirty-two thousand apple trees. The grounds contain twenty-five miles of original carriage routes and trails, now used for hiking, jogging, horseback riding, and even cross-country skiing in winter. Visitors marvel at formal rhododendron plantings, as well as mountain laurel, serviceberry, hemlock, white pines, many types of oaks and hickory, and transplanted sugar maples. The Cones' love of nature reaches out to visitors today.

Several other natural and cultural museums are accessible from the BRP, including the Museum of North Carolina Minerals (Mile Marker 331), and the Museum of American Frontier Culture in Staunton, Vir-ginia, near the BRP starting point. The Appalachian Cultural Museum at Boone (Appalachian State University) is a delight and a good intro-duction to Appalachian culture for outsiders; there is even a section to amuse and educate young children while their elders tour the main exhibits. With everything from a case filled with literally hundreds of prehistoric stone-cutting devices to a display of the local Civil War conflicts, from several full-sized weaving looms to quilts and knotted bedspreads, from a reproduced general store to displays on how the BRP was built in the twentieth century, the average tourist gets a good introduction to life in the region over a broad time period. When Al Fritsch visited in the summer of 2002, there was a sizable collection of colorful paintings by Joe Miller, a local pharmacist and storyteller. With reference to ecological matters, there is actually a display of an enormous (and unsuccessful) wind-power generator from the 1970s, and the tour guide explained clearly why it didn't work. Surrounding this mountaintop building is a garden containing many of the native plants from the region.[5]

Besides museums and folk centers, there are numerous nature centers for a more complete ecotour. South of Asheville and past the BRP headquarters are some choice viewing lookouts, all with nearby resource centers. Immediately after crossing the beautiful French Broad River, one may enter the North Carolina Arboretum, a 426-acre tract of wooded land with formal gardens and informative labels; numerous trees, shrubs, and flowers; extensive walkways; and a state-of-the-art greenhouse.[6] The well-tended grounds and the variety of plants show that this place is obviously not lacking in financial resources. Furthermore, the arboretum is part of the National Center for Plant Conservation.

Proceeding further south on the BRP along the French Broad River and past scenic Mount Pisgah, one can detour four miles downhill to the Forest Discovery Center at the Cradle of Forestry in America.[7] This property is now part of the Pisgah National Forest, but it was once the first American forestry school, founded by George W. Vanderbilt on his Biltmore Estate. One can take a tour over two miles of hard-surfaced trail, which passes numerous buildings, gardens, and artifacts, including the original schoolhouse of the Forest School. There is ample opportunity to talk with craftspeople, who pursue woodcarving, quilt making, and weaving, and to visit the Center's extensive educational displays on proper forest care and management. According to Al Fritsch, "I found this stop to be the high point of all the places I visited, in part because of the friendliness of the staff and its desire to teach and entertain at the same time."

Quite close to this is the Pisgah Center for Wildlife Education.[8] This center has the theme "Mountain streams, where water and life begin." Though part of National Forest Service property, it is run by the North Carolina Wildlife Resources Commission. The Center seeks to educate the public on both wildlife and water conservation through interior and exterior exhibits. The large fish hatchery is a favorite with children, who enjoy buying handfuls of feed and watching the trout jump to get it. The exterior walkway exhibit has many stations and recorded messages, is accessible to visitors with disabilities, and presents helpful environmental information within a wonderful canopy of vegetation. If time permits, two other nature centers are worth visiting: the Holmes Educational State Forest at Hendersonville run by the North Carolina Forest Service, and the Joyce Kilmer Memorial Forest at Robinsville, North Carolina, a remnant of original Appalachian forest located within the Nantahala National Forest.

Preserving the Blue Ridge Parkway

A pristine forested viewscape is something that must be preserved as much as possible. When development encroaches on that viewscape, the federal government should be able to take all necessary steps to reduce or eliminate it. Consider the growing number of cell-phone towers, a major threat to all viewscapes. The National Park Service is taking aggressive measures to hide these from view along the BRP. One employee said she thought there was one tower within sight, but Al Fritsch was unable to detect it. Keeping the road clear of commercial signs and free of the traces of development will be an ongoing struggle, but with determination the effort can succeed. Some have proposed creating a federal no-development zone that would cover all lands within sight of the BRP.

In order to check the high-altitude forest die-off, the best solution is still to reduce air pollution throughout the nation, especially from the coal-fired power plants to the west and southeast of the BRP. The amount of acid rain has been clearly documented with shocking pH values in the 2.0 range at very high altitudes in wintertime. The sooner the air can be purified, the safer the forests along the BRP route will be. As for new infestation of the balsam wooly adelgid, we can only hope that the up and coming generation of Fraser fir will be able to survive and continue to grow.

Great Smoky Mountains National Park

Appalachia is graced with one of America's most popular national parks, and so it is important for us to consider its ecological wealth and ecotourism potential. Can the nearly ten million visitors who come to the 850-square-mile Great Smoky Mountains National Park (GSMNP) be termed ecotourists? Certainly they come to see and appreciate spectacular mountain scenes. Many learn something about the wildlife and ecology of the region, even if only a few venture beyond the exhibit halls at visitor centers or the scenic observation points. Most want to treat the environment they visit well, and they generally do—there is little litter on the major roads, but that may be in great part due to frequent park cleanup operations. And the park both employs local residents and generates money for the local economy through nearby accommodation, dining, and shops. These sightseers can be counted as ecotourists, depending on what they are trying to get out of their trip and how well they respect the local people and landscape.

The great majority of the visitors come as sightseers and day hikers who never stray far from the Newfound Gap Road. This highway (U.S. Route 441) traverses GSMNP and runs past two visitor centers (Sugarlands near Gatlinburg, Tennessee, on the northwest side and Oconaluftee next to the Cherokee Indian Reservation in western North Carolina on the southeast). A third visitor center, Cades Cove, is approached from the west on U.S. Route 321 from Maryville, Tennessee. Visitors gaze from their cars at turn-offs to enjoy the scenes or set off on a single-day hike along various trails. And, of course, the more active of the ecotourists may bike, especially on the Cades Cove Loop Road. Opportunities also exist for fishing, horseback riding, and backcountry hiking, especially on the Appalachian Trail, which traverses GSMNP on the spine of the Great Smokies.

The Great Smoky Mountains National Park was finally established in 1934, the first national park to be assembled principally from private lands. The Smokies are a picturesque series of wooded peaks more than six thousand feet high; they contain the widest variety of flora and fauna of any temperate forest in the world—over a hundred thousand species. There are 125 species of trees (spruce-fir, basswood, beech, yellow birch, eleven species of oak, five of pine) and an equal number of shrubs, 60 fern and fern-like plants, 280 mosses, 250 species of lichens, over 200 species of birds, 40 reptiles, 80 species of fish, 50 mammals, and countless insects and soil organisms. One can count over a thousand flowering plants during the year, including nine native species of rhododendron. Much of this diversity is due to the great differences in elevation in the growing areas and the existence of a range of microclimates within the park.[9]

In its printed literature and daily presentations, the park strives to be sensitive to the Native American and Appalachian Mountain cultures that were modified or actually displaced by the establishment of the park. Besides exhibits on Native American peoples, visitors also have opportunities to view how the later inhabitants lived in the mountainous areas of the park. The GSMNP has taken pains to preserve aspects of life prior to its existence. Some 115 archaeological sites have been discovered within the park. Six churches, two schools and four gristmills have been preserved, as well as tunnels, rock walls, bridges and fire towers.[10]

Of special interest is the Mountain Farm Museum next to the Oconaluftee Visitor Center. This is a reproduction of a one-time farm in what had been an agriculturally settled valley. It gives a picture of the life of one of the 1,200 families displaced by the creation of the park, with the John E. Davis chestnut log house (built about 1900) as the centerpiece. This and other structures have been moved from other parts of the area and assembled as one farmstead. There are examples of a woodshed, bee gums (homemade beehives), meathouse, chicken house, apple house, cane mill and shed, corn crib, gear shed, barn, blacksmith shop, springhouse as well as gardens, field crops, and fencing. The well-placed descriptive signs are excellent teaching tools.[11]

Of course, one of the most-visited places in Appalachia is Gatlinburg, Tennessee, with its seemingly endless line of chain motels, theme restaurants, and tourist "attractions." Some would argue that Gatlinburg is totally out of place next to the entrance of a national park. There is a good argument for busing visitors into the park from Pigeon Forge or Maryville or Interstate 40 to eliminate the auto congestion. A drive through the main street of Gatlinburg during the midsummer peak tourist season will add converts to the anti-auto voices.

However, this strange gateway town grew up following the Depression, at a time when the park lacked financial resources and the rapidly increasing number of tourists needed places to eat and stay. From the start, park tourist developers have clashed with wilderness proponents, who won with the backing of Arno Cammerer, assistant director of the National Park Service in 1925, and Harold Ickes, FDR's Secretary of the Interior in the 1930s. Was it a mistake to concentrate the tourist areas with their shops and motels so close to GSMNP? While not a perfect world, it is doubtless better to keep Gatlinburg outside the park rather than making GSMNP "a Mecca for tourists," as early boosters openly sought. How to preserve the wilderness while attracting tourists is a challenge with a long history, and nowhere is that more evident than at the GSMNP.

The GSMNP offers visitors many opportunities to learn about the effects of human activity on the environment. No doubt the area has always been affected by humans, something that has been verified through archaeological research. However, the impacts became greater with the arrival of European-origin pioneers following the Revolutionary War and even more with the arrival of the logging companies after the turn of the twentieth century. In fact, about two-thirds of the park's area was logged during this period, with many pioneer farm families abandoning their sparse farm income for employment in these local logging operations. It was the immense devastation to old-growth forests and the subsequent soil erosion resulting from logging that moved concerned citizens to propose setting up the park as an alternative source of income. But GSMNP came and has had its problems along with benefits.

Many visitors, especially youthful ones, have been tempted to feed the unpredictable and sometimes-dangerous native black bears. These had been virtually hunted to extinction, but they have made a comeback within the park. Today, the bear population at GSMNP has climbed to about two thousand. Bears, being opportunistic feeders, can become accustomed to eating garbage and leftover food at campsites. Since such food is more easily found than natural food sources (berries, acorns, grasses, forbs, insects, and meat), behavioral changes occur and the noble black bear becomes a scavenger. In the past, the reasonable solution to keeping bears at a distance from human beings was relocation. More recently, a threatening bear is trapped and then released in the same general location after being tranquilized, marked, and studied. Bears do not like this unpleasant experience and they soon learn to avoid areas inhabited by humans.[12]

The Smokies take their name from the misty atmosphere. The Cherokees called these mountains *shaconage,* meaning "smokelike blue." However, haze from natural evergreen and other vegetative emissions has given way to haze caused by human sources both inside and outside the park boundaries. Lower visibility at scenic sites in summer and in times of high air pollution is addressed frankly in park exhibits and literature, and park research scientists are monitoring the air quality at specific locations in the GSMNP.[13] Only a small fraction of the time is the visibility such that one can see what a visitor of a half century ago would have seen, namely, a distance of 113 miles from the

Newfound Gap observational site. Now the average is 25 miles; in summer, it's only 15 miles. In a 1996 survey, 84 percent of summer visitors said scenic views and 74 percent said clean air were "extremely important."[14] The region's coal-fired power plants, including those of the Tennessee Valley Authority, are largely to blame. Still, the lowly automobile, which brings most of the ten million visitors each year, must have some deleterious effect on the forest ecosystem. Direct observation of air pollution's effects is a meaningful part of real ecotourism.

Only part of the problem is generated within the GSMNP boundaries. Some air pollutants like sulfates and other air pollutants come from fossil fuel–burning power plants and industrial sites hundreds of miles away. These may affect the health of both the human workers and visitors and the plant and animal populations. Research shows that at high elevations the soils, which teem with a wider variety of soil organisms than at any other national park, suffer from advanced nitrogen saturation. This limits the availability of forest nutrients and can harm vegetation and water quality as well. Average acidity of rainfall is ten times higher in the park than is normal rainfall, with pH values as low as 2.0 recorded at higher elevations during part of the growing season.[15]

Trees weakened by acid rain, ozone, and other air pollutants can then succumb to native or exotic stresses and parasites. This is becoming more evident to anyone traveling in the higher Appalachian elevations. Since 1963, the balsam woolly adelgid mentioned above has killed almost all of GSMNP's mature fir trees in the Clingman's Dome area.[16]

Another problem in the GSMNP is exotic plant species, plants not native to the environment brought in through human activity. Sometimes such species then "take over," driving out the native species and upsetting the ecological balance. Several factors have resulted in some 21 percent of the plant volume being non-invasive exotic and 2 percent being invasive exotic.[17] Aggressive exotics include kudzu, mimosa, multiflora rose, bush honeysuckle, Japanese grass, Japanese spirea, tree of heaven, Japanese knotweed, Johnson grass, Norway spruce, periwinkle, mullein, English ivy, and garlic mustard. These spread rapidly due to the favorable climate, rainfall, and differences in elevation. Birds and other wildlife can spread multiflora rose seed (up to one million per plant). Without natural controls, these exotics crowd out the native plants, and some have the ability to cross-pollinate and threaten the genetic integrity of the natives. GSMNP spends thousands of hours each year trying to manage exotics through prescribed burns, cutting, hand pulling, and less desirable herbicide control methods.[18]

Mammals can also invade. The coyote is an invasive species, and it has filled the predator gap in the eastern part of the U.S. during our lifetime. In the Great Smokies the European wild hog, introduced to these parts in 1912, has escaped and has done extensive damage to the forest understory due to its foraging methods. The hogs compete with native wildlife for acorns and hickory nuts, and even devour sala-mander species found only in the Smokies. On the brighter side, the peregrine falcon and river otter have been reintroduced successfully, and more recently the elk has been reintroduced and number nearly a hundred head.

The Great Smoky Mountains National Park is a treasure of which all of us, whether native Appalachians or newcomers, can be proud. During his visit Al Fritsch counted cars from twenty-five states, with 90 percent coming from within a 600-mile radius. Middle-income families find the park a wholesome vacation place with a unique variety of flora and fauna. The National Park Service is striving to maintain this fragile environment for tourists of all sorts—mainstream and ecotourists alike. GSMNP does not need to be established; it exists. The challenge is to maintain what we have. The lack of an entrance fee, the result of a promise to the displaced population, is definitely one of its drawing cards. GSMNP attracts America's rank and file, and it affords everyone a low-cost opportunity for environmental learning and enjoyment.

The Cherokee Indian Reservation

Any worthwhile ecotourist experience requires three components: an enjoyable and educational time for the tourist; benefits for the local people; and enhancement of the surrounding environment. While we have seen other places in the U.S., such as Hawai'i and Alaska, where questionable tourism practices have caused cultural and environmen-tal damage, the Cherokee Nation has taken great pains to create a sustainable tourist experience for literally millions of visitors. And this occurs within the only federally organized Indian reservation in Appa-lachia—so it is truly one of a kind. This approach can serve as a model for other locations during future tourist development in Appalachia.

The sites in and near the town of Cherokee are very enjoyable for travelers, especially in the summer and early autumn seasons. Though visitors come all year to the gambling casinos, we do not include them in this discussion—blackjack players hardly qualify as "tourists" of any description. Many Native American nations, including the Eastern Band of Cherokee, have taken advantage of this window of economic opportunity in an addicted America. It is hard to preach against gambling when the whole American economy hinges on the unpredictable fortunes of the stock exchanges.

Visitors to the reservation bring their whole families for a natural and cultural experience. They come to see the beauty of the wooded mountains and clear streams flowing through the reservation. The Museum of the Cherokee Indians and the Oconaluftee Indian Village, both just outside the town off of U.S. Route 441, are unforgettable experiences.

The Museum tells of a people who were good ecologists. For example, from their homegrown gourds they made purple martin houses to encourage the migrating songbirds to come and stay. Besides gobbling up the mosquitoes and other insects, the martins were possessive and kept away the crows, which could do considerable damage to the hills of "three sisters" (corn, beans, and squash). The Cherokee people were early natural pest-control agents, something they tell as part of their story. While describing their lifeways and appropriate technology, the museum also gives a vivid account of the early treaties and the "Trail of Tears" in the 1830s, when half the population was marched to Oklahoma, many perishing on the way. This interweaving of natural and cultural history is an excellent example of ecotourism.

The multitudes of people who visit Oconaluftee Indian Village see Cherokee culture through the eyes of the Cherokee themselves. The tribe has developed a village that gives a comprehensive picture of what life was like 250 years ago. Again, it is a learning experience for the visitor, and it employs local people in making everything from baskets, spoons, and pottery to dugout canoes and arrowheads, using their skills and traditions. Spectators find the experience fascinating, and realize that it is a wholly authentic Cherokee presentation. Outside economic interests are not dictating the direction of the Cherokee art form or style. The Eastern Band is faithful to their heritage in depicting past stories and rituals, and members earn a respectable livelihood all the while. The Cherokee themselves take part in creating and enacting summer evening performances of an outdoor drama portraying the history of their people entitled "Unto these Hills."

There is obviously some leakage of tourist spending in the local fast-food restaurants and gas stations, which are included in the mix of commercial places dotting the main street of the town of Cherokee. Unfortunately, in that respect it is like the rest of America. But some of the most prominent lodging facilities are locally owned and operated, thanks to the good sense and thrift of the reservation people. A bookstore carries the most recent Native American titles, though the publishing is done outside the area. Profits support the local economy, even if the wholesale cost is obviously leakage. However, due to ownership patterns, the leakage is lower than losses in other places.

The Cherokee have striven to keep their reservation lands intact, areas that are still covered by the forests of years ago. There are no polluting factories, burial of toxic substances, or coal or mineral mining on the land. To make a living without developing the few level places in such mountainous terrain is always a challenge. The local river runs clear, the countryside does not have the litter so often found in other parts of the region, and the forests do not undergo unsustainable logging because they are valued as viewscape and local habitat by the Cherokee. Undoubtedly, the fact there is no airport or major public transportation means that private cars will be arriving in increasing numbers with their exhaust pollutants, congestion, and need for parking areas. Just as in the GSMNP, the private mode of transportation is and will continue to be a problem. Bringing people to Cherokee by bus from a relatively short distance, such as from Asheville (one hour away), would reduce the growing problems of congestion and air pollution.

At several million people a year, the volume of tourism within the Cherokee Reservation is heavy—in fact, it is one of the heaviest on any Native land. Nonetheless, the Cherokee have handled the problems with dignified grace in order to provide a hospitable service for visitors while making a livelihood for themselves. And the reservation is a beautiful place. Some, even Native Americans, may fault one or other aspect of the reservation, but on the whole the Cherokees' practices can be a good model for future Appalachian ecotourism. A select few may go elsewhere for hard-core thrills like white-water rafting, but some places must serve as beginning lessons for the tourist crowds. Just as the Cherokees offered a welcome and performed services for early white settlers, so do they offer much to their guests today.

Ecotouring Today

This enjoyable five-day trip shows that ecotourism in Appalachia is not just a future possibility; it is an option for real-life travelers today. Though the name is not commonly applied, all the criteria for ecotourism were met in our tour: an enjoyable experience of nature, an educational component, low impact on the environment, and benefits for the local community. The only thing that's missing is the label—and the awareness that this label actually does fit experiences that are now available.

Raising visitors' awareness of the ecological treasures of Appalachia could be the first step in the development of a true ecotourism industry here. To begin developing ecotourism, what Appalachia needs is not so much new attractions and facilities as a new outlook that highlights the region's remarkable ecology and culture, and more information for travelers to help them learn about and enjoy their destination.

For now, visitors have many opportunities for environmental education, but perhaps they would benefit from contacting public agencies that can provide information for environmentally oriented vacation tours. A special focus on a single area—forests, waterways, birds, wildlife, mammals—may be helpful and make acquiring background literature worthwhile. These tours can be more than just observing and learning about natural environments, and they can also include ecological problems associated with human impacts on the environment, such as invasive species, air pollution problems, congestion at frequented place areas, and viewscape damage by development. Advice from local environmental groups would be very helpful. An organization covering portions of the tour just discussed is the Long Branch Environmental Education Center at Leicester, North Carolina, which has an informative website.[19]

We hope that our recommendations are neither too overwhelming nor too general. While we have discussed a number of federal, state, and local regulations that need to be instituted or enforced, we have also sought to honor the ingenuity of our Appalachian people in working out solutions that are right for them. It is the citizens in each local area who must shape their own destinies through community action. Outside interests must not be allowed to control the future of tourism here, though they may be invited to lend their expertise in implementing the community's decisions. What works best in one part of the region may be less successful in others. This is our message: If local folks take control of tourism development, Appalachia can remain environmentally healthy in a more prosperous future—while serving as a model for other regions in the development of true ecotourism.[20]

CHAPTER 10

Beyond Ecotourism

Transforming Travel

Throughout this book, we have seen how the current concept of ecotourism, though in some ways a promising idea, has serious drawbacks and limitations. It is inherently elitist, and because it is viewed as a specialized form of travel, it will only make up a limited segment of the commercial tourism market, with a correspondingly limited impact on the environment. We can't count on it to save the global ecology, rescue the depressed economy of a particular community, or even transform the environmental consciousness of individual travelers. Instead, we must consciously work towards changing the shape and content of all travel—jungle treks and weekend car trips, big city tours and wilderness travel. Here are our six recommendations for "re-visioning" travel in the future.

All Tourism Must Be Green

As we enter the twenty-first century, it is clear that consideration of the environmental impacts of every aspect of our daily life is vital to the health of the planet. Our recreation and travel are no exception. For a just and sustainable future, to preserve resources and share them equitably around the globe, so-called "green travel" as a separate category must disappear, and all travel must become green. Because ecotourism will never be more than a small section of the growing total market, making mass tourism more environmentally sound will in the long run have a far greater impact on our planet than any amount of whale watching or rainforest volunteer work.

One aspect of this is lessening the environmental impact of travel. The necessary measures should sound familiar, because they are similar to those in other areas of life. Transportation for travel must shift away from wasteful consumption of fossil fuels, such as those currently used in long-distance air travel. We need to emphasize more energy-efficient forms of travel that use renewable sources of energy and use fossil fuels more sparingly. The frequency and distance of pleasure travel need to be rethought. In the U.S., developing an efficient and convenient passenger rail system should be a top priority, along with greatly increased fuel efficiency in cars, and the eventual development of vehicles powered by renewable sources of energy.

Hotels, resorts, cruise ships, and all tourist facilities need to downscale their consumption of water, energy, and other resources drastically. Why is it seen as necessary for people away from home to live an absurdly luxurious lifestyle that is alien to them during the other weeks of the year? We have seen that cruise ship passengers generate twice as much solid waste daily on board the ship as they do at home. And how many people change their bedsheets every single day at home, or require imported cut flowers in their bathrooms?

Some major hotel chains have begun programs to make their accommodations more "environmentally friendly," through such measures as recycling beverage containers, installing water-conserving shower heads, and encouraging guests to reuse towels and linens during their stay rather than sending them to the laundry. All of these are praiseworthy, of course. But, not coincidentally, they also reduce costs for the hotel owners, while allowing them to trumpet to the world what good global citizens they are. A real commitment to sound environmental practice would require much more sweeping measures—including ones that do not necessarily benefit the corporate bottom line or lend themselves to brochure publicity. (For instance, it's hard to imagine resorts on Caribbean islands boasting that they have finally installed a proper sewage treatment system after decades of operation—a measure that is badly needed in many locations.)

To help travelers compare the effects of tourism choices, ecological impacts should be included in tourist literature, in much the same way that ingredients for processed foods must now be listed on packages and the energy efficiency of new refrigerators is rated on stickers. This will make travelers aware of the energy expended in flying to the destination and back, along with major outlays of resources in the country during an average tourist visit. All human activities should be considered on the basis of what the average tourist would do—namely, surface travel, lodging, food, and resource expenditures at typical resort or recreational locations (ski lodges, desert resorts, and so on)'. Of course, this is more easily calculated for a tour package than for individual travel, but guidelines could nonetheless be provided. The analysis could be made by outside consultants, which could sell the information to airlines, travel agencies, or tourism bureaus. As part of interstate commerce, tourism is open to such regulation.

Airlines, travel agencies, and hotel chains would be required to distribute such information to their customers, which could be combined with facts on the environmental treasures of the destination area. This could also describe the unique species that may be found there, along with any threatened or endangered species. In addition, rules for environmentally sound conduct could be presented on airplanes and cruise ships, in the same fashion as the reminders of safety regulations.

Learning about the environment should be an integral component of all travel, in the same way that few people today travel without finding out at least a little about the history and people of the place they visit. There are several simple ways this environmental learning could be done. A seemingly inescapable part of travel is waiting—in airport lounges, in passport lines, at bus stops. Waiting places could profit by having an "eco-corner," an area with displays and literature about the local environment and a comfortable place to sit and read. These materials and displays should illustrate the natural beauty of the destination. A number of airports already have informational displays on local endangered species and warn tourists about products containing them. In Anchorage, Alaska, air travelers have enjoyed exhibits on Alaska's wildlife.

Another useful format is environmental signage and displays at tourist sites. All types of tourists could profit from this, including those who were not specifically drawn there by natural attractions. Signs like these can be placed in parks, rest stops, information areas, museums, roadside markers, festivals, fairs, and shopping malls. Any place we visit, for whatever reason, has its ecological component, and in becoming acquainted with it, tourists broaden their perspective. Possible topics for eco-corners and signs include geographic overviews, native plants and animals, local ecosystems, geology, land use, historic highlights, topographic maps, scenic vistas, and a host of others.

An excellent example has been implemented at the Bergamo Center near Dayton, Ohio. In their descriptive corner, color photos have been displayed of a local scene, one picture for each month of the year. The seasonal variations are striking.

In sensitive natural areas that could be damaged by a large number of tourists, signage can play a crucial rule. Where an area is closed off to visitors, information should be given as to why this has been done— for example, stating that since this is a fragile area, walkways and platforms have been installed, and that visitors will be allowed to look at but not enter the fragile area. In this way, the story of the old growth forest or the natural restored wetlands is highlighted and considered with pride. This gives the tourist a sense of reverence and respect for the land, rather than making it forbidden fruit to be tasted when no one is looking.

Furthermore, signage can warn and inform about environmental problems. Most of us are familiar with beach alerts during the summer swimming season. Some waterways have so many bacteria of a harmful nature that the beaches are closed, and "No Swimming" signs appear at some of the old favorite swimming holes. This should be extended to other situations, such as signs warning that overuse of parks may necessitate their closure when they reach their carrying capacity.

All of these widely varied steps will help to make the environment an integral consideration and permanent component in all travel—not merely a marketing lure or a passing fad.

Tourism Growth Needs to Be Regulated

Many promoters of tourism bridle at the thought of added regulation. Drivers are already required to have licenses, motels have to meet safety regulations, commercial establishments have reams of forms and requirements from governmental agencies, and so on. Why would anyone say that tourist facilities need more regulation, especially since some are completely in private hands?

Our response is that if all tourism has an ecological aspect, and that component involves our global commons (air, water, and land), then places impacted by tourism should be subject to regulation for our common good and for the good of the Earth itself. We cannot turn the environment into a commodity for the wealthy to enjoy and destroy.

As we argued above, if communities are to benefit from welcoming visitors, they must take the lead in decision-making and determine what kind of tourism they wish to develop. But broader oversight and regulation are needed to ensure that decisions made by one community are not detrimental to the wider society or to the environment. For example, a single town on a big lake should not be permitted to build a speedboating marina that would inflict uncontrolled noise on neighboring towns and destroy the habitat of shore birds.

> I was talking with one promoter of private Appalachian fishing lakes about regulation. He took offense and seemed disconcerted and even a bit hostile. However, he soon admitted that some kinds of regulation could have salutary effects. He agreed that exotic fish should be prohibited, controlling noise could be beneficial, and regulations on truth in advertising would help the entire industry. Keeping the lakes healthy is likewise necessary for the continued health of the tourist industry.
>
> —Al Fritsch

Some recreational activities simply cannot be tolerated because of their effect on people (e.g., the excessive noise and danger from Jet Skis) or the environment itself (e.g., cross-country ORVs). In Appendix 2, we rank ninety-nine recreational activities by their degree of "greenness." Some, such as rock climbing with spikes, need to be highly restricted or even banned. Others can be allowed on a limited basis (e.g., horseback riding in dry times of year only) or temporarily banned to allow the ecosystem to rebound from human impact. Some, such as hunting and mountain biking, will need to be confined to carefully determined times and places. Substitutes can also be developed. For example, the urge to hunt endangered species could be satisfied by allowing tourists (for a high fee) to fire dart guns at animals needing vaccination, or anesthesia for tagging or transfer.[1]

Some land is simply too fragile to sustain the impact of people in even a limited degree, or the land may be located in places where the enforcement of regulations is not practical. For example, a high pla-teau in the Rocky Mountain National Park still has footprints made many years before, which are pointed out to visitors. In such places, the impact of even a single visitor remains for great lengths of time.

One way to safeguard such fragile areas is to put them off-limits to the visitor. Platforms may suffice if access roads and disturbances have already occurred. But the same argument for limiting access roads to forests extends to fragile areas. The development follows the road; so does the tourist trade. Limiting tourists from such areas is perhaps the most positive thing that can be done, ecologically speaking. Again, it would be good to see the fragile area close-up in a video room, where good photography has been used to capture the experience without subjecting the fragile area to the impact of every tourist who wants to see it.

Even seemingly innocuous activities can have negative effects in a particular environment. For example, few of us consider whether walking on trails will have an impact on the birds nearby. Yet Mary Hobbs reports that research done at Colorado State University on the effects of recreational trails found that certain bird populations were affected by the presence of hiking trails. Not only were more species found where no trails existed, but the number of individual birds also increased relative to the distance from the trails. In addition, nest sur-vival—the successful fledging of young birds—also increased farther from hiking trails.[2]

If the wildlife on a site is harmed by tourist intrusion, then sight-seers should be barred from the area for some part of the year, or from part of the area on a permanent basis. This means that people must not use four-wheel drive vehicles to approach for photography, and it may even mean that airplanes are not allowed to fly nearby either. In these situations, parks can be developed on some part of the land where spe-cies that are less sensitive could be presented in small numbers for people to view—a sort of theme park within a larger game preserve. An infor-mation center could present videos of the more sensitive species.

The land and the people who live on it are connected in a bond of stability, where people identify with their land. Environmental damage through any form of exploitation will weaken the bonding of that community unless extraordinary steps are taken. The Amish are able to retain a stability through the lack of use of rapid vehicles for travel—this ensures their community bonding. However, they are the first to testify that too many tourists observing their way of life have an impact that leads to a decline in the quality of that life. Communities everywhere must have the option of declaring themselves out-of-bounds for tourists.

Touring the Commons: Rediscover Local and Regional Travel

Most of us have had the experience of discovering some new aspect or attraction of our hometown for the first time while showing it to out-of-town guests. The things we take for granted close to home may be the very things that travelers cross a continent to see. How often do you make a detour to drive down a nearby country road marked as "scenic" on your state's official highway map, or visit a nearby tourist attraction? Appalachia abounds with historic and scenic attractions, such as Cumberland Gap National Historic Park, Great Smoky Mountains National Park, and countless state and local wildlife areas. And yet, as in other regions of the U.S., the majority of the cars in the parking lots there have license plates from out of state.

A real appreciation of the earth and its living systems begins close to the place we call home. If we don t know and love our own neighborhood, how can we cherish the faraway places that are home to others? We need to begin by getting intimate with the environment we ourselves live in—by touring the commons.

Historically, the term "commons" refers to property that is owned by the community as a whole, or not owned by anyone in particular, such as a pasture where all families could graze their cattle together. Commons has different meanings in various contexts, but here it refers to the natural world and its unclaimed resources, i.e., the air and upper atmosphere, outer space, the ocean, the frozen tundra and barren deserts, the wildlife and birds, the public lands and rivers, and the general resources found deep underground not yet claimed by some mining company.

Natural commons also means the things that are not exotic and exclusive but can be shared in some fashion by everyone to some degree. In this sense, a view that is accessible by large crowds is part of the commons. While some would like to emphasize the uniqueness of all beings and, especially, certain places and events, others prefer to speak of individuality in everything and thus take pride in defense of, and in sharing, the commons in a nonconsumptive, democratic, and participatory manner.

"Exotic" is in the eye of the beholder. To many of us, Central America or Nepal or even such areas of the U.S. as the Arctic region of Alaska or the islands of Hawai'i rank as exotic destinations, but there is much to see closer to home. Geographer Gene Wilhelm conducts a series of ecotours each year focusing on the rich diversity in destinations ranging from New Zealand to Maine. He has worked as a keen observer of parts of Appalachia (Virginia) and has a mastery of immense amounts of natural history, the flora and fauna of specific places. As a dedicated environmentalist, he values the global commons not as exotic but as the treasured property of all, worth sharing in a nonconsumptive manner.

Just as common resources are used to make public education available to all students for the benefit of society as a whole, touring our commons should be a component of every child's education. An understanding of our natural environment and of historic and cultural sites is central to true education, and firsthand experience of the natural and cultural wonders of our commons is the right of all children. This approach takes the elitism and status-seeking out of ecotouring and makes it an educational resource on the same plane as access to public library books or to the Internet.

It is important to combat the notion that those who go to "exotic" distant places are the most environmentally aware. In fact, the opposite might be the case, especially when the long-distance traveler is not sensitive to the amount of resources that was expended in the trip itself and in creating the infrastructure needed by travelers. Some expenditures of nonrenewable resources are socially necessary, but these need to be more evenly distributed within the whole of the society in which we live. Education consumes resources in warming buildings and in providing study materials—to this we would add travel as an integral part of education.

This is practiced on a small scale in many places already. For example, in California, each year elementary school students take trips to the Spanish Missions and other historic sites within the state to get to know and appreciate their heritage. In a broader sense, our country can become a giant classroom to teach people of all ages about the natural and man-made wonders around us. Devoting time and energy to making such travels available—especially within the local area—is as important as investing in books and school buildings.

> When I was young the Kentucky Game Conservation Club hosted middle school and high school students on an island in Dale Hollow Lake, a recently dammed facility on the Tennessee border. The camp and the food were quite simple in every sense, but the good-hearted state officials were deeply committed to giving us a sense of how to fish and hunt properly as well as basics in conservation of our Kentucky resources. It was really my first beginnings at environmental work in 1948, long before a green consciousness had arisen in our land. For most of us it was our first trip to a distant part of the state and right across the border into a second state at that. It was the beginning of tourism and yet it had an educational purpose.
>
> —Al Fritsch

An excellent current example is the Society for the Protection of Nature in Israel (SPNI), which has come close to fulfilling the ideal of tourism that has general appeal and yet is strictly regulated. The program involves over two dozen camps for seventh- and eighth-grade students from all parts of Israel. Through supervised education they have an opportunity to learn about nature and get a taste of the fragile nature of the ecology of their country. The group provides shared experiences for young people of all the nation's religions (Jews, Christians, and Muslims), and from all economic backgrounds. It gives this experience with a sense of reflection and concern for the environment.

Such educational endeavors can be designed and targeted to specific groups. A range of people from senior citizens to youths could benefit from specialized ecotouring. The Elderhostel program caters to retirees who wish to have noncredit courses in a variety of specialties involving touring, such as visiting cultural sites and museums and attending a formal educational program with lectures. People of a broad range of ages can participate in programs offering rugged experiences in nature, on the order of Naturequest, Outward Bound, or scouting programs for youth. Enrichment programs could enable inner-city children to travel to other parts of the country. Vision Quest programs combine guided spiritual reflection with experiences in nature.

Our natural commons is a vast and inexhaustible source of wonder—for those who know how to see it. Biologists tell fascinating stories about colonies of termites and ants and how insects and the microorganisms in the soil live and thrive. That upper one inch of humus, the "skin" of the Earth, contains well over 99 percent of all living organisms and is the richest and most unnoticed commons that we share. To tread upon it without ever stopping to examine it closely is a typical human mistake. Just touring our native place with an enlightened eye can be a lifetime's project.

Developing New Forms of Tourism

There are many ways we can benefit from seeing another place, many ways that travel can enrich our lives. Developing a wider array of possibilities for tourism will benefit not only travelers themselves, but also society as a whole and the environment we travel through.

Educational and Research Travel

Liberal arts students in college consider immersing themselves in another culture an important form of learning. They improve their French, German, Spanish, or other languages through actual touring and using the language in the foreign native environment. Since academic educational expenses are so very high in America, usually time spent traveling is no more costly than time spent in formal academic pursuits; thus the practice is easily justified. American educational activities may involve going to Europe or elsewhere as part of a particular course, or it may be a "junior year abroad" for college students. There is a wide variety of formats, for the students may travel abroad while matriculating in an American school; they may go to a foreign school to take advantage of the lower tuition; they may study at the overseas campus of an American college; or they may take off a year on their own, regarding it as a period of broadening their perspective through travel. An increasing number of students are opting to get their degrees in neighboring Canada and Mexico, finding educational prospects and prices inviting.

To date, Appalachia has not been a common destination for cultural-immersion study, though some research does take place at various locations in the region. Universities from countries of the Pacific

Rim (Korea and Japan) have several centers in Appalachia where their students can receive an American immersion experience.

Another form of educational travel is research tours abroad and at home, which give a chance to go beyond the usual "sights" and involve visits to places where research projects are occurring. Besides archaeological digs, programs are as diverse as scientific marine studies, tropical disease research, or installing computer systems at foreign institutions. Many participants are paid for their efforts, thus permitting touring at low cost, though they take less time than purely educational ventures. Research touring is also available in parts of the United States. These might be in places at some distance from where the person normally resides or goes to school. Summer research projects take young people to other parts of the country as well as the rest of the world, and the experience is enriching for participants, while also increasing the scientific body of knowledge.

An excellent example of overseas study with an environmental focus is offered by the Kentucky Institute for International Studies, located at Murray State University. This consortium of colleges and universities has programs in over twenty countries, ranging from a single summer month to an entire semester. Among their offerings are undergraduate and graduate programs in the rainforests of Costa Rica and Ecuador, and an environmental program in Austria for teachers.

The wilderness itself can be a uniquely valuable classroom for environmental or academic groups. Wilderness education programs include field study trips, where students have opportunities to hone critical thinking skills. An instructor accompanies the class, giving lectures and leading discussion of writings by naturalists. One two-month program features four 10- to 12-day backpacking trips, which include map reading and finding routes for travel, observing flora and fauna, and discussing wilderness policy.[3]

Social Justice Education

One form of educational tourism that has been quite common in Appalachia is social justice education in which participants learn about and take action on issues in the host region. Appalachia has been literally overrun by volunteers from high schools, colleges, and churches in recent years. Most come to do things for the local people, and they regard the host communities as opportunities for experience and for charitable giving. For two decades, Becky and Bobby Simpson and family have run a nonprofit organization called Cranks Creek Survival Center, in Harlan County, Kentucky. Houses in that county and across the border in Virginia have been built, rebuilt, or repaired. The Center has hosted youths and their chaperons for varying lengths of time and, in recent years, has increased the number of volunteer visitors to about a thousand a year. It is a noble undertaking, with the hosts furnishing a dormitory and eating place and the visitors bringing tools, food, and even building materials or money to purchase the materials.

Another example is AMERC, the Appalachian Ministries Educational Resource Center. This ecumenical operation located in Berea, Kentucky, has conducted educational tours for seminarians, seminary faculty, and church workers for the past two decades. Much hard work and planning has gone into organizing these academic winter break and June sessions. The guides are generally very dedicated people who want to pack as much as possible into these tours of the region. It is a difficult assignment because the people coming have a short time to jell as a group, adjust to the region, learn something somewhat alien to them, and take back this experience in such a manner that they get academic credit for it. Much depends on the seminary students' commitment to rural ministry and their openness to what lies in store.

AMERC focuses on the Appalachian experience, but that can have so many different interpretations. The guide or educational team is crucial in its organization of the program and interaction with the tourists/learners. The AMERC program is educational in scope, not a volunteer program to provide a little work in exchange for the experience. However, the relationship of tourist and host remains ambiguous, with few wanting to concede to the other party an intellectual superiority. Balancing the welfare of the visitor, the adequate treatment of the host, and the proper amount of information to process is often quite difficult to achieve.

All travel can be beneficial and educational if it is properly planned and the experience properly processed. The same is true of those who come to Appalachia for social justice experiences. The ultimate aim is clearly good. But if local guides try to impose some other agenda on the visitors and/or host organizations, the whole experience may be distorted and fail to convey the situation accurately. And if visitors are only passive spectators, their learning is necessarily incomplete. Making the most of the experience requires a commitment to action.

Roots Tourism

In the autumn of 2002, Al Fritsch went to France and Germany with his brother and sister-in-law to explore their family roots. They went both to the border village of Damback in Alsace (Al's paternal roots) and ten kilometers away to Schönau in the Pfalz region of Germany. The forested, hilly terrain is very similar to that of Central Appalachia. Both areas are noted for tourism. Alsace has its much-traveled "Route du vin" and the harvesting of grapes each autumn, and hundreds of hikers walk in the woods and gather mushrooms in Germany. The experience gives him hope for what Appalachia could become. Lodging, restaurants, and tourist activities are for the most part operated by local people. Few tourists arrive by air, most being domestic or from neighboring countries. And the incredibly beautiful countryside shows few marks of environmental degradation.

An interest in ethnic roots can take two forms. Some travelers want to answer questions about where their ancestors came from, lived, or are buried. Others have a more general interest in the ethnic roots of groups who may or may not be related, such as travelers interested in African American culture or the cultures of various Native American nations.

Searching for one's family roots in "the old country" is like a pilgrimage or an investigative trip; it can bring a deeper understanding of who one is, and even of why ancestors left and migrated elsewhere. Understanding why they emigrated broadens our perspective of people who are not immediate family and yet are part of our lives in some ways. This quest for roots may involve considerable travel during vacation time; it can be a satisfying experience, though too serious to be mere entertainment. Searching for roots has become quite popular in recent years, due to easier access to court records and the development of Internet tools. Many people are fascinated with the project of tracing genealogy and family history. As these family histories expand with information, interesting names and places, the enthusiast wants to know more and more. Cheaper air travel and rising incomes have made a personal quest for those roots possible for many. When the opportunity presents itself, the individual or family decides that it's time to return and visit the old home place. The descendants may no longer speak the original family language, creating some hurdles. But most travelers in search of their personal heritage are able to find hosts in the original home who can lower the barriers.

There are many Americans in distant places who regard Appalachia as home, and the Appalachian culture as a distinct "ethnic group." So the idea of "roots travel" is also very relevant to Appalachia. Returning to one's roots within Appalachia is easier than going overseas. Much of the travel to Appalachia will be by interstate highway and does not require passports or currency exchange. However, one should prepare for differences, for the culture of the region has a subtle character well worth savoring and which requires some sensitivity.

Appalachia invites its millions of sons and daughters and their descendants to return, visit, linger, and maybe even resettle. Searching out the old family cemeteries and sprucing them up can be a worthwhile family activity. The region's ethnic enclaves still have their own celebrations, which can prove entertaining and educational, especially for visitors who share the roots of these pioneers and settlers. The native foods, music, and customs tell us much about the great melting pot that now makes up the "American."

The Cherokee people who managed to escape the mass deportation to Oklahoma of the 1830s have remained visible in western North Carolina. This is perhaps the best-known Native American site in the Appalachian region, though other tribes have some presence, especially in the outer fringes of the region. Due to its close proximity to the Great Smoky Mountains National Park with its millions of visitors, the town of Cherokee, North Carolina, has been altered from its original appearance, though it does maintain a flavor of Native American culture. Demonstrations, crafts, and other attractions of all sorts are available. Some of the other sites of the Cherokee Nation, such as those in eastern Tennessee and Georgia, are now open for touring.

The white settlers of Central and Southern Appalachia were generally descendants of migrants from the British Isles who came to America via the Virginia and Carolina coastal ports. Due to poverty and overcrowding, the families later crossed the mountains in hopes of a better life. Northern Appalachia, which has a rather defined boundary across the upper third of West Virginia, is more Germanic than British. People of Scottish descent have retained their Highland Games in parts of the region, including North Carolina, Georgia, Kentucky, and Pennsylvania. These are major yearly festivals and perhaps the best-known ethnic events in many parts of the region.

With rare exceptions, the eastern and southern Europeans who migrated to Appalachia were ethnically scattered, poor, and oppressed. Many moved on as soon as better opportunities arose in other parts of America. Generally, these immigrants arrived at a particular coal mine in small numbers, over time transferring to larger colonies of their countrymen, thus depleting the scattered clusters of Italians, Hungarians, Poles, and others. These groups developed only a handful of local customs, such as the return of the Italians each year to the cemetery at Jellico, Tennessee. A few groups retained some connection with the motherland, such as the Swiss-Americans in East Bernstadt, Swiss Colony, and Ottenheim, Kentucky; some have returned to Europe and some musicians have come from Europe to the respective colonies.

Central Appalachia has traditionally had few African American residents, except in some coal mining towns. When looking at county racial statistics in Appalachian states (Virginia, Kentucky, Tennessee, and North Carolina), one generally finds the lowest percentage of African Americans in the mountain counties. Few of these groups have ethnic celebrations.

Travel in search of one's roots can be quite satisfying, and it is an educational opportunity for entire families, even for those members who do not travel. Such travel is generally on an individual basis, making it possible to follow a very specific itinerary; the trip may require the researcher to enlist local resources to help find graveyards or family home places and thus is an opportunity to develop connections. It can bring back healing memories. On the negative side, revisiting the past may prove quite a traumatic experience for elderly members of a family. Mindful planning is essential.

Agritourism

Which is a more meaningful form of ecotourism: teaching about the resplendent quetzal in the Costa Rican cloud-forest or helping children milk a Holstein cow?

This is the question posed by David Moon in a thoughtful article on environmental education. Though most of us would be more inclined to favor the foreign venture, Moon has personally done both, and he opts in favor of the cow. The sheer mass of the cow, the unpredictable tail rising and the warm teat all are fascinating to the nonrural visitor. At Stonewall Farm in New Hampshire, visitors have direct contact with living creatures and learn the facts behind the milk that they all have tasted for most of their lives. Such farm-based educational centers are now scattered across the U.S.[4]

A growing number of activists believe that agritourism is an ideal way to save family farms by enticing tourists, especially parents and children, to come and experience farm life, and pet and observe farm animals firsthand. For example, an article in *Back Home* magazine describes Ioka Valley Farm in Hancock, Massachusetts, and its guests as they make maple syrup. Some twenty-five miles away is the Hale farmstead, with a house built about 1703, catering to tourists at their bed-and-breakfast. Another nearby farm supplies apples and pumpkins to the B & B and makes homemade doughnuts and other goodies at their bakery. Their orchard supports three farm families. Such New England farms are part of a network that promotes a low-cost, no-tax way of supporting family farms. Massachusetts has an active agritourism program, with highway signs, a farm directory, a website (massgrown.org), a calendar, conferences, and farm tours.[5]

Not all farming is fun and games. In fact, serious agriculture is a difficult occupation requiring planning and long hours of work. Agritourism may be something like playing soldier in Civil War reenactments. Both lack the major ingredient—the sweat in one case, and the blood in the other. The unfortunate fact is that farming is a somewhat risky occupation, and if the visitor is not made aware of this, the experience is a poor imitation of the real thing. Those who actually make a living farming or orcharding know that a flood of people inundating their territory can spell disaster to the crops. For that reason, rules and restrictions are needed, including limits on areas of the farm visited, restricted visiting times, and places where crops can be picked. And all of this has to be done in a manner that won't offend the customers.

But well-planned agritourism can be immensely beneficial for both farmers and visitors. The time is right for different state agriculture departments to work together with county extension agencies and tourism bureaus to promote agritourism within their respective boundaries, and to work with neighboring states for coordinated tours of regional farmland. Free publicity in newspapers is one of the best advertisements. Flyers can go to schools, local libraries, market bulletin boards, and civic centers in the local and more distant towns, both in the state and beyond. Farms participating in agritourism in Massachusetts have received visitors from New York and Connecticut as well. Individual sites can offer their own special events or coordinate them with festivals in the vicinity. The list of possible specialties is endless, from making fresh cider to husking corn to picking ripe peaches to walking in the fields.

Appalachia has the potential to lead the way in developing these innovative forms of tourism and could provide a model for other regions and nations seeking to transform their own approaches to tourism.

5. Alternatives to Travel: Is This Trip Necessary?

For many of us, the appearance on the horizon of two weeks off from work is our cue to pick up the phone and call the travel agent. A vacation means getting as far away from home as we can possibly afford (or, if our credit card limit permits, farther than we can really afford). This can mean anything from taking the kids for an exhausting week at Disney World to a safari in South Africa. But how many of us have thought through this impulse to get away?

In its most fundamental meaning, a vacation is a set-aside period of time that differs from our daily routine and refreshes us. The actual forms this can take are limited only by our imaginations. Vacations can be long or short, at home or away, alone or with others, active or tranquil—and can include a wide range of activities. Yet few of us have ever contemplated a vacation that does not include travel.

Thanks to the travel industry, most of our annual breaks are centered on going to a faraway place, which we hope will entertain and refresh us. But we should ask ourselves whether this is the only, or even the best, way to fulfill these hopes. For stressed-out workers, does battling highway congestion or hauling heavy bags through a series of jam-packed airports really increase our well-being? For nature lovers, is a pricey trip to a national park on the other side of the country that much better than a relaxed camping sojourn in a state park close to home?

It's time to examine our motivations for traveling, and to give serious consideration to alternative ways of using our annual breaks. Do we have a reason for traveling to a destination—to learn, experience, or take part in some activity that can be done only in that specific place? For example, are we fascinated by Civil War battlefields? Do we want to see the manatees of Florida's rivers and springs in their natural homes? Or do we just want to relax in a pleasant place, surrounded by family or friends—or do something totally different from the usual daily grind? Is there another, and possibly better, way to fulfill those wishes besides travel?

There are a number of alternatives to a traveling vacation. People can relax and renew themselves at home, or close to home, by doing volunteer work, taking an educational workshop or course, or undertaking a spiritual retreat. Another possibility is a house-swap with friends or family. City dwellers might enjoy a week or two closer to nature in the country, while rural people might like to take advantage of the cultural opportunities of an urban area. Despite the blandishments of the travel industry, an enjoyable vacation need not involve spending large amounts of travel time, resources, or cash.

In our present-day economy in North America, virtually all long-distance travel involves consumption of large amounts of nonrenewable fossil fuels. For a green future, we need to rethink the frequency of travel. Local travel is obviously the greenest of all and should be undertaken as often as desired—while expending modest amounts of resources, it puts money into our local communities and increases our understanding of the environment we live in. National touring, though more consumptive of resources, has other benefits, bringing us in touch with the beauty and diversity of our country. This is worthwhile for all, but should be done less frequently. International travel is of greater moment, and should be done with careful consideration and planning, and much more infrequently.

Another suggestion that has been made is to make fewer, but longer, trips. For example, a New Yorker who flies to Guatemala to spend two months studying Spanish and learning about the rainforest will expend the same amount of fossil fuels (and possibly the same amount of cash) as someone who flies to Las Vegas for a weekend of "fun." And which trip will produce more in the way of lasting benefits?

Rather than dividing the annual vacation time into a number of short "getaways," as more and more Americans are doing, it may be more valuable to consolidate available free time for an in-depth type of travel over longer periods. Examining the issue in the light of energy consumption for air travel, the German environmental group BUND has recommended that long-distance travel (i.e., to another continent) should involve a minimum stay of three weeks.[6]

Truly green travelers should examine their motivations for trips they are contemplating and consider whether there may be alternative ways to attain the same ends while consuming fewer resources. Though travel can convey many benefits and enrich us immeasurably, the travel industry has largely brainwashed us into believing that "getting away" is the only thing to do when we want to relax during our days away from work. We need to be clear about our purpose in every trip and plan it carefully to maximize what we get out of it.

It is also useful to consider travel within the broader perspective of all our personal recreational choices. Traveling vacations are just one of the ways that we relax and refresh ourselves. Recreation may be done at home or nearby, or it may be done through travel, and differences in resource use can be vast. The recreation one chooses depends on numerous factors: age (mud pies or shuffleboard), economic status (yachting or checkers), talents of one's peers or parents (golf or tennis), physical ability and endurance (rock climbing or strolling in the countryside), residential location (sledding or surfing), or time and energy (reading or jogging). Where one undertakes recreation also depends on many factors: proximity to children or parents, the time available for travel, and financial resources.

Recreation choices may be affected by changing stages of life. These changes may be welcome or they may be dictated by other circumstances, including body health, physical stamina, location, age, or time constraints. The average person of a given background does not have the same recreational activities in Alaska as in Florida. People generally shift their major recreational activity several times in a lifetime, depending on the factors already listed, though some few pride themselves on continuing practices begun many years before, e.g. jogging far past middle age or going on annual fishing expeditions with the same group of friends.

So often recreation has more to do with associations and environment than with a inherent love of the activity itself. People within the culture of recreation tend to change the mix of their recreational spectrum year by year to fit their changing circumstances and changing friends. If some activity is too costly, too hard on the physique, or too time-consuming, people move to less demanding alternatives while remaining within the cultural framework in which they find themselves. They are often drawn to reconsider existing activities and are influenced by friends or relatives to change to a more appropriate alternative.

In all of our life choices, we need to consider the environmental effects of our actions. The truly green traveler will look at the entire spectrum of his or her leisure choices and at the resources they use and the ways in which they affect the environment. Benign recreation involves minimal use of resources in getting to the site, proper safety equipment for the execution of the activity, the lowest possible impact on the environment, and maximum relaxation and well-being without harming the human body or other people, plants, or animals. Moderate-impact recreation includes a reasonable expenditure of resources for travel to and from the site, upkeep of a facility used by a reasonable number of people, and moderate heating and cooling of the facility. Heavy-impact recreation involves the operation of fuel- and resource-intensive motor vehicles, exotic and distant travel, high maintenance and operation costs, high-risk health and safety factors, and severe environmental damage resulting from the recreation activity.

Some recreational activities are far greener than others—that is, they consume fewer resources and cause less pollution. Choosing activities with ecology in mind can be quite complicated, because a pursuit that is normally quite benign, such as bird watching, can also involve extensive travel to an exotic place. In fact, the birder may have a minimal impact in the actual recreational activity and demonstrate great concern for the environment of the valued species, and yet consume vast amounts of fuel going to New Zealand or the African rainforest for the expedition. Thus the activity, which is inherently green, takes place in a framework that is decidedly not green. From an ecological standpoint, some forms of recreation are quite wholesome; others are threatening and risky to the health and safety of both participants and the natural world. Some use very little equipment, have low travel costs, and consume little nonrenewable energy; others put heavy demands on the Earth's limited resources.

The recreation seeker may have a right to entertainment, but not at the expense of the Earth or its people. A motorboater's right to access to the common lake does not allow him to race through a children's swimming area or roar around late at night disturbing others. The enthusiast's claim to leisure or reduction of stress is hardly sufficient if that person disturbs the peace. But this negative approach is not enough. We need to promote positive alternatives to intrusive recreation forms or practices. Agencies that promote activities for economic or commercial reasons are biased—and speedboating has more commercial interests than walking or jogging. Society should favor simpler recreational forms, for they have less environmental impact, require less security, less reclamation, less ongoing maintenance, and pay back more in fees from the potential volume of intensive users using less resources. In other words, the same Earth can support many more hikers than it can ORV users. If private and public tourist entities promote low-impact recreational activities, our overall quality of life will improve.

The challenge to the individual ecologically conscious recreation-seeker is to discover and champion low-impact activities, and ultimately to replace resource-intensive activities with environmentally friendly ones. Low-impact activities tend to be local and nonmechanized, and use common or public property with few capital-intensive facilities. Resource-intensive activities involve long distances, short duration travel, complex facilities with a low rate of occupancy, and damaging internal-combustion engines. Appendix 2 is an analysis and ranking of ninety-nine common recreational activities according to their impacts.

Finally, more public awareness is needed of the impact of our recreational choices. Participants in particularly "green" activities could be encouraged to wear green symbols showing their pledge to conserve resources while undertaking leisure activities. These pledges could be printed in different formats such as scouting merit badges, labels at sports stores, caps and jackets for those participating in low-impact recreational events and meets, and stickers for bikes and other low-impact sports equipment. We need to peel away the layers of peer pressure and advertising propaganda and take responsibility for our own recreation choices.

6. Mindful Travel: Making the Most of Every Trip

"If it's Tuesday, this must be Belgium." That was the title of a comedy movie a number of years ago, but the joke still hits home. For too many of us, travel is a lightning series of experiences and impressions that we race through, with no time to process or understand. It's like a restaurant buffet with too many dishes, whose flavors all run together on our plate. In trying to see more and more, we understand less and less and risk becoming jaded.

World Expeditions, an ecofriendly tour operator with an excellent reputation, has among its offerings a trip called "Nepal Panorama," featuring a trek in the Annapurna region, two days of white-water rafting, a wildlife safari in Chitwan National Park, and two days touring Kathmandu—all packed into two weeks. Any one of these experiences would be the trip of a lifetime for many people—and yet here they are, crammed into a breathless marathon of hurry. And the concept is so popular that the trip is offered every week from September to May. Who could possibly take this all in and let it change their understanding and vision of the world?

Contrast this with the old-timey practice of spending one's vacation at the family summer cottage—whether rented or owned. Every year, there is the same enjoyable routine of eager anticipation, of packing and preparations and looking forward to the first dip in the lake or river, the first catch of fish frying in the pan. Over many summers, vacationers of different ages got intimately acquainted with the most promising spots for berry picking, the calls of the different birds, where to find the prettiest wildflowers to give to Mom, the best fishing location for each time of day and type of weather. Even years of summers could not exhaust the pleasures of a single well-loved spot.

Instead of traveling more and more, "consuming" ever more distant places, we should strive to travel better—getting the most from every trip we take, letting each place we visit teach us and change us. Here are some points for more mindful travel.

Planning

One of the key elements for a successful trip is planning. There are many things that, when thought out in advance, make life far easier for the traveler just down the road. This is especially true for infrequent travelers who do not have the experience of the seasoned globetrotter. However, seasoned globetrotters don't always have the most fun, for the anticipation of seeing new and unfamiliar sights is a big part of the fun of travel.

While some people prefer to think through every detail of their trip in advance, others find more joy in keeping options open. Nonetheless, at least the basic outline of the trip needs to be sketched out in advance, in order to prepare for the conditions travelers will encounter. The potential tourist can benefit from advice from better-traveled friends, along with maps, travel literature, and websites for further details. The Internet, especially, can be very attractive to those travelers who enjoy planning every detail beforehand. For example, there are several sites where you can get a detailed driving itinerary by entering your starting point and destination; the site then lists each stretch of road (down to the tenth of a mile) and where and what the next road will be.

A knowledgeable travel agent can also be invaluable for such tasks as working out the most convenient and inexpensive airline routing. But let the buyer beware! Travel agencies make their money by selling things, which is often presented in the guise of pure helpfulness. Many of them focus on the most common destinations, and they dispense some very good tips and suggestions to the inexperienced traveler. But their business is to encourage you to travel. An agency can be to the potential tourist what a realtor is to a potential homeowner. If you know exactly what you want, they can be very helpful in finding it for you—but if you don't know, they can end up selling you something far more elaborate than you need (or can afford). Their goal is to stir up the craving to travel, and then sell you something to satisfy it. Cultures and even environments too easily become high-priced status symbols to add to the collection—one more commodity to consume.

One factor that people too often forget in their travel planning is the human factor. Plan with companions and places in mind. Be honest with yourself: is my desired timetable too hard for my companions to keep up with? Will a lack of language skills make a major difference to our trip? Do the friends we want to see truly have time for us, or will this visit be an imposition? Could bad weather make a major difference in our plans? Are we prepared for the small inconveniences that will undoubtedly arise? Are our expectations of the place reasonable? Are we harming plant and animal life unduly? Do we have the means to cope with the ruggedness of the terrain? Have I broken in the hiking boots and the backpack?

Give some thought, also, to just how much you want to see and do. While on a trip, do you feel obliged to take in every last sight? Might it be better to allow free hours or free days to take off, take a peaceful stroll and see what happens? The unplanned is often both the least stressful and the most rewarding. As you think about the trip, don't overplan so that it becomes like every other overloaded day at home. Allow for the possibility of changing your schedule without remorse, and regard this as part of having control over your life.

A major operation for many travelers is packing. Many people feel insecure about traveling to an unknown place, and they try to calm this anxiety by bringing along every object that they might possibly need, no matter how remote the chances are that it might actually be used. But traveling with an excess of heavy baggage is exhausting, expensive, and unnecessary. Any true necessity that has been forgotten can most likely be purchased at the destination. Besides, is it really necessary to iron your pants or style your hair on vacation? On the other hand, there are also travelers who pack too little and regularly find them- selves missing important items—for example, a sweater for that unex- pectedly cool day in summer. It's not fair to your travel companions to borrow from them constantly, and it's a waste of money and vacation time to go shopping repeatedly for things you should have brought from home.

Experience is the best teacher when it comes to packing, and people who have traveled little can take advantage of the packing lists suggested in guidebooks to the area you will visit. Keep a copy of your own packing list, and after you return home, cross off the items you didn't use, and add any others you wish you had brought. Then leave the list in your bag for the next time you travel.

Learn Before You Go

Knowing the stories behind a place can make all the difference in how you experience it. To someone unfamiliar with history, the area around Antietam Creek in Maryland looks like a pretty piece of rolling farm- land, dotted with woods. A little reading tells you it was the site of the bloodiest day in America's history, a tragic Civil War battlefield where twenty-two thousand soldiers lost their lives.

> When we were little, my sister and I adored *Little House in the Big Woods* and the whole series of children's books on pioneer life by Laura Ingalls Wilder. A couple of summers ago, we took a trip to visit the sites Wilder wrote about. Though some have been modernized into tourist attractions, Plum Creek in western Minnesota hadn't changed a bit. We followed the description in the story down to a little creek, still lined with wild plum trees, and even located the big rock where the heroine used to stand watching the fish. It staggered me. This plain, muddy, flat rock that looked like a million others was the actual place where my heroine stood with her toes in the water!
>
> —Kristin Johannsen

Spend the weeks before your trip investigating what you will see, and how it got to be that way. Find out about the history of a place, the events that happened there. Who lives there? How did they get there? What do they do? How did this city, village, settlement come into being? How has it changed? What challenges do its people face now?

In addition to books on the history and environment of the place, it's worth looking for novels set in that location, particularly those by native authors. And what do local activists have to say about problems in their society? Visitors to the Caribbean will never look at the islands the same way after reading Jamaica Kincaid's *A Small Place,* which is about corruption and racism in her native island of Antigua. And don't overlook the present day. The Internet makes it easy for prospective visitors to follow the news in the local press. Even non–English speaking countries often have an English newspaper for foreign residents, many of which are online.

Bring some of your background reading matter along on the trip to review as you move from one place to another. It's too easy to pass right by a sight of interest and not realize it until later. Spend some quiet time during the evening while in transit reading up on what you will see the next day and telling your travel companions what to look for as well.

Travel with a Guide

One of the best ways to enter into a place fully is by visiting it in the company of a knowledgeable local guide. Non-native guides can give very enjoyable commentary, but few can equal the trained native with an awareness of land and people, a manner of thinking shared with others in the area, and a firsthand grasp of the problems, which outsiders can hardly match. This unity of person and place comes through to the visitor. A commitment to the area often outweighs the enthusiasm and dedication brought by outsiders who come as tour guides only during the vacation season.

The personality of the guide is paramount. Guides assist the tourist in basic daily needs—room, food, and so on—while controlling the pace of the trip and dispensing information. This is not unlike acting as both chaperon and schoolteacher for a disparate collection of mature adults. One hardly expects these abilities to be found in a single person. Most teachers are busy enough just teaching; looking out for the physical needs of their charges is another job. The best guide may be most successful as part of a team, where different people are responsible for imparting knowledge and satisfying immediate travel needs.

A skillful guide understands that people come to experience, not to listen to lectures. A happy medium between total freedom and a deluge of information requires involving all parties in preparing the tour/educational process—hosts, guides (as intermediaries), and visitors. The tour group becomes a learning community, and the guide is not so much a lecturer as a facilitator for those of equal status. This eliminates the tedious (and common) experience of sitting for a length of time listening to a lecture, asking only pertinent questions, and listening dutifully to other travelers' silly comments. If visitors are drawn into local issues, deepen their concern, and learn about evolving solutions, then the tour will be more worthwhile and truly educational.

Pause and Reflect

It's no coincidence that travel reminiscences make some of the most enjoyable reading around, from Marco Polo's chronicles of unknown Asia to the memoirs of astronauts who have been to the moon. When we travel, everything is fresh and immediate, and we are opened to a new world and a new way of being. For the mindful traveler, it can be a lot to take in, and time is needed to think it all through. One of the best ways to do this is to keep a record of your trip. While doing it, you are choosing the parts of the trip—the places, people, experiences— that have been the most significant for you, as well as preserving the trip for further reflection in the future. Later on, well after returning home, too many travelers wish they had kept a better record of what they saw and experienced.

There are many different approaches to capturing the trip. Some travelers prefer cameras, and snap those goofy shots of friends and companions standing in front of a rock, which the professionals have photographed a million times. Never mind—it's one way to preserve the fleeting moment. Other travelers like to use camcorders, perhaps adding their spoken commentary to the scenes they film. Travel journals of differing types are a very common approach—from elaborate diaries to notepads to a series of scribbles in the margins of a guidebook. The more artistic travelers like to record favorite scenes in a pocket sketchbook, or may even bring tiny watercolor sets for portable painting. And some people like to amass a collection of ticket stubs, postcards, and other bits of paper to make into a collage, as a visual record of their travels.

The important thing is to keep a record in whatever form suits you, to capture what you see, hear, taste, touch, and smell, to record your impressions and the things you learn. Most of what we take in vanishes quickly if we do not use it in some way, by writing it down, explaining it to someone else, or putting it into tangible form. Taking the time to pause, reflect, and capture your thoughts and impressions is one of the best ways to profit from travel. Al Fritsch once took a trip and recorded cryptic notes each day; later he found that even this brought back a flood of memories. He was wise to jot down even a little each day, for the memories are so fleeting.

Share and Act on What You've Learned

We spent a month traveling in Vietnam, and I was stunned to find that not only do people there not hate Americans, we were welcomed everywhere we went. The Vietnamese feel that the war is a tragic part of their country's past—of course, to them it's the American War—and they think it's more important now to look to the future. When I got back home, everyone I told this to was just amazed. They never imagined Vietnamese people could feel that way.

—Kristin Johannsen

Not all of us are fortunate enough to travel, and even those who do can never hope to visit every corner of this vast earth. We owe it to nontravelers to share with them the surprising things we've seen first-hand, the discoveries we've made that will never be printed in a book or shown on TV. Beyond your snapshots of gorgeous sunsets and historic buildings, share your impressions of the people and cultures you encountered.

As part of the tiny percentage of people on this planet who are fortunate enough to be able to travel for pleasure, we also have a responsibility to take action on those situations and issues we have observed. If one has practiced responsible touring and has seen environments that will be destroyed by future development, we must act to preserve the good things we have seen to future generations. If we have witnessed injustice or exploitation, we must make other people aware of the situation.

We went to Burma in 1992 as a side trip from Thailand, not really knowing what was going on there, and found a police state! There were huge, Nazi-like propaganda billboards everywhere, and everyone was too afraid to talk to foreigners, except for the Buddhist monks. Young monks kept coming up to us and saying, "Do people in your country know what's happening here?" They told us the government was using forced labor to build a lot of new tourist facilities in Mandalay. They destroyed the entire town of Pagan so there would be no people there to talk to the tourists. I felt so guilty for paying money to that government that after the trip, I told everyone I knew all about what we'd seen and heard.

—Kristin Johannsen

Here sharing is a communal enterprise and we fulfill the need to act responsibly after our experience is ended. Furthermore, consider writing a report or a story for the local newspaper or some magazine about what you have learned, or some action that should be taken by the public.

Appalachia's Welcome Mat Is Out

Travel expands everyone, if the traveler is truly open to what is seen and experienced. Too many folks come with fixed ideas to a given place—and that includes visitors to Appalachia—and never truly see the beauty and hues and tints of the region. The destination can become a sacred site, a place set apart as one in which the Spirit can be encountered—and for us, Appalachia is a holy land. Travelers must open themselves to being moved and changed by the different places they pass through. By always staying in one place, we may not have the opportunities to welcome that diversity. And Appalachia offers so much. By going about, we encounter new situations that can change us and remake our way of being in the world—and we are afforded the opportunity to respond with a humble and open mind. And by being mindful of our impact on the places that host us, we open up the possibility of truly leaving them better for our having been there. Appalachia, by being host to visitors from afar, opens itself to being enriched by people who have come to know and love the land and its people.

A Parting for Now

Let's return to the question we asked in our introduction: Will ecotourism enhance the well-being of Appalachia's people, its visitors, and the land itself? We hope this journey has been both a critique and a realistic picture of ecotourism, its inherent possibilities and weaknesses, and how it could apply to Appalachia. We have tried to do this from the perspective of environmentally concerned travelers, who see the fallacy of greenwashing and tying nature tourism into the large-scale corporate economy.

Rather, sound ecotourism must provide a healthy nature experience for visitors to the region, showing both the natural beauty and the human threats to the environment. All forms of tourism must be green, and the criteria for so-called "ecotourism" should be applied to all travel. We welcome visitors who come to Appalachia with respect for this fragile landscape and for the residents they will meet.

We hope that our recommendations are neither too overwhelming nor too general. While we have discussed a number of federal, state, and local regulations that need to be instituted or enforced, we have also sought to honor the ingenuity of our Appalachian people in working out solutions that are right for them. It is the citizens in each local area who must shape their own destinies through community action. Outside interests must not be allowed to control the future of tourism here, though they may be invited to use their expertise in implementing the community's decisions. What works best in one part of the region may be less successful in others. This is our message: If local folks take control of tourism development, Appalachia can remain environmentally healthy in a more prosperous future—while serving as a model for other regions in the development of true ecotourism.

Co-op America's Travel Guidelines

Guidelines for Responsible Travel

1. Travel in a spirit of humility and with genuine desire to meet and talk with local people; travel to meet, not conquer.

2. Reflect daily on your experiences; seek to deepen your understanding. "What enriches you may rob or violate others."

3. Be environmentally friendly; use energy, water and other resources efficiently and in keeping with local practices. Only bring necessary technological gadgetry. Participate in local recycling programs where available. Try not to bring into the country any containers that you don't plan to take out.

4. Don't create barriers; take advantage of opportunities to walk, bicycle, and use other forms of nonmotorized transport.

5. Acquaint yourself with the local customs. Be culturally sensitive, especially with photography; people will be happy to help you.

6. Realize that the people in the area you visit often have time concepts and thought patterns different from your own; not inferior, just different.

7. Be economically beneficial. Spend money so that it stays in the community. When buying, remember that a bargain may be obtained because of low wages paid to the producer. Don't purchase products made from endangered species.

8. Cultivate the habit of listening and observing, rather than merely hearing and looking. Discover the enrichment that comes from seeing another way of life.

99 Recreational Activities Ranked by Impact

Abbreviations

HR   Health risk
SR   Safety risk
ED   Potentially high environmental damage
RE   Moderate to high resource expenditure (water, land, energy)

Socially beneficial—low resource use

1. Nature Observation
2. Wildlife Preservation
3. Organic Gardening (vegetables, herbs, flowers)
4. Home Rehabilitation and Repair
5. Solar Energy Development
6. Nature Trail Building and Maintenance
7. Environmental Writing and Publicity
8. Environmental Education
9. Visual Arts and Crafts (with safe materials)
10. Singing, Dancing, Music Playing, Performing Arts

Local—low resource use

11. Entertaining Children with Simple Toys
12. Board Games (nonelectronic)
13. Bird Watching and Nature Observation

14. Walking, Hiking, Jogging, Running (cross-country)
15. Swimming, Wading, Beach Play (natural setting)
16. Snow Play, Sledding, Cross-Country Skiing, Ice Skating (natural setting)
17. Reading
18. Picnics, Potluck, Social Events (local)
19. Fishing (natural areas)
20. Home Exercising, Weightlifting

Local—outdoor—with equipment

21. Playground Activities (swing set, volleyball, sandbox, flying kites)
22. Canoeing, Rowboating
23. Softball, Soccer, Baseball
24. Track and Field, Jogging, Running
25. Biking (hard surface)
26. Basketball, Tennis, Handball
27. Dry Land Skiing, Roller Skating SR
28. Antiquing, Collectible Assembling
29. Gym Activities (acrobatics, handball, karate, judo, racquetball, basketball)
30. Model Planes, Electric Toys

Moderate travel—outdoor—with equipment

31. Camping and Backpacking (low impact)
32. Photography
33. Sailing, Crew, Rafting
34. Rappelling, Rope Work
35. Summer Camp Games
36. Horseback Riding (on trails)
37. Lawn Croquet, Badminton, Lawn Tennis
38. Spectator Sports (outdoors)
39. Spelunking SR

Indoors—with equipment— energy-consuming

40. Home Decorating (lights)
41. Wrestling, Fencing, Boxing
42. Moviemaking, Home Video
43. Amusement Parks
44. Writing (computer)
45. Television-Watching RE
46. Electronic and Video Games RE
47. Computer Hacking RE
48. Private Gym Activities (low-use) RE
49. Private Swimming (low-use pool) RE

Indoors—with equipment—energy-consuming—some travel

50. Opera, Concert, Festival, Movie (by auto) RE
51. Spectator Basketball
52. Bowling (automated) RE
53. Ice Skating (artificial ice) RE

Outdoors—with equipment   human safety factors

54. Surfing, Surf Sailing SR
55. Ice Sailing SR
56. Scuba Diving SR
57. Target Practice, Archery SR
58. Hunting (for meat consumption) SR
59. Contact Sports (football, rugby) SR
60. Ice Hockey (natural setting) SR

Outdoors—with equipment—travel

61. Camping, Backpacking (distant) RE
62. Touring, Sightseeing RE
63. Mountain Biking ED
64. Horseback Riding, Fox Hunts, Polo RE, ED

Outdoors—with equipment—human safety factors—travel

65. Skiing or Snowboarding Downhill (mechanical lift) SR, RE
66. White-Water Rafting SR
67. Motorcycling SR
68. Rock Climbing, Mountain Climbing SR, ED
69. Snowmobiling RE, ED
70. Auto Racing, Drag Racing, Demolition Derby SR
71. Rodeo Riding SR
72. Hang-Gliding SR
73. Bungee Jumping SR

Outdoors—environmental threat

74. Lawn Care, Gardening (pesticides) ED, RE, HR
75. Landscaping (with exotic species) ED
76. Wildflower Picking, Wildlife Gathering ED
77. Beachcombing
78. Golfing (lawn chemicals) ED, RE
79. Amateur Archeology ED

Outdoors—heavy energy use

80. Overseas Vacationing RE
81. Auto-Cruising RE
82. Ocean Cruising RE
83. Horse Racing (with jockey) RE
84. Deep-Sea Fishing (small numbers) RE
85. Motorized Camping RE
86. Yachting RE
87. Airplane Touring RE
88. Hot-Air Ballooning SR, RE

Outdoors—damage to bodily and psychic health

89. Sunbathing (UV damage to skin) HR
90. Gambling, Cockfighting HR
91. Malling, Compulsive Shopping RE

Heavy impacts of multiple kinds

92. Parachuting, Skydiving SR, RE
93. Wildlife Hunting for Sport SR, ED, RE
94. Touring Fragile Lands, Dune Buggy Operation SR, ED, RE
95. Off-Road Vehicles (cross-country) SR, ED, RE
96. Motorboating, Water-Skiing SR, ED, RE
97. Big Game Hunting (distance) SR, ED, RE
98. Smoking Tobacco HR, RE
99. Substance Abuse (drugs, alcohol) HR, RE

Notes

Introduction

1. Quoted in Lisa Mastny, *Traveling Light: New Paths for International Tourism.* (Washington: Worldwatch Institute, 2001).

2. See http://www.wttc.org/resourceCentre/mediaCentre/releases/000511tsaforecasts.asp.

3. Despite the Cold War connotations of the term Third World, in this book we use it in preference to more current terms like "developing world" or "lessdeveloped countries" to express our skepticism that these countries are actually experiencing worthwhile development, or that so-called developed countries are a worthy model for them to emulate.

4. Travel Industry Association of America; see http://www.tia.org/Travel/EconImpact.asp.

5. See http://www.tia.org/Press/pressrec.asp?Item=127.

6. US Census Bureau, *Statistical Abstract of the United States,* 2000.

7. David A. Fennell, *Ecotourism: An Introduction* (London: Routledge, 1999).

8. Pamela Wight, "Ecotourism: Ethics or Eco-Sell?" *Journal of Travel Research* (Winter 1993), 3.

9. Robert W. McIntosh, Charles R. Goldner, and J.R. Brent Ritchie, *Tourism: Principles, Practices, Philosophies,* 7th ed. (New York: Wiley, 1995), 368.

10. Tensie Whelan, "Ecotourism and Its Role in Sustainable Development." In Tensie Whelan, ed., *Nature Tourism: Managing for the Environment* (Washington, DC: Island Press, 1991), 9.

11. Valene L. Smith, "Boracay, Philippines: A Case Study in 'Alternative' Tourism." In Valene L. Smith and William R. Eadington, *Tourism Alternatives: Potentials and Problems in the Development of Tourism* (Philadelphia: University of Pennsylvania Press, 1992), 157.

Chapter 1
The World's Biggest Industry

1. Martha Honey, *Ecotourism and Sustainable Development: Who Owns Paradise?* (Washington, DC: Island Press, 1999), 9.

2. Quoted in John A. Jakes, *The Tourist: Travel in Twentieth-Century North America* (Lincoln: University of Nebraska Press, 1985).

3. *Kentucky Explorer,* May 2001.

4. Horace Sutton, *Travelers: The American Tourist from Stagecoach to Space Shuttle* (New York: Morrow, 1980), 134.

5. Ibid., 184.

6. Quoted in Deborah McLaren, *Rethinking Tourism and Ecotravel: The Paving of Paradise and What You Can Do to Stop It* (West Hartford, Conn.: Kumarian, 1998), 11.

7. See http://www1.iata.org/pr/pr01junc.htm.

8. David Zurick, *Errant Journeys: Adventure Travel in a Modern Age* (Austin: University of Texas Press, 1995), 157.

9. Valene L. Smith, introduction to Valene L. Smith, ed., *Hosts and Guests: The Anthropology of Tourism* (Philadelphia: University of Pennsylvania Press, 1977).

10. Davydd J. Greenwood, "Culture by the Pound: An Anthropological Perspective on Tourism as Cultural Commodification." In Smith, *Hosts and Guests,* 136.

Chapter 2
Mountain Mist

1. Quoted in Harry M. Caudill, *Theirs Be the Power: The Moguls of Eastern Kentucky* (Urbana: University of Illinois Press, 1983).

2. Calculated by extrapolating from the $1.58 billion tourist industry in wholly Appalachian West Virginia, which has a population of 1.8 million. Estimates for the population of Appalachia range from 5 to 10 million, depending on how broadly the area is defined.

3. Joe Kane, "Arrested Development," *Outside* (May 2001), 68–78.

4. See http://www.tia.org/Press/trends.asp.

5. "Globalization Threat to World's Cultural, Linguistic and Biological Diversity"; see http://www.unep.org/gc_21st/NR%20_18.doc.

Chapter 3
On the Wrong Track

1. United States Consumer Product Safety Commission, *All-Terrain Vehicle Exposure, Injury, Death, and Risk Studies,* April 1998.

2. See http://www.bluewaternetwork.org/reports/rep_pl_offroad_atvreport.pdf.

3. Personal communication. The personal communications cited in this chapter were e-mail messages and phone calls collected by Appalachia-Science in the Public Interest over twelve years of advocacy on environmental issues surrounding ATV use.

4. Personal communication. The source asked to remain anonymous for fear of retaliation by ATV riders.

5. See http://www.outdoorsite.com.

6. Personal communication.

7. See http://www.kybiz.com/lanereport/issues/may01/coverstory501.html.

8. See http://magazine.audubon.org/incite/incite0003.html.

9. Personal communication.

10. See http://www.atvsource.com/articles/press releases/2001/honda/013101.

11. National Survey of Hunting, Fishing and Wildlife-Associated Recreation Activities, 1996.

12. Consumer Product Safety Commission, data from 1995. National Electronic Injury Surveillance System (NEISS).

13. Personal communication.

14. Personal communication.

15. Personal communication.

16. Personal communication. The officer asked to remain anonymous.

Chapter 4
Going Green

1. Smith, *Hosts and Guests.*

2. See http://www.ecotourism.org/textfiles/stats.txt.

3. Megan Epler Wood, *Ecotourism: Principles, Practices, and Policies for Sustainability* (Paris: United Nations Environment Programme, 2002), 12.

4. Kenneth E. Silverberg, Sheila J. Backman, and Kenneth F. Backman, "A Preliminary Investigation into the Psychographics of Nature-Based Travelers to the Southeastern United States," *Journal of Travel Research* (fall 1996), 19–27.

5. Robert Christie Mill and Alastair M. Morrison, *The Tourism System: an Introductory Text* (Englewood Cliffs, N.J.: Prentice-Hall, 1985), 4.

6. Ibid., 6.

7. *Utne Reader,* May/June 2001.

8. Honey, *Ecotourism and Sustainable Development,* 51.

9. Anita Pleumarom, "Ecotourism: A New 'Green Revolution' in the Third World"; see http://www.twnside.org.sg/title/eco2.htm.

10. Bryan R. Higgins, "The Global Structure of the Nature Tourism Industry: Ecotourists, Tour Operators, and Local Businesses"; see http://www.ecotourism.org/textfiles/higgins.pdf.

11. David Cruise Malloy and David A. Fennell, "Ecotourism and Ethics: Moral Development and Educational Cultures," *Journal of Travel Research* (Spring 1998), 47–56.

12. Eugenio Yunis, "The Evolution of Accreditation and Certification," presentation given at International Adventure Travel and Outdoor Sports (IATOS) 2002 World Congress on Adventure and Eco Tourism.

13. Personal communication, at IATOS 2002 World Congress on Adventure and Eco Tourism.

14. Megan Epler Wood, "Ecotourism in an Uncertain World," presentation at IATOS 2002 World Congress on Adventure and Eco Tourism.

15. Data from 2000 US Census, and US Department of State; see http://travel.state.gov/passport_statistics.html.

Chapter 5
Lessons for Appalachia 1

1. David N. Zurick, "Adventure Travel and Sustainable Tourism in the Peripheral Economy of Nepal," *Annals of the Association of American Geographers* 82:4 (1992), 608–28.

2. Sanjay K. Nepal, "Tourism in Protected Areas: the Nepalese Himalaya, *Annals of Tourism Research* 27:3 (2000), 661–81.

3. Gary Walder, "Sagarmatha National Park and the Annapurna Conservation Area Project, with special reference to Upper Mustang," Master's Thesis, Bournemouth University, 2000.

4. Nepal, "Tourism in Protected Areas and the Annapurna Conservation Area Project."

5. Walder, "Sagarmatha National Park and the Annapurna Conservation Area Project."

6. Nepal, "Tourism in Protected Areas."

7. Stanley F. Stevens, *Claiming the High Ground: Sherpas, Subsistence, and Environmental Change in the Highest Himalaya* (Berkeley: University of California Press, 1993), 378.

8. Nepal, "Tourism in Protected Areas."

9. M. N. Sherpa, quoted in Jai N. Mehta, "Problems and Prospects of Ecotourism in Nepal"; see http://www.geocities.com/jaimehta223/article1.html.

10. See http://www.nepalnews.com.np/archive/2002/september/arc466.htm#13.

11. Linda Mastny, *Traveling Light: New Paths for International Tourism* (Washington DC: Worldwatch Institute, 2001), 22.

12. See http://www.kanantik.com.

13. Linda Baker, "Enterprise at the expense of the environment?" Environmental News Network, 21 November 2000; see http://www.enn.com/features/2000/11/11212000/belize_40273.asp.

14. Honey, *Ecotourism and Sustainable Development,* 52.

15. Caroline Arlen, "Ecotour, Hold the Eco," *U.S. News,* 29 May 1995, 61–63; Mary-Lou Weisman, "Confessions of a Reluctant Eco-Tourist," *New York Times,* Travel section, 1 March 1998.

16. Cited above, 43.

17. Jill M. Belsky, "Misrepresenting Communities: The Politics of Community-Based Rural Ecotourism in Gales Point Manatee, Belize," *Rural Sociology* 64:4 (1999), 641–66.

18. Kreg Lindberg, Jeremy Enriquez, and Keith Sproule, "Ecotourism Ques-

tioned: Case Studies from Belize," *Annals of Tourism Research* 23 (1996) 543–62.

19. Belsky, "Misrepresenting Communities," 661.

20. Ibid.

21. Frank Brennan and Garth Allen, "Community-Based Ecotourism, Social Exclusion, and the Changing Political Economy of KwaZulu-Natal, South Africa." In David Harrison, ed., *Tourism and the Less-Developed World: Issues and Case Studies* (Wallingford, U.K.: CAB International, 2001), 218–19.

22. Epler Wood, "Ecotourism in an Uncertain World."

Chapter 6
Lessons for Appalachia 2

1. Hawaii Tourism Authority, *Competitive Strategic Assessment of Hawaii Tourism,* 1999; see http://www.hawaii.gov/tourism/pwccsa.pdf.

2. Hawaii Tourism Authority, *Hawaii Tourism Product Assessment,* 1999, section 4–5; see http://www.hawaii.gov/tourism/kpmgtpa.pdf.

3. Hawaii Tourism Authority, *Hawaii Tourism Product Assessment,* 1999, section 4–4.

4. Kaleo Patterson, "Aloha! Welcome to Paradise," *New Internationalist* (July 1993) xx.

5. Haunani-Kay Trask, "Tourist Stay Home," *The Progressive* 57:7 (July 1993), 32.

6. Ibid.

7. Patterson, "Aloha! Welcome to Paradise."

8. Luis H. Francia, "Ka Lahui Hawai'i," *Village Voice,* 20 June 1995.

9. Ian McIntosh, "Ecotourism: A Boon for Indigenous People?" *Cultural Survival Quarterly,* 23:2; see http://www.culturalsurvival.org/newpage/index.cfm.

10. Quoted in Ken Ross, *Environmental Conflict in Alaska* (Boulder: University Press of Colorado, 2000).

11. Gabriel Scott, "Ecotourism Discovers the Last Frontier," *Clearinghouse for Reviewing Ecotourism* 8; see http://www.twnside.org.sg/title/eco8.htm.

12. Ross, *Environmental Conflict in Alaska,* 79.

13. Nichols Gilstrap, "Strategic Market Analysis and Planning for Alaska Tourism," 2000; see http://www.dced.state.ak.us/cbd/toubus/pub/marketinganalysis2000.pdf.

14. Alaska Wilderness Recreation and Tourism Association, *Guiding Alaska Tourism: Strategies for Success,* 2002; see–http://www.guidingalaskatourism.org/GATworkbook.pdf.

Chapter 7
The Bottom Line

1. Sue Wheat, "Visiting Disaster," *Guardian Weekly,* 20 June 2002.

2. RTP, INSO, CICE, "Background Paper: Escaping Ecotourism" (St. Paul, Minn.: Rethinking Tourism Project, 2001).

3. Clearinghouse for Reviewing Ecotourism; see http://www.twnside.org.sg/ title/iye.htm.

4. Rosaleen Duffy, *A Trip Too Far: Ecotourism, Politics, and Exploitation* (London: Earth–scan, 2002); see http://www.earthscan.co.uk/ samplechapters/1853837598Chapter1.htm.

5. Epler Wood, "Ecotourism in an Uncertain World."

6. Sarah Marriott, "Is Ecotourism a Greenwash?" *Irish Times*, 26 May 2001.

7. Honey, *Ecotourism and Sustainable Development*, 296.

8. Ibid., 132–33.

9. Mastny, *Traveling Light*, 43.

10. Honey, *Ecotourism and Sustainable Development*, 391.

11. Marriott, "Is Ecotourism a Greenwash?"

12. Brian Wheeller, "Tourism's Troubled Times: Responsible Tourism is not the Answer," *Tourism Management* (June 1991), 91–96.

13. Honey, *Ecotourism and Sustainable Development*, 108.

14. See http://www.twnside.org.sg/title/iye3.htm.

15. See http://www.ecotourism.org/textfiles/stats.txt.

16. Anita Pleumarom, "Ecotourism: A New 'Green Revolution' in the Third World."

17. See http://www.sierraclub.org/ico/louisville/

18. McLaren, *Rethinking Tourism and Ecotravel*, 98.

19. "The Oil Crisis and You," *Auto-Free Times*, Spring 2001, 24–27.

20. Arlen, "Ecotour, Hold the Eco," 61–63.

21. Weisman, "Confessions of a Reluctant Eco-Tourist."

22. Kutay and Kagan comments from "Business Models for Developing Ecotourism Programs," symposium at IATOS 2002 World Congress on Adventure and Eco Tourism.

23. Carol Patterson, "The Future of Ecotourism in an Uncertain World," at IATOS 2002 World Congress on Adventure and Eco Tourism.

24. See http://www.twnside.org.sg/title/iye1.htm.

25. Personal communication.

26. Pleumarom, "Ecotourism."

27. Richard Butler, "Alternative Tourism: The Thin Edge of the Wedge." In Smith and Eadington, *Tourism Alternatives*, 41.

28. Pleumarom, quoted in Marriott, "Is Ecotourism a Greenwash?"

Chapter 8
2020 Visions

1. Jane L. Brass, ed., *Community Tourism Assessment Handbook*, Western Rural Development Center, 1996; see http://www.montana.edu/wwwwrdc/.

Chapter 9
Our Own Backyard

1. Horace Kephart, *Our Southern Highlanders* (1913; reprint, Knoxville: University of Tennessee Press, 1976).

2. The Blue Ridge Parkway has more visitors than any other National Park Service entity, peaking at almost 25 million in 1988 and attracting almost 22 million in 2001.

3. Victoria Logue, Frank Logue, and Nicole Blouin, *Guide to the Blue Ridge Parkway* (Birmingham, Ala.: Menasha Ridge Press, 1997).

4. Folk Art Center and Allanstand Craft Shop; see http://www.southern highlandguild.org.

5. See http://www.museum.appstate.edu.

6. See http://www.ncarboretum.org.

7. See http://www.cradleofforestry.com.

8. See http://www.ncwildlife.org.

9. "Smokies Guide," newspaper of Great Smoky Mountains National Park, Summer 2002, 1.

10. "Historic Preservation," *GSMNP Management Folio #-5*, 2000.

11. Tom Robbins, "A Mountain Farm Museum" (Gatlinburg, Tennessee: Great Smoky Mountains Natural History Association).

12. "Black Bears," *GSMNP Management Folio #-1*, 1996, 2002.

13. "Air Quality," *GSMNP Management Folio #2*, 1997.

14. "Smokies Guide," 8.

15. "Air Quality," 3.

16. Daniel S. Pierce, *The Great Smokies: From Natural Habitat to National Park* (Knoxville: University of Tennessee Press, 2000), 204.

17. "Exotic Plants," *GSMNP Management Folio #-4*, 1999.

18. "Fire Management," *GSMNP Folio #-3*, 1997.

19. See http://www.main.nc.us/LBEEC/.

Chapter 10
Beyond Ecotourism

1. See http://www.jackhanna.com/africa99/sableranch.htm.

2. "Science Briefs," *Biodiversity Notes: A Newsletter from the Biodiversity Project*, Spring 2001.

3. Greg Gordon, "Wilderness U," *Orion Afield*, Spring 1999, 10–14.

4. "Teaching the Human Habitat: Environmental Education Down on the Farm," *Orion Afield*, Summer 1998, 20–23

5. *Back Home*, March/April 2001, 48–51.

6. See http://www.tourism-watch.de/dt/26dt/26.energieverbrauch/content.html.

Index